The Old English Poem *Seasons for Fasting*
A Critical Edition

MEDIEVAL EUROPEAN STUDIES XV
Patrick W. Conner, Series Editor

OTHER TITLES IN THE SERIES:

The Book of Emperors:
A Translation of the Middle High German Kaiserchronik
Translated and edited by Henry A. Myers

Sir Gawain and the Green Knight
Translated by Larry Benson
with a foreword and Middle English text edited by Daniel Donoghue

Perspectives on the Old Saxon Hêliand:
Introductory and Critical Essays, with an Edition of the Leipzig Fragment
Edited by Valentine A. Pakis

Cross and Cruciform in the Anglo-Saxon World:
Studies to Honor the Memory of Timothy Reuter
Edited by Sarah Larratt Keefer, Karen Louise Jolly, and Catherine E. Karkov

The Cross and Culture in Anglo-Saxon England
Edited by Karen Louise Jolly, Catherine E. Karkov, and Sarah Larratt Keefer

Cædmon's Hymn and Material Culture in the World of Bede
Edited by Allen J. Frantzen and John Hines

The Power of Words: Anglo-Saxon Studies Presented
to Donald G. Scragg on his Seventieth Birthday
Edited by Jonathan Wilcox and Hugh Magennis

Innovation and Tradition in the Writings of the Venerable Bede
Edited by Scott DeGregorio

Ancient Privileges: Beowulf, Law, and the Making of Germanic Antiquity
Stefan Jurasinski

Old English Literature in its Manuscript Context
Edited by Joyce Tally Lionarons

Theorizing Anglo-Saxon Stone Sculpture
Edited by Catherine E. Karkov and Fred Orton

Naked Before God: Uncovering the Body in Anglo-Saxon England
Edited by Benjamin C. Withers and Jonathan Wilcox

Hêliand: Text and Commentary
Edited by James E. Cathey

Via Crucis: Essays on Early Medieval Sources and Ideas
Thomas N. Hall, Editor, with assistance from Thomas D. Hill and Charles D. Wright

The Old English Poem

Seasons for Fasting

A Critical Edition

Edited by

Mary P. Richards

with the assistance of

Chadwick B. Hilton, Jr.

WEST VIRGINIA UNIVERSITY PRESS
MORGANTOWN 2014

Copyright 2014 West Virginia University Press
All rights reserved
First edition published 2014 by West Virginia University Press

    21 20 19 18 17 16 15 14   1 2 3 4 5 6 7 8 9

PB: 978-1-938228-43-8
PDF: 978-1-938228-44-5
EPUB: 978-1-938228-45-2

Library of Congress Cataloging-in-Publication Data:
Richards, Mary P.
The Old English poem Seasons for fasting : a critical edition / Mary P. Richards; with the assistance of Chadwick B. Hilton Jr.
    pages   cm
Includes complete text of the poem and its translation in English.
Includes bibliographical references.
ISBN-13: 978-1-938228-43-8 (pbk.)
ISBN-13: 978-1-938228-44-5 (pdf)
ISBN-13: 978-1-93-822845-2 (epub)

1. Seasons for fasting (Old English poem) I. Hilton, Chad B. II. Seasons for fasting (Old English poem) III. Seasons for fasting (Old English poem). English. IV. Title.
PR1773.S383R53 2014
829'.1--dc23
2013042729

Front cover image: Laurence Nowell's transcript of MS Cotton Otho B.xi, original now destroyed. British Library MS Additional 43703, fol. 157r.
© The British Library Board.

Contents

Acknowledgments	vii
Short Titles and Other Abbreviations	ix
Introduction	
Description of The Poem	1
Manuscripts and Editions	2
Metrical and Linguistic Features	20
Sources and Influences	36
Style and Structure	60
Principles of This Edition	83
Seasons for Fasting	
Text	87
Translation	103
Commentary	111
Glossary	139
Bibliography	159
Index to Manuscripts	178
Index	179

Acknowledgments

This edition began almost thirty years ago as the dissertation project of Chadwick B. Hilton Jr. at the University of Tennessee, where I served as his advisor. Chad and his wife, B. Jane Stanfield, who also worked with me, participated in research projects of mutual interest that led to several publications. They now have completed successful careers at the University of Alabama, where Chad served as the associate dean for International Business Programs and Bennett faculty fellow in International Business, Management, and Marketing, and Jane retired as the associate provost for International Education and Global Outreach. Having entered the field of business communications, Chad discontinued his work on *Seasons for Fasting* and passed the project along to me. Numerous obligations of my own intervened, delaying its completion until now.

The present edition owes much to the interest and support of colleagues through the years. Along with Chad and Jane, scholars who have been especially helpful include Carl T. Berkhout, Mary Blockley, David Bright, Tom Cable, Patrick Conner, the late James Cross, Richard Dammery, James Dean, John H. Fisher, Rob Fulk, Jim Hall, Tom Hall, Toni Healey, the late Connie Hieatt, Joyce Hill, Aaron Kleist, Gay Marie Logsdon, Eric Stanley, Paul Szarmach, and Joseph Trahern. Additionally, the staffs at the British Library and at the University of Delaware Library were instrumental to my work. To all of these individuals, I offer sincere gratitude. Any mistakes or infelicities, however, are solely my responsibility.

Final preparation of the text has been aided by my husband, Bob Netherland, and our close friends, Buddy and Jack.

Short Titles and Other Abbreviations

(Entries are keyed to the bibliography)

Bethurum	*The Homilies of Wulfstan*, ed. Dorothy Bethurum
BL	London, British Library
BT, BTA, BTS	*An Anglo-Saxon Dictionary*, ed. Joseph Bosworth and T. Northcote Toller; *Supplement*, ed. T. Northcote Toller; *Addenda*, ed. A. Campbell
Caie	*The Old English Poem "Judgement Day II,"* ed. Graham D. Caie
Campbell	*An Old English Grammar*, A. Campbell
CCCC	Cambridge, Corpus Christi College
CH I	*Ælfric's Catholic Homilies: The First Series*, ed. Peter Clemoes
CH II	*Ælfric's Catholic Homilies: The Second Series*, ed. Malcolm Godden
Concordance	*A Microfiche Concordance to Old English*, ed. Antonette diPaolo Healey and Richard L. Venezky
D, Dobbie	"Seasons for Fasting," *The Anglo-Saxon Minor Poems*, ed. Elliott Van Kirk Dobbie
DOE	*The Dictionary of Old English A to G on CD Rom*, ed. Angus Cameron, Ashley Crandell Amos, and Antonette diPaolo Healey
EETS	Early English Text Society
Gen A,B	*Genesis A and B*, an Old English poem, ed. George P. Krapp
G, Greeson	"Two Old English Observance Poems: 'Seasons for Fasting' and 'The Menologium'—an Edition," ed. Hoyt St. Clair Greeson Jr.
Hil, Hilton	"An Edition and Study of the Old English 'Seasons for Fasting,'" ed. Chadwick B. Hilton Jr.

Short Titles and Abbreviations

Holt, Holthausen	F. Holthausen, "Ein altenglisches Gedicht über die Fastenzeiten"
JDay II	*Judgment Day II*
J, Jones	"Seasons for Fasting," *The Old English Shorter Poems*, ed. Christopher A. Jones
lOE	late Old English
lWS	late West Saxon
Maldon	*The Battle of Maldon*, an Old English poem, ed. Donald G. Scragg
MED	*Middle English Dictionary*, ed. Hans Kurath, Sherman A. Kuhn, John Reidy, and Robert E. Lewis
Nw	British Library Additional MS. 43703
OE	Old English
OED	*Oxford English Dictionary*
Ot	British Library MS. Cotton Otho B.xi
PL	*Patrologia Latina*, ed. J.-P. Migne
Pope, Æ *Hom*	*Homilies of Ælfric: A Supplementary Collection*, ed. John C. Pope
Skeat	*Ælfric's Lives of Saints*, ed. W. W. Skeat
Wan, Wanley	Humfrey Wanley, *Catalogus Historico-Criticus*
Whe, Wheelock	Abraham Wheelock

Introduction

1. DESCRIPTION OF THE POEM

Seasons for Fasting is a stanzaic poem composed in Old English probably in the early eleventh century by an anonymous poet. Its language, style, metrics, and sources place *SF* in the company of late Old English ecclesiastical poetry and prose, especially poetry translated from the Latin, such as *Creed* and *Judgment Day II*.

As implied by its modern title, the first topic of the poem is the dating of the four seasonal fasts known as Ember fasts, or Ember days. The poet argues for the English dates, traditionally ascribed to a dictum from Pope Gregory the Great, which he fears are under threat from the continental practice. To bolster his case, the poet draws upon statements in the laws of Æthelred, Byrhtferth's *Enchiridion*, and the writings of Ælfric and Wulfstan, all prose materials composed in Latin and Old English, roughly contemporary with the composition of the poem. The poet continues with a more traditional discussion of fasting focused on the Lenten season, followed by an attack on priests who neglect to teach and practice proper fasting.

Among the poem's more interesting features are its stanzaic structure, three-part organization, argumentative stance, and use of the complaint. Many of these elements typify the writings of Archbishop Wulfstan, the Anglo-Saxon author of hortatory sermons in a rhetorical style that relied on alliteration, rhythm, doublets, and even rhyme. Wulfstan also was responsible for ecclesiastical and royal law codes, along with other regulatory materials, some of which may have inspired our poet. The homilist Ælfric was another important influence, both in his didactic methods and his criticisms of the contemporary clergy. Beyond the poem's situation within the current literary scene, the form

Introduction

and stance of *Seasons for Fasting* look forward to such Middle English poems as *Piers Plowman* and *Cleanness*, where complaint and satire against the clergy animate the portrayals of contemporary social and ecclesiastical issues.

2. MANUSCRIPTS AND EDITIONS

2.1 MS Cotton Otho B.xi

The unique copy of *Seasons for Fasting*, found in British Library MS Cotton Otho B.xi [Ot], was destroyed in a fire at Ashburnham House, Westminster, in 1731, where Sir Robert Cotton's library was housed.[1] Although some portions of the manuscript survived, nothing remains of the last three articles, including *SF*.[2] Besides the remaining fragments, two sources of information help shed light on the lost original. First, from a transcript made in 1562 by the antiquary Laurence Nowell (British Library MS Add. 43703) [Nw] and a description of Ot by the librarian and paleographer Humfrey Wanley, completed by the early eighteenth century before the fire, there emerges a sense of the full contents and, hence, the manuscript context of *SF* as originally preserved.[3] Second,

---

1   Colin G. C. Tite, *The Manuscript Library of Sir Robert Cotton*, The Panizzi Lectures 1993 (London: British Library, 1994), 38. More on the destruction of the library and the efforts to save the manuscripts can be found in Andrew Prescott's essay, "'Their Present Miserable State of Cremation': The Restoration of the Cotton Library," in *Sir Robert Cotton as Collector*, ed. C. J. Wright (London: British Library, 1997), 391–454.

2   See the description by N. R. Ker, *Catalogue of Manuscripts Containing Anglo-Saxon* (Oxford: Clarendon Press, 1957), 230–34; repr. with 1976 supplement from *Anglo-Saxon England* 5 (1990). Ker's item 5 is no longer assumed to have been part of the original manuscript.

3   For a description of Nowell's transcript, see Richard Dammery, "The Law-Code of King Alfred the Great: A Study, Edition and Translation" (Ph.D. diss., Cambridge University, 1991), 84–95; also, *The British Museum Catalogue of Additions to the Manuscripts 1931–1935* (London: British Museum, 1967), 196–97. A useful facsimile is available in *Old English Verse Texts from Many Sources: A Comprehensive*

2

Manuscripts and Editions

using these and related materials, modern paleographers can reconstruct the foliation, assembly, layout, and hands of Ot, such that we can make reasonable inferences about the original physical text of *SF*.[4]

As is well known to many scholars of Anglo-Saxon, when Ot was assembled during the first half of the eleventh century it contained the following works: (1) a mid-tenth-century copy of the Old English translation of Bede's *Historia Ecclesiastica*; (2) the West Saxon genealogy to Alfred; (3) version G of the Anglo-Saxon Chronicle; (4) a list of popes to Damasus and of archbishops of Canterbury and bishops of Rochester, Essex, Sussex, Wessex, and Sherborne, with later additions; (5) an early version of *II Æthelstan*, the Grately code;[5] (6) the laws of Alfred and Ine [*Alfred-Ine*] appended by a short text on adultery;[6] (7) an early version of the Burghal Hidage, listing the fortifications across southern England and the number of hides of land required to support the men needed

---

Collection, ed. Fred C. Robinson and E. G. Stanley, Early English Manuscripts in Facsimile 23 (Copenhagen: Rosenkilde and Bagger, 1991), item 33. The BM catalogue entry is especially useful for its cross-references to published editions drawing on Nowell's transcriptions. An excellent and appreciative introduction to Wanley's career and achievements appears in Kenneth Sisam's essay, "Humfrey Wanley," in Sisam's *Studies in the History of Old English Literature* (Oxford: Clarendon, 1953), 259–77. Milton McC. Gatch describes Wanley's cataloguing methods in "Humfrey Wanley (1672-1726)," in *Medieval Scholarship: Biographical Studies on the Formation of a Discipline, 2: Literature and Philology*, ed. Helen Damico, with Donald Fennema and Karmen Lenz (New York and London: Garland, 1998), 52–53. Wanley's description of MS Cotton Otho B.xi appears in his catalogue of Anglo-Saxon manuscripts, *Librorum Veterum Septentrionalium, qui in Angliae Bibliothecis extant, nec non multorum Veterum Codicum Septentrionalium alibi extantium Catalogus Historico-Criticus, cum totius Thesauri Linguarum Septentrionalium sex Indicibus*, vol. 2 of George Hickes's *Linguarum Veterum Septentrionalium Thesaurus* (Oxford, 1705), 219.

4   See especially the work of Roland Torkar, to be cited below.

5   Felix Liebermann, ed., *Die Gesetze der Angelsachsen* (Halle: Niemeyer, 1903; repr., Aalen, 1960), 1:150–67.

6   Liebermann edits the text recoverable from the remaining fragments of *Alfred-Ine* in *Die Gesetze*, 1:74–76, 118–22. Wormald translates and discusses the addendum, *Ymb Æwbricas*, in *The Making of English Law: King Alfred to the Twelfth Century*, vol. 1, *Legislation and Its Limits* (Oxford: Blackwell, 1999), 372–73.

to maintain them, with an additional note;[7] (8) a poem, *Seasons for Fasting*; (9) and a collection of medical recipes, many known from the Leechbook.[8] Items 2, 3, 4, and 6 (excepting the appendix) are closely related to and probably copied from texts in the Parker manuscript, Cambridge, Corpus Christi College, MS. 173 [CCCC 173]. Item 5 seems to have been a slightly later addition, possibly in a third hand, compressed into a tight space.[9] As stated previously, items 7, 8, and 9 have completely disappeared, and are known mainly through Wanley's description of the manuscript and Nw. Ker has assigned dates of mid-tenth and first half of the eleventh century to the two main hands of Ot, with Winchester as the place of origin.[10] These attributions have been confirmed by more recent examinations, including those of the present editor.[11]

Wanley was not the first to mention the manuscript or the poem. For his 1643 edition of the Old English version of Bede's *Historia Ecclesiastica*, Abraham Wheelock cited variants from the text in Ot.[12]

---

7   For a transcription of these texts as well as the preceding statement on adultery, see Robin Flower, "The Text of the Burghal Hidage," *London Mediæval Studies* 1 (1937): 62–64.

8   See Roland Torkar, "Zu den ae. Medizinaltexten in Otho B.xi und Royal 12 D. xvii. Mit einer Edition der Unica (Ker, No. 180, art. 11a-d)," *Anglia* 94 (1976): 319–38.

9   Wormald, *Making of English Law*, 177.

10   Ker, *Catalogue*, 231–34.

11   Helmut Gneuss, *Handlist of Anglo-Saxon Manuscripts: A List of Manuscripts and Manuscript Fragments Written or Owned in England up to 1100*, no. 357 (Tempe: Arizona Center for Medieval and Renaissance Studies, 2001), 67. Angelika Lutz in *Die Version G der Angelsächsischen Chronik*, Texte und Untersuchungen zur Englischen Philologie 11 (Munich: Wilhelm Fink, 1981), xxx–xxxi, states that Hand 2's items 2 and 3 in Otho B.xi—the West-Saxon genealogy and version G of the Anglo-Saxon Chronicle—were copied in Winchester between 1001 and 1012/13.

12   Peter J. Lucas gives a full account of Wheelock's career as an editor and publisher in "Abraham Wheelock and the Presentation of Anglo-Saxon: From Manuscript to Print," B*eatus Vir: Studies in Early English and Norse Manuscripts in Memory of Phillip Pulsiano*, ed. A. N. Doane and Kirsten Wolf, Medieval and Renaissance Texts and Studies 319 (Tempe: Arizona Center for Medieval and Renaissance Studies, 2006), 383–439. Lucas does not discuss the accuracy of Wheelock's Old English transcriptions.

Manuscripts and Editions

He made reference to *SF* following Book I, chapter 27, known as the *Libellus Responsionum*, an exchange of questions and answers between St. Augustine of Canterbury and Pope Gregory the Great on matters of Christian practice to be conveyed to the recently converted English people.[13] Wheelock must have looked through the entire manuscript and read at least the first part of the poem, for he alludes to the authority of Gregory's *dictum* conveyed therein and quotes *SF* stanza XII, lines 87–94, wherein Gregory's message to the English is summarized.[14] Here are Wheelock's comments preceding the quoted passage:

> *Quanti hinc auctoritatem Beati Gregorii Majores nostri fecerint, analecta præsentes indicabunt.*
> *Miscel. Sax. ad finem Bedæ Sax. MS. Cot. pag. 353. lin. 6.*
> [Just how highly our forebears respected the authority of Blessed Gregory, this collection of quotations will indicate. Miscellaneous Saxon materials at the end of the Saxon Bede Cotton manuscript, p. 353, line 6.]

The citation could suggest that the medical texts following *SF* were missing by the time Wheelock examined Ot, but as Torkar argues, it may only indicate the place where the poem and quoted passage are to be found.[15] One suspects that the poem's stanzas were marked in such a way that the unit caught Wheelock's eye, since it did not begin on the first line of the page. In Nw, stanza XII is set off by an opening capital and his distinctive sign at the close, to be discussed below.

---

13   Abraham Wheelock, *Historiæ Ecclesiasticæ Gentis Anglorum Libri V. a Venerabili Beda Presbytero scripti . . .* (Cambridge 1643, reissued 1644).
14   This material is included in R. J. S. Grant, "A Note on 'The Seasons for Fasting,'" *Review of English Studies* 23 (1972), 303. There is a misprint in line 91b (line 5b by Grant's numbering) of the quotation from *SF*: geþyrþe should read gewyrþe.
15   Roland Torkar, *Eine altenglische Übersetzung von Alcuins De Virtutibus et Vitiis, Kap 20 (Liebermanns Judex). Untersuchungen und Textausgabe,* Texte und Untersuchungen zur englischen Philologie 7 (Munich: Wilhelm Fink, 1981), 145.

Introduction

The first printed catalogue of the manuscripts in the Cotton library, compiled by Thomas Smith in 1696, preceded Wanley's work by nearly ten years but did not provide a useful description of items following *Alfred-Ine* in Ot:[16]

> 10. R. Ælfredi leges.
> 11. R. Inæ leges, & aliæ,
> in unum corpus collectæ; Saxonice. p. 305.
> [10. Laws of King Alfred.
> 11. Laws of King Ine, and other items,
> collected in one body; Old English. 305 pages.]

It is not even clear whether Smith examined the full codex, since he mentions only 305 pages of the total 362 (as reconstructed by Torkar). Wanley's description of Ot, published in 1705, is more extensive but still problematic.[17] For one thing, Wanley opens with the statement that Ot consisted of two components combined, raising the specter of Sir Robert Cotton's possible interference with the structure of the manuscript. However, Wanley goes on to note that the first item, the OE translation of Bede, concluded with a Southwick Priory ex libris, suggesting to him, perhaps, a division in Ot. Paleographic evidence to be discussed shortly indicates that Ot was completed as a single unit in the first half of the eleventh century.

The last item cited in Wanley's description of Ot, the poem, is introduced as follows:

> XIV. fol. 351. Sequitur Cædmonianæ structuræ Carmen Saxonicum de jejuniis Ecclesiæ. sc. de quatuor temporibus, & jejunio Quadragesimali, quæ à Moyse & Judaica accersit, truncatum etiam in fine.
> [XIV. fol. 351. There follows a Saxon poem of Caedmonic structure

---

16   Thomas Smith, *Catalogue of the Manuscripts in the Cottonian Library 1696*, ed. C. G. C. Tite (Cambridge: D. S. Brewer, 1984), 71.
17   Wanley, *Librorum Veterum Septentrionalium*, 219.

Manuscripts and Editions

on the fasts of the Church, namely on the four seasons and the Lenten fast, which it derives from Moses and Jewish tradition; but it is also cut off at the end.]

Thereafter Wanley quotes the first six and one-half lines of *SF*, in keeping with his general practice of construing an incipit from the first statement in an item. In the description, he states that the last portion of the poem has already disappeared, and he mentions no further texts. Wanley's omission of the recipes that once followed *SF* suggests that they, too, had been lost, but Torkar proposes that the cataloguer could have overlooked them or the printer omitted the item inadvertently.[18] Because *SF* broke off at the foot of a verso side and the recipes began at the top of the facing recto, even Nowell continued copying without break before he realized that he had begun another text.[19] However, since Wanley noted correctly that *SF* lacked an ending, it is unlikely that he would have missed the following text if it had still been attached in the early eighteenth century.[20]

Given that the full range of prose materials copied together in Ot—laws, chronicle, genealogies, hidage, ecclesiastical lists, and recipes—can be found associated in other manuscripts, the inclusion of

18   Torkar, *Eine altenglische Übersetzung*, 145.
19   Torkar, "Zu den ae. Medizinaltexten," 319–20. See also the analysis by Audrey L. Meaney, "London, British Library Ms. 43703," *Old English Newsletter* 19, no. 1 (Fall, 1985): 34–35.
20   It is remotely possible that Wanley did miss the break between the texts and interpreted the recipes as being incomplete, for those pieces copied by Nowell in Add. 43703 are often excerpted from longer leechdoms, as compared to the same recipes in the Leechbook in British Library MS Royal 12 D. xvii. See Ker, *Catalogue*, 233, for a table of equivalences. Furthermore, the recipes in Nw conclude with a short excerpt addressing hair loss, published in book 1, no. 87, p. 154, lines 17–22, of *Leechdoms, Wortcunning, and Starcraft*, ed. Oswald Cockayne, vol. 2, Rolls Series 35 (London: Longman, Green, 1865). This final excerpt, which Torkar believes came at the bottom of p. 362 in Ot, is a complete statement, but could possibly have been interpreted by Wanley as a fragment of a recipe. See Torkar, *Eine altenglische Übersetzung*, 144.

a poem there presents a conundrum.²¹ As illustrated in the quotation above, Wheelock linked the Gregorian message of *SF* to Bede's history. When Wheelock inserted his description after the *Libellus Responsionum* and quoted only stanza XII, he was implying that the first part of *SF* concerning Gregory's directive to the English people accounted for its inclusion in the collection. Patrick Wormald expands this idea, observing that "the poem's emphasis on a distinctively English spiritual heritage" reflects the dominant focus of the manuscript collection on the history and traditions of the nation.²² Wormald's conclusion is useful as far as it goes, but reconstructing the physical text helps further explain how *SF* came to appear in Ot.

Here is what we know with some certainty. First, Ot was copied in three hands. Hand 1, from the mid-tenth century, copied the Bede text with the exception of the autobiographical note copied by Hand 2, dated to the first half of the eleventh century. Hand 2 also copied the royal genealogy, the Chronicle at least as far as the annal for 1001, the papal and Episcopal lists, *Alfred-Ine* with its appendix, the Burghal Hidage and additional note, *SF*, and the medical texts. Hand 3, also from the first half of the eleventh century but slightly later than Hand 2, copied *II Æthelstan*. Despite the loss of the last portion of Ot, Nowell's transcript provides good evidence of Hand 2's work. Torkar first pointed out certain peculiarities of script and orthography that Nowell seems to have adopted from his original. Specifically, an f-shaped *y* and the digraph *-ng* for *-nc* (as in *dreng*) link *SF* to the medical recipes that follow, as well as to the other texts in Ot copied by this scribe.²³ These features tell us that the materials relating to the Burghal Hidage, *SF*,

---

21 On the manuscript relationships of these texts, see Wormald, *Making of English Law*, 178–79.
22 Patrick Wormald, "BL Cotton Ms Otho B.xi: A Supplementary Note," *Legal Culture in the Early Medieval West: Law as Text, Image and Experience*, ed. Patrick Wormald (London: Hambledon, 1999), 78–79.
23 Torkar, *Eine altenglische Übersetzung*, 152–53. Lutz discusses the y forms as they may have appeared in the Chronicle portion of Ot in *Die Version G*, xliii–iv. Ker, *Catalogue*, also mentions the f-shaped y, 234.

Manuscripts and Editions

and the medical recipes were purposely assembled with the historical and legal texts copied from CCCC 173 during the first half of the eleventh century.

One other graphic feature probably derived from Ot is a distinctive sign [⁓] that Nowell used to conclude many of the individual laws from *Alfred-Ine*. Each of these signs appears prior to the Roman numeral of the rubric for the subsequent law. The same feature appears in the poem, marking the conclusion of fifteen (out of twenty-eight) complete stanzas within *SF*. It also follows some of the medical recipes, but does not occur in the Burghal Hidage. The source of this sign is not clear. A slightly different version appears in CCCC 173 at the end of most Chronicle entries and of the individual laws in *Alfred-Ine*, which may indicate that the feature was copied from there into Ot by Hand 2, and thence by Nowell.[24] But the picture is complicated by two factors. Places where the signs have been omitted from the laws in CCCC 173 and in Nowell's transcription do not fully match.[25] Furthermore, on the basis of her examination of the few remaining fragments of version G of the Chronicle in Ot, Lutz believes that the signs appeared sparingly in the Ot copy as compared to CCCC 173. Nowell's transcript of the G Chronicle bears this out. Nowell uses a bold paragraph sign to mark the opening of each annal but generally does not mark the conclusion distinctively.[26] However, beginning with *Alfred-Ine*, something in his exemplar must have caused Nowell to institute the sign regularly and then to continue using it in *SF* and the medical recipes. Given that he seems to follow his source in reproducing the three kinds of *y* that he saw in Hand 2, for example, we can infer that he may have followed suit, albeit not absolutely consistently, with

---

24   *The Parker Chronicle and Laws (Corpus Christi College, Cambridge 173)*, facsimile ed. by Robin Flower and Hugh Smith, Early English Text Society o.s. 208 (1941 for 1937; repr., London: Oxford University Press, 1973).
25   A different sign marking the end of Chronicle entries in CCCC 173 is not found in Nw. Rather, Nowell uses a bold paragraph sign in the margin to mark the beginning of many entries.
26   Lutz, *Die Version G*, xlvi.

the division markers. This would confirm that in Ot, a number of stanzas within *SF* were marked graphically at the end, just as they probably all opened with a capital, as reproduced by Nowell.[27]

By comparing the number of lines per page in Nw with surviving portions of Ot and using Wheelock's details about the position of stanza XII, we can also estimate the number of pages *SF* occupied in the destroyed part of the manuscript. An undamaged leaf from Ot containing the West Saxon regnal list—now London, British Library, Add. MS. 34652—detached prior to 1562 when Nowell made his transcription, is especially helpful for reconstructing the original details.[28] This leaf measures 244 mm x 177 mm, with a written space 207 mm x 144 mm containing twenty-six lines on the recto and twenty-one lines on the verso.[29] *SF* would have been copied with the same script into roughly equivalent writing blocks. According to Wanley's description of Ot, the poem began at the top of page 351. Stanza XII (*SF*, line 87) began on line 6 of page 353, indicating a rate of about forty lines of poetry, copied as prose, per page. The text broke off in the middle of line 230 (stanza XXIX) at the bottom of page 356.[30] On the basis of this physical evidence and the three topical and stylistic divisions in the poem, detailed in "Style and Structure," one can estimate the extent of the missing portion. The first of the divisions ends with stanza XIII, the second with stanza XXIII. If the poet maintained a rough symmetry in the divisions, the complete *SF* would have run to about thirty-five stanzas, or 280 lines, and would have ended on page 358.

---

27   On the basis of similarities between Nowell's treatment of the medical texts and the arrangement of such compilations in other Old English manuscripts, Audrey Meaney believes that he made a conscious attempt to reproduce the text he copied. See Meaney's essay "Variant Versions of Old English Medical Remedies and the Compilation of Bald's Leechbook," *Anglo-Saxon England* 13 (1984): 247.
28   Lutz, *Die Version G*, xli–xlii.
29   Dammery, "The Law Code of King Alfred," 40. See also Neil R. Ker, "Membra Disiecta, Second Series," *British Museum Quarterly* 14, no. 4 (1940): 81–82.
30   Torkar, *Eine altenglische Übersetzung*, 142. I follow Torkar in giving the page number rather than folio.

Manuscripts and Editions

As to how and why *SF* came to be incorporated into Ot by Hand 2, one can only make an educated guess. The analysis in "Sources and Influences" will show that *SF* has close connections to a variety of materials associated with Worcester and Archbishop Wulfstan. Texts and collections akin to those that influenced *SF* did travel to Winchester, as evidenced by the presumed route of Cambridge, Corpus Christi College, Cambridge, MS. 201, part 1, which contains—among other items related to *SF*—the unique copy of *JDay II*.[31] If Anglo-Saxon historical and cultural texts were the object of the compiler, as Wormald argues, the first topic of the poem—the English dates for Ember fasts—could account for its inclusion in the collection. This theory remains a strong possibility but ignores the majority of *SF*, which continues with an extended explication of the Lenten fast and concludes with an attack on lax priests. Then again, if the scribe found the Burghal Hidage materials, *SF*, and/or the recipes in the same exemplar, he might have included the block without a thorough perusal of the poem. It is remotely possible that he did not realize that *SF was* a poem, since it would have been written as prose marked off in units that resembled paragraphs. Certainly Wheelock printed stanza XII as prose and made no mention of the text being a poem.[32] Wanley was the first to indicate a poem, though he printed the opening lines as prose. Nowell copied the poem in prose paragraphs, without title, and never indicated that he was transcribing a poetic work.

---

31   See Wormald, *Making of English Law*, 209–10. Donald Scragg also proposes Winchester, New Minster as the source of additions and corrections in CCCC 201, in *A Conspectus of Scribal Hands Writing English, 960–1100*, Publications of the Manchester Centre for Anglo-Saxon Studies 11 (Cambridge: D. S. Brewer, 2012), 12–13, Hands 125–37. The earliest of these hands, 125, dates from the beginning of the eleventh century.

32   As Danielle Cunniff Plumer points out in "The Construction of Structure in the Earliest Editions of Old English Poetry," *The Recovery of Old English: Anglo-Saxon Studies in the Sixteenth and Seventeenth Centuries*, ed. Timothy Graham (Kalamazoo: Medieval Institute, Western Michigan University, 2000), 253–54, Wheelock did not always recognize poetry in Old English manuscripts. Plumer makes the point in reference to the Chronicle poems.

But wherever the Ot scribe found the text of *SF*, he would have seen that it was a work written in paragraphs and that it related graphically and perhaps topically to his other materials.

The three items (Burghal Hidage, *SF*, and recipes) copied into Ot following *Alfred-Ine* likewise share a regulatory aspect that could have interested a compiler when he broadened the scope of the collection taken from CCCC 173. A small but telling piece of evidence to support this explanation lies in the unique statement on forfeitures assigned to cases of adultery added without break to *Alfred-Ine*, as indicated by Nowell's transcript. Wormald theorizes that the piece had been excerpted from an earlier, longer letter or treatise and intentionally made part of the *domboc* in Ot. He concludes that the stipulation of penalties for fornication is "an official record [added to *Alfred-Ine*] on the initiative of a scribe or his judicially involved director."[33] In context with the subsequent texts, this legal statement suggests that the issue of guidance for the social, economic, spiritual, and physical well-being of the English people could have motivated the inclusion of all the new materials. If this were the case, the copier signaled a change in emphasis when he left CCCC 173 and began adding a group of texts not so directly related to the national identity of the Anglo-Saxons but more practical for their lives.

2.2 British Library Add. 43703: Nowell's Transcript

When he completed the transcript of Otho B.xi in 1562, the date entered twice in his copy, antiquary Laurence Nowell was working in William Cecil's house in the Strand, London.[34] The year previous, he

---

33   Wormald, *Making of English Law*, 372–73. He implies that this addendum was intended to bring *Alfred-Ine* up to date in this one area, where it would reflect contemporary practice.

34   This brief account of Nowell relies on information provided by Carl T. Berkhout in "Laurence Nowell (1530–ca. 1570)," in *Medieval Scholarship: Biographical Studies on the Formation of a Discipline, 2: Literature and Philology*, ed. Helen Damico, with Donald Fennema and Karmen Lenz (New York and London: Garland, 1998), 3–17. Berkhout's bibliography provides a splendid guide to sources and scholarship on

had undertaken the study of Old English, and the transcription may have been an early assignment as he entered the employ of Cecil. Nowell remained attached to the household until 1567, when he departed for travel and study in Europe, a trip from which he never returned. He left his papers and books for safekeeping with his friend and fellow scholar, William Lambarde, in 1567, and Lambarde drew upon them as he developed his own translations and editions thereafter.[35]

As a student of Old English, Nowell's main interests seem to have been the Anglo-Saxon Chronicle and the laws of the Anglo-Saxon kings. He continued to work with his transcripts in Nw and to copy and collate other versions of these texts as they came to hand. Along the way, he also worked with the Exeter Book, in which he began an interlinear gloss of *Christ I*; the *Beowulf* manuscript (now also called the Nowell codex) wherein he inscribed his *ex libris*; the Chronicle poems; *Cædmon's Hymn* from the Old English translation of Bede; and, of course, *SF*. But, as Berkhout observes, he had little affinity for Old English poetry. Whereas Nowell may have recognized from the diction and alliteration of a text that he was copying poetry, he made errors in transcription that reveal an incomplete grasp of poetic meter and compounds.[36] These shortcomings, among others, can be seen in his transcriptions of *SF*, *Cædmon's Hymn*, and the Chronicle poems copied into Nw.[37] Although he rarely

---

Nowell and his work. For such details as are known of his lineage and life, see Carl T. Berkhout, "The Pedigree of Laurence Nowell the Antiquary," *English Language Notes* 23, no. 2 (1985): 15–26.

35   For more on this point, see Berkhout, "Laurence Nowell," 8, 11–12, and Rebecca Brackmann, *The Elizabethan Invention of Anglo-Saxon England* (Cambridge: D. S. Brewer, 2012), 96–8. Lambarde used Nw for his own editions after Nowell's disappearance.

36   Berkhout, "Laurence Nowell," 10–11.

37   Nowell's textual variants are indicated by Elliott Van Kirk Dobbie in his edition of *Cædmon's Hymn* in *The Anglo-Saxon Minor Poems* (New York: Columbia University Press, 1942), 106. For the Chronicle poems, see Lutz, *Die Version G*, 84–87 for *The Battle of Brunanburh*; *The Capture of the Five Boroughs*, 87–88; *The Coronation of Edgar*, 90–91; *The Death of Edgar*, 91–93. In Nw, all five poems are copied as prose. The Chronicle poems, however, show pointing after many half-lines in patterns

Introduction

overlooked words and never transposed them in poetry (where other copies survive for comparison), Nowell omitted some inflectional endings, separated simplexes and compounds he did not recognize, and occasionally combined words by running them together.[38] As a result, editorial challenges abound in his copies of poetry, but usually the meter and alliteration are discernible.

Nowell's copy of Ot in Nw preserves nearly all of the original contents including the unique version of *SF*, yet this work was unknown to modern scholars until March 1934, when the British Museum received eight volumes of Nowell transcripts plus a number of printed books owned and annotated by him.[39] When the deputy keeper of manuscripts, Robin Flower, recommended—on behalf of Idris Bell, the keeper—that the Museum trustees accept the items offered by collector Lord Howard de Walden, he stressed the importance of the transcript of Ot and especially "the poem on the fasts of the church." The recommendation added that "the poem has hitherto only been known from the quotation of the first few lines in Wanley's catalogue of Anglo-Saxon MSS. The transcript thus restores a long Anglo-Saxon poem in alliterative verse, with the lines arranged in twenty-nine eight-line stanzas, a metrical form hitherto without parallel in Anglo-Saxon poetry."[40] Flower announced the gift to the public later that year and continued to study Nowell's

---

that closely resemble those found in the corresponding poems in CCCC 173, the presumed exemplar for Ot.

38   The one exception in *SF* occurs in line 220b, where Nowell transposed *me* and *þingað*, but then corrected the problem with insertion marks.

39   The transcripts are now BL Add. 43703–43710. In Add. 43703 Nowell did not copy a portion of the Bede text, the West Saxon royal genealogy, or the lists of Episcopal figures; see Torkar, *Eine altenglische Übersetzung*, 43, 47.

40   Details of the transaction, including the full contents of the recommendations to the trustees of the British Museum, appear in Andrew Prescott, "Robin Flower and Laurence Nowell," *Old English Scholarship and Bibliography: Essays in Honor of Carl T. Berkhout*, ed. Jonathan Wilcox, Old English Newsletter Subsidia 32 (Kalamazoo: Medieval Institute, Western Michigan University, 2004), 41–61.

work, one of his many interests.⁴¹ He planned to publish an edition of *SF*, but the project never reached fruition.

Nw contains 277 paper leaves, into which *SF* is copied on pages 257r–260v. The leaves measure 202 x 154 mm, but the size of the written space (approximately 155 x 100 mm) and the number of lines per page varies a bit.⁴² The poem begins with a large capital *wynn* about six lines from the top, with a total of twenty lines of text. The succeeding pages contain twenty-five lines of text until 260r, where a twenty-sixth line is squeezed in at the foot to complete stanza XXVI. The final page 260v ends with nineteen lines. The first word of each stanza begins at the left margin with a capital. The stanzas often conclude in the middle of a line with the remainder left blank, and they always end with a period. Sometimes the period is followed by Nowell's distinctive division mark described previously. Given Nowell's general fidelity to his source and his uneasy grasp of Old English poetry, it is probable that he imitated the format he saw in Ot, although he did not reproduce the *SF* text line for line.⁴³

Nowell seems likewise to have adopted some elements of script from his exemplar. As can be seen on fol. 257r, he alternates f-shaped *y* [ƪ], fan-shaped *y* [ẙ], hooked *y* [ẏ], and straight-limbed *y* [y]. He uses a minim for *i* that is hooked to the left at the top in certain environments, for example, following *h* and before *n*.⁴⁴ At times, he employs a

---

41   In his published essay devoted to the gift, Flower continued to feature *SF*: "Laurence Nowell and a Recovered Anglo-Saxon Poem," *British Museum Quarterly* 8 (1934): 130–32. In his 1935 address to the British Academy, Flower set the wider context for Nowell and his achievements: "Laurence Nowell and the Discovery of England in Tudor Times," *Proceedings of the British Academy* 21 (1935): 47–73.

42   Dammery, "The Law Code of King Alfred," 86.

43   *SF* filled six larger pages in Ot, as opposed to the eight pages used by Nowell in Nw. Meaney argues, however, that when copying the medical texts, Nowell tried to reproduce the line and possibly the page divisions of the original. See Audrey L. Meaney, "Variant Versions," 247.

44   This confusing feature is noted by Roy F. Leslie, "Textual Notes on *The Seasons for Fasting*," *JEGP* 52 (1953): 558; and Torkar, "Zu den ae. Medizinaltexten," 332.

high-backed *e* before *n* and occasionally elsewhere. He also uses three distinctive forms of abbreviation: ⁊ for *ge*, normally but not always as the prefix; a vertical line over the preceding letter to indicate a nasal, *m* or *n*; and ƥ for *þæt*. Although these forms appear consistently with few exceptions, it is difficult to know whether Nowell always found them in his exemplar. When Grant compared some of the surviving Bede text (in Hand 1) to Nowell's transcript, he found evidence of these three types of abbreviation, but Nowell seems not to have included them as consistently there as he did in his transcript of texts in Hand 2.[45]

Nowell corrected his work in *SF*, but of course not against other copies of the poem as he clearly did for some other texts, such as *Alfred-Ine*.[46] He may have had some difficulties reading Hand 2, especially the vowels *a*, *e*, and *o*. He corrects his transcription of the poem at least eight times for this type of confusion. There are two instances of an omitted *r* and one of *n* corrected to *r*. Spellings of *i* and *y* are the biggest problem, with Nowell correcting to *i* three times and to *y* six times. These and other examples, such as his corrections of false starts, omissions of letters, and misreading of letters and words, merge into the issue of Nowell's accuracy as a copyist. An early assessment by Alistair Campbell in appendix 1 of his edition of the Chronicle poem, *The Battle of Brunanburh*, published in 1938, points out that Nowell was careless in inserting or omitting final *e* and made minor mistakes such as those he corrected for in *SF*; however, Campbell believed that the *i/y* confusion lay in Otho B.xi. He judged Nowell's transcription of the Chronicle to be a generally accurate, diplomatic copy.[47] Sisam's analysis published in 1953 mentions the *i/y* problem as well as Nowell's *i* spellings for the expected *e* as in *ni* and *rædi*, "which are unlikely in

---

45 Raymond J. S. Grant, "Laurence Nowell's Transcript of BM Cotton Otho B.xi," *Anglo-Saxon England* 3 (1974): 118–20.
46 See the commentary by line for more specifics of Nowell's corrections.
47 Alistair Campbell, *The Battle of Brunanburh* (London: W. Heinemann, 1938), 133–44.

Manuscripts and Editions

a pre-Conquest MS."[48] Sisam observed that Nowell's errors tended to occur on the level of letter confusion and misreading.

As scholars have continued to work with Nw to produce editions of texts partly or completely lost from Ot, a consensus about Nowell's strengths and problems as a transcriber of Ot has emerged. There is general agreement that Nowell tried to reproduce what he saw in that manuscript. He sometimes omits letters, words, and even phrases, usually due to eyeskip, but these mistakes are relatively minor. Occasional examples of metathesis, dittography, and spelling anomalies appear, but confusion of letter forms is more frequent. In the course of his work on *Alfred-Ine*, Grant provides a useful summary of Nowell's mistakes, some of which—as in *SF*—result from difficulties reading Ot Hand 2.[49] Grant cites the vowel confusion, notably *e* and *a*, *o* and *u*, *a* and *o*, and *a* and *u*. Nowell interchanged þ and ð, as he did not seem to recognize a difference between the two. The written forms of certain consonants also misled him. The most common of these examples found in *SF* are *n/r* (Nowell's *fon* instead of *for*), *s/r* and *r/s* (*gewesed* for *gewered*), and *s/f* (*sæsten* for *fæsten*). In *SF*, Nowell also struggled with the letter *h*, copying it at least three times where it did not belong: line 85a *hæt* for *æt*, line 119 *hus* corrected to *us*, and line 205 *tæchð* for *tæcð*. In these cases, it appears that he wrote what he anticipated rather than reproducing the word or spelling before him. The variation in unstressed vowels of inflectional endings is a separate matter that could reflect the state of the language in Ot and/or Nowell's interventions. Individual examples of these and other anomalies are identified and discussed in the commentary.

---

48   Sisam, "Seasons of Fasting," in *Studies in the History of Old English Literature* (Oxford: Clarendon, 1953), 59, 59n1.
49   Raymond J. S. Grant, *Laurence Nowell, William Lambarde, and the Laws of the Anglo-Saxons*, Costerus New Series 108 (Amsterdam and Atlanta: Rodopi, 1996), 27–28. Grant's earlier work, "Laurence Nowell's Transcript," identifies many of the same types of errors in Nowell's copy of the Bede text written by Hand 1.

2.3 Previous Editions of Seasons for Fasting

With its unusual history and obvious flaws, *SF* has offered interesting challenges for editors. The poem was first edited by E.V.K. Dobbie in 1942, in volume 6 of the Anglo-Saxon Poetic Records.[50] He emended the text conservatively by correcting some of the obvious copying errors and the endings on nouns and verbs (and one definite article). His notes are primarily linguistic, supplemented by Biblical citations and liturgical information. Some ten years later, F. Holthausen re-edited the poem, numbering the stanzas and inserting macrons over long vowels and diphthongs.[51] He adopted many of Dobbie's emendations and contributed some of his own. Among other "improvements," Holthausen regularized the use of *i* and *y* spellings, corrected the accidence, and substituted "better" readings (for example, *beorhtlic* for *þeodlic*, line 86) for those he thought weak. His notes offer additional Biblical citations and source suggestions and query the meaning of certain words and phrases. These pointers indicate new areas of investigation that scholars have pursued over the years, such as the possible allusion to Malachi 2:7 in *SF*, line 136.[52] However, Holthausen often fails to explain his new readings, such as the example cited for line 86, so we are left to guess the reasoning behind the substitution.

In 1970, the first of two doctoral dissertations with editions of *SF* appeared. Hoyt Greeson's work (University of Oregon) pairs *SF* and the *Menologium*, which he describes as "observance poems."[53] Pioneering at the time, his research on manuscripts and language is now, understandably, out of date. Greeson's commentary on the historical milieu,

---

50 Elliott Van Kirk Dobbie, *The Anglo-Saxon Minor Poems*: introduction, xcii–xciv; bibliography, clxx; text, 98–104; nn pages 194–98.
51 Ferdinand Holthausen, "Ein altenglisches Gedicht über die Fastenzeiten," *Anglia* 71 (1952–53): 191–201.
52 See the commentary to lines 136–38.
53 Hoyt St. Clair Greeson Jr., *Two Old English Observance Poems: 'Seasons for Fasting'* and 'The Menologium' (PhD diss., University of Oregon, 1970). As shown in "Sources and Influences," the poems in fact have little in common.

structure, and art of the poem, however, provides a thorough analysis of the controversy over the dates of Ember fasts. He also considers the issue of clerical abuses that may tie *SF* to the circle of Archbishop Wulfstan. Greeson's stanza-by-stanza analysis, which lacks a conclusion to bring the observations into focus, remains useful for the additional sources and influences identified. He presents the text of *SF* in numbered stanzas covering about half of each page, followed by a prose translation below. In the textual notes, Greeson comments on the emendations of Dobbie and Holthausen, as well as of other scholars such as Sisam who published suggestions before 1970. Greeson's use of this material is thoughtful and often enlightening, as indicated in the commentary to the present edition. He also includes a thorough glossary and a bibliography.

Chadwick Hilton's 1982 dissertation (University of Tennessee), which provided the genesis of the present edition, adds some new aspects to the consideration of the poem.[54] In a section on the style of *SF*, he provides numerous examples of variation, compounding, and analogy, the last defined as a more complex type of metaphor. In a novel reading of the structure of the poem, Hilton shows how groups of stanzas work together and argues that the transitions between topics are more logical than had been appreciated by previous commentators. He also demonstrates an "exemplum and response" pattern that he believes accounts for the internal structure of the three large sections of the poem. His analysis of the literary context of *SF* is especially strong, as he delineates its debts to the prose writers Ælfric and Wulfstan and its uniqueness within the Anglo-Saxon poetic tradition. Hilton also includes a verse-by-verse translation and commentary.

Soon after the appearance of Greeson's dissertation, Anita L. Puckett wrote a master's thesis (University of North Carolina, Chapel Hill, 1973) presenting a translation of *SF* based on Dobbie's edition, with copious references to Holthausen's and Greeson's works. Most of the introductory material is derived from previous scholarship,

---

54   Chadwick Buford Hilton Jr., *An Edition and Study of the Old English 'Seasons for Fasting'* (PhD diss., University of Tennessee, 1983).

but Puckett adds some useful observations about metrical stress and style, calling attention to the poet's effective use of verbal transition. The translation is accompanied by textual notes, based primarily on earlier editions.[55]

In 1981, Maria Grimaldi published an edition of *SF* in which she used Dobbie's text but drew upon the more recent scholarship of Sisam, Whitbread, Ker, Holthausen, Schabram, Greeson, and Grant, for an introduction and textual notes.[56] Another edition and translation of *SF* appeared in a 2012 anthology entitled *The Old English Shorter Poems*, edited by Christopher A. Jones.[57] Jones adapts his text from Dobbie's edition with some modifications, many based on more recent scholarship, and collates it with Nw. To this he adds a brief commentary primarily explicating some points of his translation. Besides these editions, a number of scholars, including Hilton and Richards, have published notes and articles concerning textual and interpretive issues in *SF*. References to such works appear throughout the present edition, especially in the commentary.

3. Metrical and Linguistic Features

Although the poem's present state can challenge metrical and linguistic analysis, *SF* has many interesting features to compare with other late Old English poetry. As noted in this study and elsewhere, especially in work by Sisam, Stanley, and Whitbread, the poem's greatest affinity is with the Old English metrical *Creed*, all the more striking because *Creed* is only fifty-eight lines long and has a single source, the Apostles' Creed

---

55   Anita M. Puckett, *The Old English Seasons for Fasting: A Translation* (master's thesis, University of North Carolina, Chapel Hill, 1973).
56   Maria Grimaldi, "The Seasons for Fasting," *Annali Istituto Universitario Orientale Napoli, Filologia Germanica* 24 (1981): 71–85.
57   *The Old English Shorter Poems*, ed. and trans. Christopher A. Jones, vol. 1, *Religious and Didactic* (Cambridge: Harvard University Press, 2012), 156–73, 359–61, 402–406.

Metrical and Linguistic Features

from the Benedictine Office.[58] These and related poems—such as *JDay II* and, more distantly, *Menologium*—give evidence of a late tenth/early eleventh-century school of ecclesiastical poetry derived from Latin sources in verse and prose as well as Old English religious prose. The poems share many features characteristic of late Old English poetry with *The Battle of Maldon* but do not employ a heroic vocabulary and, in fact, offer little narrative action. Rather, they present basic Christian doctrine and information about observance, and their artistry is unique.

One special feature is the use of stanzas. The *SF* poet crafted the structure of the poem with eight-line stanzas, a feature that *SF* shares in part with *Creed*.[59] In *SF*, this plan is followed regularly with the exception of three stanzas, one of six lines (stanza IV), one of nine (stanza XV), and the last stanza (XXIX), which breaks off after line 230a. It appears that a copyist, possibly Nowell, omitted the final two lines of stanza IV.[60] Regarding stanza XV, the poet may have lost count of the lines, as the ninth line (119),

gif us þære duguþe hwæt   dryhten sylleð
[if the Lord gives us the means of salvation]

adds little meaning to the previous eight.[61] The stanzas themselves observe a syntactical regularity that reinforces their function as a unit

---

58 James M. Ure's analysis of *Creed* in *The Benedictine Office: An Old English Text* (Edinburgh: University of Edinburgh Press, 1957) is the most thorough to date. See esp. 55–56, 71, and 124–25. Ure edits the poem on 87–89.

59 *Creed* has six stanzas of eight lines separated by lines of Latin verse. The poem concludes with eleven lines of macaronic verse. E. G. Stanley recognizes the SF poet's innovation in "Old English Poetic Vocabulary: 'The formal word precise but not pedantic,'" in *Essays on Old, Middle, Modern English and Old Icelandic*, ed. Loren C. Gruber, Meredith Crellen Gruber, and Gregory K. Jember (Lewiston, ME: Edwin Mellen, 2000), 178.

60 See the commentary for lines 25–30. Three stanzas—V, XVII, XXVI—conclude with such a couplet.

61 This line could be the work of the poet; see commentary to line 119.

Introduction

of thought. That is, thirteen of the twenty-eight complete stanzas, as punctuated in this edition, are comprised of one full sentence.[62] Three additional stanzas have two or three independent clauses that break in the middle of a line, with the final clause concluding at the end of the stanza.[63] The poet's heavy use of parataxis complicates decisions about punctuation, but no stanza begins with *And*, as might be the case if the conjunction were used as a syntactic marker.[64] This means that clauses beginning with *and* are set off by commas within larger syntactical structures (in modern editions). As visual reinforcement, capitals in Nw open each stanza but appear elsewhere only for *Sancte* in line 100. Nowell probably adopted the format he found in Ot, for the same practice is followed in *Creed*, found uniquely in Oxford, Bodley MS Junius 121, where only *Sanctan* (line 30) is otherwise capitalized.[65] This attention to form may have been customary in copies of stanzaic poetry from the eleventh century, but in the case of *SF*, the careful presentation belies its prosaic subject matter.

3.1 Meter and Alliterative Patterns

Despite the many indications of loosening metrical restrictions in the early eleventh century and of problems in Laurence Nowell's transcription process, his copy of *SF* has very few defective verses—five in

---

62   These are stanzas I, IV (short), VI, VII, VIII, IX, X, XII, XV (long), XVI, XXII, XXIII, and XXIV. This edition corrects my statements in "Prosaic Poetry: Late Old English Poetic Composition," in *Old English and New: Studies in Language and Linguistics in Honor of Frederic G. Cassidy*, ed. Joan H. Hall, Nick Doane, and Dick Ringler (New York and London: Garland, 1992), 65. Stanley, "Old English Poetic Vocabulary," 182, takes the one-sentence stanzas as evidence that verse paragraphs persisted until the end of the Old English period.
63   Stanzas XI, XIII, and XXI divide in this manner.
64   Of the nine instances of *ac* "but," in contrast to *and*, two of these begin stanzas: V and XXVII.
65   See Junius 121, fols. 46r, line 10–47r, line 18.

Metrical and Linguistic Features

all.[66] Based on his general fidelity as a copier of poetry in that he rarely omitted and, as the comparative evidence indicates, never transposed words without correction, one can make a reasonably accurate metrical description of *SF*. The analysis that follows takes into account problematic readings in the text, and in the few cases where these may interfere with the description, they are left aside. What emerges are a number of features associated with late verse, especially *Maldon*. Whereas *SF* has elements of form and vocabulary in common with poems such as *Creed* and *JDay II*, the fact that these are translated from Latin makes an original poem such as *Maldon* a more useful comparator in respect to rhythm. There are, for example, twenty-one A3 verses in *SF* as it now stands, some of these short—that is, alliterating on a short syllable. Type A3 always appears in the on-verse, in *SF* comprising 9 percent of the on-verses, or 4.5 percent of total verses in the poem. As Hutcheson has shown, *Maldon* also has a high proportion of A3 verses, one of that poem's "metrical peculiarities," but its 3.7 percent falls short of the usage in *SF*.[67]

In all, there are some 202 type A verses in *SF* excluding the A3 verses and three defective verses where part is missing but the second foot is clearly type A. The majority of type A appears in the off-verse (162 instances).[68] In fact, stanzas XV and XVII have only A types in the

---

66   Four defective verses (lines 23a, 44b, 70b, 173b) result from omission of one or more words, probably copying errors. The fifth example, the defective line 92a, possibly resulting from another such problem,

    ac þu þæt sylf heald

is remedied to a B verse with the emendation to *sylfe*. Thus a caveat: enumerated examples, percentages, and descriptive statements about the versification and language of *SF* must always be considered approximate. The five verse types defined by Eduard Sievers in *Altgermanische Metrik* (Halle: Niemeyer, 1893) and refined by subsequent theorists as noted shortly, underlie the metrical analysis offered in this edition.

67   B. R. Hutcheson, *Old English Poetic Metre* (Cambridge: D. S. Brewer, 1995), 38, 198–99.

68   This figure bears out Puckett's observation in "A Translation," 27 that "around 75 percent of the b lines scan as Siever's type A."

off-verses. There are 118 B verses and seventy-four C verses in the poem. A total of thirty-one examples of D1, D2, and D3 appear, but only six of type E. The total of C, D, and E verses amounts to 26.5 percent of the poem, a figure slightly higher than the 24.5 percent in *Maldon*, according to Cable's figures.[69] Approximately 8 percent of the *SF* verses are types D and E, even fewer than the 10 percent Scragg cites for *Maldon*.[70] The comparisons suggest that the traditional dating of *SF* to the early eleventh century is correct, metrically speaking.

As Scragg has noted, A3 verses appear in *Maldon* along with verses of other types that alliterate only on the second lift, symptomatic of late poetry.[71] He cites B, C, and E examples, whereas *SF* has A and D verses—a total of five—showing this pattern.[72] For the *SF* poet, the A3 verses seem to have been integral to the process of composition, which partly explains their higher frequency than found in *Maldon*. Although not limited to the role, the A3 verses in *SF* often carry formulaic information about fasting. For example, the phrase *on þam monþe* appears as *SF* lines 49a, 61a, and 69a; *on þære wucan* serves as *SF* lines 58a, 67a, and 72a. A further stipulation appears in the A3 verse *butan hine unhæl*, line 84a. Recounting Moses's role in the Lenten fast, A3 verses are used in lines 111a and 117a. In fact, the *SF* poet seems to resort to A3 usage when he is striving to make a point, as indicated by the emphasis on specific times in the previous examples. While composing, he selects the word needed in the on-verse and then builds the rest of the line. This method is not limited to A3 verses, as can be seen in stanzas VII, VIII, IX, and X, where strings of on-verses convey the specifics of the dates for Ember fasts, but in fact A3s make up at least one-third of each string in these stanzas as well.[73]

---

69   Thomas Cable, "Metrical Style as Evidence for the Date of *Beowulf*," in *The Dating of Beowulf*, ed. Colin Chase, Toronto Old English Series 6 (1981; repr., Toronto: University of Toronto Press, 1997), 79–80.
70   D. G. Scragg, ed., *The Battle of Maldon* (Manchester: Manchester University Press, 1981), 30.
71   Scragg, *Battle of Maldon*, 30, 53n148.
72   A: lines 17a, 89a, 91a, 100a; D1: line 225a.
73   See *SF*, lines 58–62, 67–70, 72–73.

Metrical and Linguistic Features

Several features of A-type verses in *SF* testify further to its late date of composition. Scragg observes that in *Maldon* most such verses in the first half-line employ double alliteration.[74] This trend holds true for *SF* in twenty-eight instances out of a total forty-three (excluding A3 verses). The situation in *SF* is, however, more complicated than that Scragg describes for *Maldon*. Beyond the use of double alliteration in type A on-verses (xx/xy), in *SF* we find crossed alliteration (xy/xy) in a variety of rhythmical patterns: in line 9 with paired A verses; in line 110 with B and A verses; in line 169 with A and C verses; and in line 192 with C and A verses. Then, among the fifteen type A on-verses with only one alliterating syllable, there are six instances in *SF* (lines 17a, 65a, 73a, 88a, 91a, 169a) of Bliss's Type IA*1a verse, which violate his requirement of double alliteration.[75] This type has one or more extra unstressed syllables between the feet of the on-verse and normally alliterates on both stresses; the lack of double alliteration here is another symptom of late Old English poetry. Finally, Russom's observation that very late Old English poetry like *Maldon* shows "wholesale displacement" of two-word A1 verses to the second half of the line helps explain the preponderance of type A in off-verses in *SF*.[76] Some 96 percent of two-word A1 examples in *Maldon* occur in the off-verse, comparable to 90 percent (fifty-eight out of a total sixty-four) in *SF*. As Russom explains, owing to complications caused in the on-verse by a growing reliance on anacrusis to carry function words, poets responded by "shift[ing] metrically simpler variants to the b-verse."[77]

Maldon's relatively loose hierarchy of alliterating forms is paralleled in the *SF* poet's practice of employing a finite verb in the head-stave. This

---

74 Scragg, *Battle of Maldon*, 30.
75 A. J. Bliss, *The Metre of Beowulf* (Oxford: Blackwell, rev. ed. 1967), discusses such verses as a feature of late Old English verse on 100–103. .
76 Geoffrey Russom, "Dating Criteria for Old English Poems," in S*tudies in the History of the English Language: A Millennial Perspective*, ed. Donka Minkova and Robert Stockwell (Berlin and New York: Mouton de Gruyter, 2002), 248–49.
77 Russom, "Dating Criteria," 249.

happens fourteen times in *SF*, so frequently that it becomes a metrical feature of the poem.⁷⁸ The heaviest use of finite verbs to set the alliteration occurs in the final section of the poem, with seven examples in a total of sixty-two lines serving part three's distinctive hortative style. Describing such effects in *Maldon*, Griffith argues that such "irregularities might be an aspect of the poet's artistry and integral to his composition."⁷⁹ That said, there are twenty-four examples of stressed auxiliary verbs in *SF*, including ten forms of *sculan* and five of *hafan*, which seem to result from necessity rather than artistry. Moreover, fourteen pronouns carry stress, including three different forms of the personal pronoun that set the alliteration for the line in 61b, 69b, and 180b. These are not pronouns displaced for emphasis, as one finds in *Maldon*. Rather, the *SF* poet composes in his own rhythmic style, different from that of classical Old English poetry but not identical to any other.⁸⁰

Just as he revises the traditional hierarchy of ictus-bearing words in the alliterative line, the *SF* poet weakens the caesura by separating nouns and their modifiers and the constituents of verb phrases. This feature, also seen in *Maldon*, seems to result from privileging metrical requirements over syntax, though occasionally it may have an aesthetic purpose.⁸¹ Of the nine instances of noun/modifier separation in *SF*,

---

78   E. G. Stanley discusses the feature in "Verbal Stress in Old English Verse," *Anglia* 93 (1975): 307–21. The *SF* verses with finite verbs setting the alliteration are lines 5, 15, 16, 18, 90, 153, 156, 194, 206, 215, 217, 221, 222, 225.
79   M. S. Griffith, "Alliterative Licence and the Rhetorical Use of Proper Names in *The Battle of Maldon*," in *Prosody and Poetics in the Early Middle Ages: Essays in Honour of C. B. Hieatt*, ed. M. J. Toswell (Toronto: University of Toronto Press, 1995), 61. The essay's focus on proper names allows for little comparison with *SF*, which has few of these.
80   Thomas Cable revises the hierarchy of lexical categories of stress in Old English verse in *The English Alliterative Tradition* (Philadelphia: University of Pennsylvania Press, 1991), 22. Pronouns and auxiliaries fall under "Nonictus-bearing . . . but promotable."
81   R. D. Fulk, *A History of Old English Meter* (Philadelphia: University of Pennsylvania Press, 1992), 260. See also Scragg, *Battle of Maldon*, 29.

Metrical and Linguistic Features

of style and vocabulary with *SF*, only hints at rhyme.[91] The rhyming phrase *fæsten gelæsten* (*SF*, line 71a) is weakened in *Creed*, line 40, to

   and mid fæstum sefan   freode gelæstan

where *fæstum* is used as an adjective and falls within the on-verse. *SF* has a similar example, but with noun and finite verb separated, in line 150, where the effect is more assonance than rhyme:

   gif we þæt fæsten her   fyrena gelæstað

Among later ecclesiastical poetry, *JDay II* has a remarkable number of rhymes, as Stanley points out, in lines 3, 6, 82, 147, 266, with inexact rhymes in lines 28, 126.[92] However, even more examples appear in *SF*, involving at least ten rhyming elements. In addition to lines 6–7a, there are rhymes at lines 36–37 (near), 71b, 85a, 150, 153, 174 (near), 193b, 202a–203a, and 203b–204. The last examples involve repetition, but the phrases do rhyme. In fact, echoes of sound are so prevalent in *SF*, as in line 187a *folce gynd foldan*, that it can be difficult to distinguish assonance from rhyme. There may be little subtlety in the poet's use of sound, but he clearly made an effort to enhance his work aurally.

3.3 Syntactical Elements

Beyond the syntactical features of *SF* already covered, most prominently those related to the caesura, two further kinds of syntactic

---

91   Richard Dance describes the artistry of the sound effects in *Maldon* in "'Þær wearð hream ahafen': A Note on Old English Spelling and the Sound of *The Battle of Maldon*," in *The Power of Words: Anglo-Saxon Studies Presented to Donald G. Scragg on his Seventieth Birthday*, ed. Hugh Magennis and Jonathan Wilcox (Morgantown: West Virginia University Press, 2006), 278–317.

92   E. G. Stanley, "Rhymes in English Medieval Verse: from Old English to Middle English," in *Medieval English Studies Presented to George Kane*, ed. Edward Donald Kennedy, Ronald Waldron, and Joseph S. Wittig (Wolfeboro, NH: D. S. Brewer, 1988), 25.

Introduction

developments characteristic of late Old English poetry appear in *SF*. One such feature is the decline in the use of poetic compounds, which Fulk describes as possibly attributable to a decline in secondary stress.[93] Owing to Nowell's uncertain copying of compounds, a few examples in *SF* remain doubtful, but overall the situation is clear. Although there are at least twenty-one compounds (plus two repeats) in the poem, including seventeen nominal compounds, this number represents about one-half the frequency that Fulk calculates for other late poems such as *Maldon* and *Menologium*.[94] Several factors may contribute to the *SF* poet's lexical choices, but mostly he seems to have had problems incorporating compounds into the line. In all except two of the twenty-three instances, the compound appears in the on-verse, suggesting that he had to build the line with it, just as he did with other essential words relating to the specifics of fasting.

Second, about 50 percent of the lines in *SF* are end-stopped, a prominent feature of the poet's work and one consistent with a late date of composition. By comparison, Scragg cites "more than a third [in *Maldon*], twice the proportion found in earlier poems."[95] Caie states that more than 200 of the 305 lines in *JDay II* have this feature, which he suggests may result from its Latin source, which is composed in end-stopped hexameters.[96] While not influenced by a single source or model, the syntactical features in *SF* once again suggest that the poet's message, incorporating both Latin and Old English prose sources, drove the creative process. Aesthetics and poetics, including the deployment of compounds and variety in metrical and syntactical structures, were secondary considerations. Simply put, the poet of *SF* may have held a different view of poetry from his contemporaries who composed heroic

---

93   Fulk, *History*, 253–56.
94   Fulk, *History*, 254–55. Scragg, *Battle of Maldon*, 32, cites "more than sixty" nominal compounds in the 325-line poem, or one in five lines. The figure in SF is about one in twelve lines.
95   Scragg, *Battle of Maldon*, 53, 53n142.
96   Caie, "*Judgement Day II*," 51.

Metrical and Linguistic Features

poems (*Maldon*) or who translated from a single Latin source (*JDay II, Creed*), and he certainly had a different set of challenges in his material.

3.4 Linguistic Features

The two areas to be considered here are phonology and accidence, both from the perspective of dating and assigning dialect features to *SF*. Despite a textual history that has led to some obvious errors and certain problems more difficult to interpret, *SF* is remarkably consistent in many aspects of its language. Furthermore, because the poet employs a fairly restricted vocabulary and repeats key words and phrases, there are often several internal witnesses to consult when questions of usage arise. The best external comparators for the language of *SF* are *Maldon* and *JDay II*. As will be clear, both the sounds and inflections in *SF* are those of late Old English (lOE) and late West Saxon (lWS):

(1) *i* and *y*: there is significant confusion between these in *SF*, evidenced, for instance, by the alternate forms of pret. 3. sing. of *dihtan*, *dyhte* (line 95b) and *dihte* (line 123b); nevertheless, specific examples of lWS developments can be seen
    a. Rounding between labials and *l*: *abylgþ, wyle*
    b. Rounding before *r*: *fyra*[97]
    c. *y* for *e* in the group *sel*: *syllan* (all forms), *sylf* (all forms)[98]
    d. *i* for *y* before palatal consonants and nasals: *hicganne, hige, higefæste, mihta, nihta, þinceð*[99]
(2) Smoothing: *egum, mihte* < *magan, nehstan*, possibly *nanuht* < *nanwiht*[100]
(3) Parasiting: *æbyligþe, fyligan, þegen*[101]

---

97   Karl Luick, *Historische Grammatik der englischen Sprache* (Leipzig: Tauchniz, 1921) 1:§285.
98   A. Campbell, *Old English Grammar* (Oxford: Clarendon, 1959), §325.
99   Scragg, *Battle of Maldon*, 23; Campbell, *Old English Grammar*, §301, §316.
100   Campbell, *Old English Grammar*, §767; Scragg, *Battle of Maldon*, 23; Greeson, *Two Old English Observance Poems*, 17.
101   Campbell, *Old English Grammar*, §365.

(4) Loss of palatal *g*: *asæde*
(6) Weakening of unstressed vowels: *atele, æreste < ærist, besyredon, hlutter, dogera*
(7) Velar *ng* for *nc*: *dreng, þingað, wlangum*

With the exception of *asæde* and *nanuht,* the examples given here represent multiple citations, so we can be fairly confident that they reflect linguistic features rather than copying errors. In addition to the *i/y* alternation, there is confusion in the treatment of OE diphthongs—*bearn/ beorn, læran/ leoran, helpan/ heolp, heoldan/ healdaþ, heowan/ hewan*—in numerous attestations, affecting stressed vowels and diphthongs in several environments. These problems may result from Nowell's difficulty in reading and copying vowels, but in any case they are not helpful to a linguistic description of the text.

Pronouns, nouns, and adjectives offer some additional evidence for lWS dating. Third-person plural pronoun forms in *SF* of note are: nom. pl. *hi*; gen. pl. *hyra, hiora*; dat. pl. *heom*.[102] The accidence of nouns and adjectives is generally conservative with only slight indication of leveling. Among nouns showing leveling are acc. sing. masc. *andfenge*; nom. pl. neut. *mægena*; acc. pl. masc. *stæppon*; dat. sing. neut. *fæstenne*. The dat. fem. of strong adjectives shows special confusion: sing. *eallum, full*; pl. *ure*. Other adjectives with non-standard endings are strong acc. sing. masc. *hali* (lWS);[103] weak nom. sing. fem. *mære*; strong acc. pl. neut. *wancule*. Although adjective endings in particular may reflect Nowell's mistakes, overall these examples are evidence of lWS.

Among verb forms, the evidence for dating and dialect is somewhat more pronounced, with variation in unstressed vowels that reflects Marckwardt's findings for late Old English.[104] To wit, in *SF* the present

---

102 Campbell, *Old English Grammar*, §289.
103 Campbell, *Old English Grammar*, §267.
104 Albert H. Marckwardt, "Verb Inflections in Late Old English," in *Philologica: The Malone Anniversary Studies*, ed. Thomas A. Kirby and Henry Bosley Woolf (Baltimore: Johns Hopkins University Press, 1949), 79–88.

Metrical and Linguistic Features

plural subjunctive endings of the verb divide between *-an* (twelve examples) and *-on* (five examples). These subjunctives are the forms in which changes seem to occur the earliest. By contrast, in *SF* the pret. indic. 3 sing. shows possible vowel confusion only in two instances of *-ude* for *-ede* (*firude*) and *-ode* (*costude*). The pret. indic. pl. has *sohtan* and *leordun*, but otherwise shows the standard Old English endings. The pres. indic. 3 sing. of *þincan* occurs once as *þingað* and once as the expected *þinceð*. In the past participle, we find three unusual weak forms: the inflected *forþegide* < *forþecgan*; *gestrangud* < *gestrengan*; *gewered* < *gewerian*; and a fourth strong, lWS *cymene* < *cuman*. All of the infinitives in *SF* end in *an*, the last part of the verb to be affected by leveling, according to Marckwardt.[105] Among auxiliaries, forms of *beon/wesan* are standard with the exception of pret. sing. subj. *wese*, used twice, a lWS form.[106] Inverted pl. *hæbbe we* is a WS form of *habban*, as is pres. 3 sing. *hafað*, a form that may derive from WS prose.[107] Pret./pres. *magan* has lWS pret. 3 sing. *mihte*.[108] Forms of *sculan* and *willan* follow the expected patterns, although there are numerous examples of WS *sceo-* in the present and the preterite of *sculan*.[109]

In summary, confusion of unstressed vowels and case endings in *SF* is less prevalent than might be anticipated, given the presumed date of composition and transmission history of the text. Of course, one should not draw conclusions from individual examples, but overall, the language of *SF* seems to allow substitution of *u* for *e* and *o* in weak preterite endings. Furthermore, evidence of lOE and lWS changes is sufficiently spread throughout the grammatical categories to support an early eleventh-century date of composition for *SF*.

---

105   Marckwardt, "Verb Inflections," 87.
106   Campbell, *Old English Grammar*, §768.
107   Campbell, *Old English Grammar*, §762.
108   Campbell, *Old English Grammar*, §767.
109   Campbell, *Old English Grammar*, §179–80, §767.

4. Sources and Influences

Seasons for Fasting emerges from a school of late Old English ecclesiastical poetry best known by the poems translated from the Benedictine Office, *JDay II*, and *Menologium*. *SF* is also topical in part, with connections to late historical poetry such as *Maldon*. Its sources, however, appear primarily in ecclesiastical prose, especially materials associated with the homilists Ælfric and Wulfstan. In general, the types and contents of these sources support the poem's three-part structure. Even the Biblical references, documented in the commentary, support this model and appear only in the first two sections. As the analysis that follows makes clear, we cannot identify the exact manuscripts, or even the precise texts in some cases, used by the *SF* poet, but we can achieve a very good sense of the ecclesiastical and textual culture that inspired his work.

4.1 The Ember Dates Controversy (lines 1–102)

The title bestowed by editors in the twentieth century highlights the first and, some would say, most interesting portion of *SF* devoted to the proper celebration of Ember fasts. Known in Anglo-Saxon England as *ymbrendagas* or *ymbrenfæstena*, these seasonal fasts were celebrated on Wednesday, Friday, and Saturday of designated weeks in late February or March, June, September, and December.[110] The *SF* poet addresses the controversy, current at the time, over the dates of the spring and summer fasts. According to English practice, first ascribed to the authority

---

110   For the origin and significance of Ember days, see Amalarius, *De ecclesiasticis officiis (Liber officialis)*, ed. J. M. Hanssens, *Amalarii Episcopi Opera Liturgica Omnia*, Studi e Testi 138–40 (Vatican, 1948–50), 1:II, pp. 201–205. For the specifics of days, readings, and English dates of the four fasts, see *Ælfwine's Prayerbook*, ed. Beate Günzel, Henry Bradshaw Society 108 (London: Boydell, 1993), 108–109. Although never used by the *SF* poet, the English term *ymbre* and its variants refer to the four seasonal fasts. The *OED* suggests that it could be a corruption of OE *ymbrene*, meaning "period or revolution of time," more specifically, "season or time of year." Ælfric uses *ymbre* and *ymbrene* with their different senses in his writings; citations can be found in the Concordance.

Sources and Influences

of Pope Gregory the Great by Ecgberht, Archbishop of York (735–66), the spring fast was to be observed in the first week of Lent and the summer fast in the week following Pentecost Sunday.[111] Continental practice differed from this schedule in fixing the spring and summer dates to the first week of March and second week of June respectively. Both calendars agreed on the third and fourth Ember fasts in the week of the autumnal equinox and the week prior to the Nativity.[112]

The English dates persisted without dispute until the aftermath of the Benedictine Revival, when calendars reflecting the continental usage began to appear at centers such as Worcester and Winchester.[113] Such was the level of resistance to the new practice that English legal and computistical materials drawn up in the late tenth/early eleventh century specified Gregory's dates as the correct ones to follow.[114] In royal legislation drafted by Archbishop Wulfstan about 1008–1009, a

---

111   For the ascription to Gregory, see Ecgberht's *Dialogus ecclesiasticae institutionis* (first and second seasonal fasts) in A. W. Haddan and W. Stubbs, *Councils and Ecclesiastical Documents Relating to Great Britain and Ireland*, (Oxford, 1869–71; repr. Oxford: Clarendon, 1964) 3:411–12. PL 139:441. A spurious canon stating Gregory's rule for the English on the Ember fasts is printed in Haddan and Stubbs, *Councils and Ecclesiastical Documents*, 3:52–53.

112   The regulations governing Ember days are discussed by C. G. Willis in *Further Essays in Early Roman Liturgy*, Alcuin Club Collections 50 (London: SPCK, 1968), 227–29. See also Heinrich Henel, *Studium zum altenglischen Computus* (Leipzig: Tauchnitz, 1934), 6064; and Sisam, "Seasons of Fasting," 49, 49n1.

113   Sisam, "Seasons of Fasting," 48–50.

114   For an enlightening discussion of the spiritual ties between Anglo-Saxon England and Rome, especially the conversion history originating from Gregory the Great, see Nicholas Howe, "Rome; Capital of Anglo-Saxon England," *Journal of Medieval and Early Modern Studies* 34 (2004): 147–72. Veronica Ortenberg details the liturgical and devotional exchanges between England and Rome in *The English Church and the Continent in the Tenth and Eleventh Centuries* (Oxford: Clarendon, 1992), 160–84, with reference to the Ember days at 160. Given the historical background to the English dates for the Ember fasts and the factors that provoked the controversy, Sarah Downey's suggestion that unease with excessive fasting lies behind the reference to Breton and Frankish influences seems off the mark. See "Too Much of Too Little: Guthlac and the Temptation of Excessive Fasting," *Traditio* 63 (2008): 124–26.

Introduction

directive about the observance of festivals and fasts includes the following statement about Ember fasts: *7 ymbren fæstena, swa swa Sanctus Gregorius Angelcynne sylf hit gedihte* (and Ember fasts, just as St. Gregory himself prescribed it for the English) (*Æþelred VI. 23*).[115] This injunction is amplified in texts for determining the Anglo-Saxon calendar, wherein computistical tables and charts often present information about the seasonal fasts. The highly influential computus—compiled about 978 in Winchester with surviving copies in BL Cotton Tiberius B.v, fols. 2r–19r, and in the contemporary Leofric Missal (Bodleian Library, MS. Bodley 579, fols. 38r–58r)—prescribes the English dates for Ember fasts. The Leofric Missal introduces them with a reminder of their origin: *Haec sunt ieiunia quae Sanctus Gregorius Genti Anglorum predicare precepit* (These are the fasts which St. Gregory prescribed publicly for the people of England).[116]

In the first section of *SF*, two works dealing with the Ember dates served as probable sources for the poet: Byrhtferth of Ramsey's *Enchiridion*, a commentary in Latin and Old English written to accompany his own version of the computus, and a Latin text on the Ember fasts associated with Archbishop Wulfstan. Byrhtferth composed the *Enchiridion* about 1011 as a means to instruct young priests on the basics of the computus.[117] While setting forth the English dates for Ember fasts

---

115   Liebermann, *Die Gesetze*, 1:252, §22.3–§23. The same admonition appears in the Latin version of this text.

116   Quoted from *The Leofric Missal*, ed. Nicholas Orchard, vol. 1, Henry Bradshaw Society 113 (London: Boydell, 2002), 92.

117   Peter S. Baker and Michael Lapidge, eds., *Byrhtferth's Enchiridion*, EETS s.s. 15 (Oxford: Oxford University Press, 1995). For a broader discussion of the sources and structure of *SF*, see Mary P. Richards, "Old Wine in a New Bottle: Recycled Instructional Materials in *Seasons for Fasting*," in *The Old English Homily: Precedent, Practice, and Appropriation*, ed. Aaron J. Kleist (Turnhout: Brepols, 2007), 345–64. Philippa Semper analyzes Byrhtferth's innovative presentation of his material in "Doctrine and Diagrams: Maintaining the Order of the World in *Byrhtferth's Enchiridion*," in *The Christian Tradition in Anglo-Saxon England: Approaches to Current Scholarship and Teaching*, ed. Paul Cavill (Cambridge: D. S. Brewer, 2004), 121–37.

in a diagram, Byrhtferth urged priests to know the correct dates and to observe the fasts accordingly:

Þæt sceolon preostas witan mid fullum gerade þæt feower ymbrenfæstenu beoð on twelf monðum. (lines 388–89)[118]
[Priests must know with perfect understanding that there are four Ember fasts in the twelve months.]

And ic þe bebeode þæt þu þa twelf ymbrendagas gehealde, and ealle þa ymbrendagas glædlice gehealde þe ealde uðwitan gesetton eallum folce to ecere blisse. (Postscript, lines 38–40)[119]
[And I exhort you to hold the twelve Ember days, and to joyously observe all the Ember days that scholars of old established for all people (as a means) to eternal bliss.]

Beyond admonitions resembling these in the first part of the poem, *SF* suggests a link to the *Enchiridion* through two technical terms in stanza VI. When he introduces Gregory's directions to the English, the poet uses the word *mearc*, meaning a "term" or, more precisely, "a lunar date from which a feast is calculated":[120]

*and we þa mearce sceolan
heoldan higefæste [ ] mid Anglum,
swa hie gebrefde us   beorn on Rome,
Gregorius,   gumena papa.* (*SF,* lines 43b–46)
[And we must keep those occasions resolutely among the English, just as the man in Rome, Gregory, the people's pope, wrote them down briefly for us.]

Mearc appears twice in Byrhtferth's explication of Latin mnemonic verses for determining the term of Easter. By using *mearc* in reference

---

118   Baker and Lapidge, *Enchiridion,* 81.
119   Baker and Lapidge, *Enchiridion,* 245.
120   Baker and Lapidge, *Enchiridion,* 452.

Introduction

to the Ember dates, the poet is able to convey the precise distinction between the English and continental practice.[121] The rarely-used *gebrefde* from this passage, literally "written down briefly," also appears in the *Enchiridion* in reference to directions for determining Leap Year and for the proper conduct of the Passover feast.[122] By employing this verb to characterize Gregory's prescription to the English nation, our poet likewise emphasizes the connection between the lunar calendar and the spiritual imperative. It seems, therefore, that the *SF* poet knew some of the terminology employed in Byrhtferth's handbook and probably a version of the computus as well. It is even possible that the traditional association of computistical materials with Latin mnemonic poems for reckoning the dates of Easter and Lent could have offered a model for poetic treatment of the seasonal fasts.

A Latin text on the Ember fasts, preserved in five manuscripts of the so-called Commonplace Book associated with Archbishop Wulfstan, may also have served as an important source for the *SF* poet.[123] *De ieiunio quattuor temporum* was first fully described and edited by James Cross in 1992.[124] This text occurs in two versions, the shorter of which is comprised of the introduction expanded by a statement of Gregory's prescription for the English.[125] Copies of the short version appear in Cambridge,

---

121 Richards, "Old Wine," 351–52.

122 Baker and Lapidge, *Enchiridion*, 437.

123 An important study of the collection appears in Hans Sauer, "The Transmission and Structure of Archbishop Wulfstan's 'Commonplace Book,'" in *Old English Prose: Basic Readings*, ed. Paul E. Szarmach with Deborah A. Oosterhouse, Basic Readings in Anglo-Saxon England 5 (New York and London: Garland, 2000), 339–93.

124 Cross expanded on Sauer's work, first published as "Zur Überlieferung und Anlage von Erzbischof Wulfstans 'Handbuch,'" *Deutsches Archiv für die Erforschung des Mittelalters* 36 (1980): 341–84. See J. E. Cross, "A Newly-Identified Manuscript of Wulfstan's 'Commonplace Book,' Rouen, Bibliothèque Municipale, MS 1382 (U. 109), fols. 173r–198v," *Journal of Medieval Latin* 2 (1992): 63–83.

125 The shorter version in CCCC 190, collated with the copy in Cotton Nero A.I, is printed by Bernhard Fehr, *Die Hirtenbriefe Ælfrics in altenglischer und lateinischer Fassung*, Bibliothek der angelsächsischen Prosa 9 (Hamburg: Henri Grand, 1914; repr. with

Sources and Influences

Corpus Christi College MS. 190, pp. 225–27, and BL, Cotton Nero A.i, part B, fols. 173r–174r.[126] Addressed to *fratres mei* (my brothers), the piece opens with the Old Testament origins of the seasonal fasts and closes with an exhortation to the audience to observe the fasts, avoid scandal, and comport themselves properly on fast days. Whereas none of the additional material in the longer version occurs in *SF*, this shorter text offers some close parallels to passages in the poem and shows the poet drawing from its descriptions of both the continental and English practices. The result in *SF* is a highly unusual fusion of the lunar dates with specific months, as can be seen in the description of the first Ember fast, which features the English date but also mentions March:

> *We þæt forme sceolan   fæsten heowan*
> *on þære ærestan   wucan lengtenes*
> *on þam monþe   þe man Martius*
> *geond Romwara   rice nemneð* . . . (*SF*, lines 47–50)
>
> [We must observe the first fast in the first week of Lent, in the month which is called March throughout the kingdom of Rome.]

---

a supplement by Peter Clemoes, (Darmstadt: Wissenschaftliche Buchgesellschaft, 1966), Anhang III: 14, 240–41. Cross, in "A Newly-Identified Manuscript," believed that the longer version was expanded "under the direction, at least, of Archbishop Wulfstan," 66. See further Thomas N. Hall, "Wulfstan's Latin Sermons," in *Wulfstan, Archbishop of York: The Proceedings of the Second Alcuin Conference*, ed. Matthew Townend (Turnhout: Brepols, 2004), 98–99, 99 n14.

126   H. R. Loyn, ed., *A Wulfstan Manuscript Containing Institutes, Laws and Homilies: British Museum Cotton Nero A.I*, Early English Manuscripts in Facsimile 17 (Copenhagen: Rosenkilde and Bagger, 1971), 53, attributes the text to pseudo-Theodore. According to Helmut Gneuss, *Handlist*, 33, CCCC 190, pp. 1–294, was copied in the first half of the eleventh century, possibly at Worcester, but moved to Exeter by the middle of the eleventh century. Cotton Nero A.i, fols. 70–177, dates from 1003x1023 from Worcester or York. An important study by Cristopher A. Jones, "Two Composite Texts from Archbishop Wulfstan's 'Commonplace Book': the *De ecclesiastica consuetudine* and the *Institutio beati Amalarii de ecclesiasticis officiis*," *Anglo-Saxon England* 27 (1998): 237–38, discusses the Ember Day selections in the context of their affiliations with other pieces in the collections.

Introduction

Comparable statements from the Latin source make similar points about the timing of this fast, the influence of Rome, and the month, "which the Romans call March":

> *Sed sanctus Gregorius hęc ieiunia genti Anglorum sic predicare precepit: Ieiunium primum in prima ebdomada quadragesime . . .* (Cross, p. 75)
> [But St. Gregory prescribed these fasts to the people of England thus: the first fast in the first week of Lent . . .]
>
> *Quae tempora ieiuniorum ita praecepit Romana auctoritas obseruare, ut in primo mense, quem Martium uocant* (Cross, p. 73)
> [The Roman authority undertook to observe times of fasting, as in the first month, which they call March]

In the Latin text, the first of these statements occurs in the interpolated passage about Gregory's prescription for the English. The second statement comes in a description of the rival continental practice, just preceding the interpolation.[127] Oddly enough, the poet seems to have taken wording from both, hence his confusing ascription of the English date to the Romans. Moreover, his subsequent references to the months of June (second fast) and September (third fast) echo those in the Latin source text stipulating the continental dates, while neither the poem nor the Latin text mentions December by name.

Still, the wording of parallel passages regarding the fourth (December) fast is very close. From *SF*:

> *We þæt feorþe sceolen   fæsten gelæsten*
> *on þære wucan   þe bið ærur full*
> *dryhtnes gebyrd . . .* (*SF*, lines 71–73a)
> [We must perform the fourth fast in the full week which will be complete before the birth of the Lord.]

---

127   The passages here are quoted in reverse order of their appearance in the Latin text to show how they are used by the *SF* poet.

Sources and Influences

Here the poet versifies the more concise statement of the interpolated Latin text, translating phrases for "the full week" "before the Lord's birth":

Ieiunium quartum in integra ebdomada ante natale Domini. (Cross, p. 75)
[The fourth fast (is) in the full week before the birth of the Lord.]

When the poet goes on to specify the days of the week for the four seasonal observances,

*On þissum fæstenum   is se feorþa dæg
and sixta samod   seofoþa getinge
to gelæstanne . . . (SF,* lines 79–81a)
[During these fasts, the fourth day and the sixth, together with the seventh immediately following, is to be performed . . .]

he may be drawing upon another directive in *De ieiunio*:

iiii et vi feria et sabbato ieiunandum sit. (Cross, p. 73)
[the fourth and sixth days and Saturdays should be observed as fast days.]

Noting that the autumn equinox as well as Christmas could fall on any day of the week, hence the need to specify that each fast should be observed for a full week, Sisam traces the difference in wording between *SF* lines 67b for autumn *(on þære wucan   þe ærur byð)* and 72b for Christmas *(on þære wucan   þe byð ærur full)* to the omission of *plena* from the corresponding passage on the autumnal fast as copied in CCCC 190.[128] His observation thus specifies the version of the source drawn upon by the poet.

In sum, this brief Latin text on Ember fasts seems to have supplied wording for some of the poet's key points in the first portion of *SF*,

---

128   Sisam, "Seasons of Fasting," 52–53.

Introduction

although he struggled to assimilate and convey the essentials. For basic information about the computus, he probably turned to Byrhtferth's handbook or a similar source, from which he adopted Old English terminology for determining movable feasts.[129] These contemporary materials in Latin and Old English offer a crucial view of the poet's working methods as he created poetry from prose.

4.2 Lenten Materials (lines 103–83)

SF's technical sources are relatively easy to trace, since the controversy over dates for Ember fasts—though alive from the tenth through the mid-eleventh century—did not receive extensive written coverage in Latin or English, as far as surviving materials indicate.[130] The Ember issue, however, accounts for just the first topic of *SF*, after which Lenten fasts and then lax priests move to the fore. As the poem proceeds, links to possible sources become more diffuse—and indeed, the poet may occasionally have worked from memory when his topic was less specific—yet many of the identifiable strands lead to two collections of texts treating similar themes: Wulfstan's Commonplace Book again, and a related set of manuscripts containing homilies and ecclesiastical materials, Oxford, Bodleian Library, MSS. Hatton 113–114 and Junius 121.[131] Sauer describes

---

129 Richards, "Old Wine," 355. Henel, *Studium*, 61, prints and collates two brief Old English texts, one presenting the continental dates (two copies) and the other the English dates, from mid-eleventh century manuscripts.

130 For background to continental influences during the reign of King Athelstan (924x929) and resistance to ensuing Benedictine reforms with Frankish roots, see Caroline Brett, "A Breton Pilgrim in England in the Reign of King Athelstan," in *France and the British Isles in the Middle Ages and Renaissance: Essays by Members of Girton College in Memory of Ruth Morgan*, ed. Gillian Jondorf and D. N. Dumville (Woodbridge, Suffolk: Boydell, 1991), 43–69, esp. 44–48.

131 On the role of memory in late Old English homiletic composition, see Mary Swan, "Memorialized Readings: Manuscript Evidence for Old English Homily Composition," *Anglo-Saxon Manuscripts and Their Heritage*, ed. Phillip Pulsiano and Elaine M. Treharne (Aldershot, UK: Ashgate, 1998), 205–17. Greeson, *Two Old English*

Sources and Influences

the Commonplace Book as a collection of canonical, liturgical, and homiletic writings assembled by the archbishop to help with his spiritual and administrative duties.[132] Nine of the eleven copies were produced during the eleventh century, most by mid-century. Hatton 113–114 and Junius 121, companion volumes copied at Worcester in the second half of the eleventh century, comprise another, slightly later, penitential and homiletic compilation for use in teaching and preaching. Hatton 113–114 contains one of five surviving collections of Archbishop Wulfstan's homilies, while Junius 121 is a version of the Commonplace Book.[133] The bulk of the materials were written by Wulfstan (d. 1023) and the homilist Ælfric (d. c. 1010) but collected in Hatton/Junius for Wulfstan II of Worcester, bishop from 1062–95.[134] The *SF* poet did not necessarily consult any of the specific manuscripts to be discussed; in fact, the Hatton/Junius collection probably postdates the poem. Rather, these compendia are indicative of the types of ecclesiastical writing and concerns that influenced the last two sections of *SF*.

The same two copies of the Commonplace Book preserving the key Latin text on the Ember dates also contain a rare Lenten source for the

---

Observance Poems, 82, 82n57, calls attention to the fact that "the order of exemplars for fasting reverses the order found in Missals for the Masses during Lent." Christ normally precedes Moses and Elijah, but the poet has chosen to begin with the Old Testament figures.

132   Sauer, "Transmission and Structure," 339. Sauer describes eleven manuscripts related to the Commonplace Book, 340–43. Wormald, *Making of English Law*, Table 4.4, 214–15, provides a comparative analysis of blocks of material in six of the manuscripts.

133   See Jonathan Wilcox, "The Dissemination of Wulfstan's Homilies: the Wulfstan Tradition in Eleventh-Century Vernacular Preaching," *England in the Eleventh Century: Proceedings of the 1992 Harlaxton Symposium*, ed. Carola Hicks, Harlaxton Medieval Studies 2 (Stamford, UK: Paul Watkins, 1992), 202; Sauer, "Transmission and Structure," 341.

134   Elaine Treharne, "Bishops and Their Texts in the Later Eleventh Century: Worcester and Exeter," in *Essays in Manuscript Geography: Vernacular of the English West Midlands from the Conquest to the Sixteenth Century*, ed. Wendy Scase (Turnhout: Brepols, 2007), 20–23.

Introduction

poem. In this case, the *SF* poet has adopted a complex image expressed in the Old English and Latin versions of an anonymous sermon for Ash Wednesday found in CCCC 190, part A, p. 247 (Latin), and part B, pp. 351–53 (OE), and Cotton Nero A.i, part B, fol. 189 (Latin).[135] The problematic passage in *SF*:

> *Sint for englas geteald   eorþbugendum*
> *þa þe dryhtnes word   dædum lærað.* (*SF*, lines 136–37)
> [Angels are considered as earth-dwellers who teach the word of God by deeds.]

becomes clear when compared with corresponding statements from the Latin and Old English versions of the sermon in CCCC 190:

> *quia angelus id est nuntius dei uocatus est sacerdos.*
> *forðan se sacerd is gecyged godes engel, þæt is godes boda.*[136]
> [therefore the priest is called God's angel, that is, God's messenger.]

With his translation of the *SF* verses, adopted in this edition, Schabram notes the allusion, inspired by Malachi 2:7, to priests who serve both as God's angels and his messengers on earth.[137] The appearance of this uncommon double image in a sermon marking the beginning of the Lenten season as well as in *SF*'s treatment of Lent links the two works, even though the poet adopted the image awkwardly.

---

135 Hans Schabram, "Zur Interpretation der 18. Strophe des alteenglischen Gedichts *The Seasons for Fasting*," *Anglia* 110 (1992): 296–306. For manuscript information on the Ash Wednesday sermon, see Ker, *Catalogue*, 73, item 20. The Latin version also appears in a pontifical from the first half of the eleventh century, probably from Ramsey, BL Cotton Vitellius A.vii, fol. 64. The OE version is designated HomS 9 in the Concordance to the *DOE*. Gneuss, *Handlist*, 33, states that the portion of CCCC 190 preserving the Old English text is a later addition from the third quarter of the eleventh century made at Exeter.
136 Schabram, *18 Strophe*, 305.
137 Schabram, *18 Strophe*, 306. See further, Richards, "Old Wine," 357–58.

Sources and Influences

Connections to materials found in Hatton 113–114 and Junius 121 are just as striking.[138] A very important one is the Old English version of the Benedictine Office in Junius 121, with three poems from the same circle as *SF*. These include *Gloria I*, found in one other manuscript, along with uniquely preserved copies of *Lord's Prayer III* and *Creed*.[139] Each poem has some stylistic correspondences with *SF*, but *Creed* shares half-lines, exclusive vocabulary, and a stanzaic structure, all of which indicate direct influence if not common authorship between the two poems.[140] Again in Junius 121, an excerpt from the OE "Confessional of Pseudo-Egbert" rubricated *Be þeódores gesetnysse hu man sceall fæsten alýsan* "Concerning Theodore's directives as to how a person can redeem a fast" provides instruction about proper fasting as well as alternate ways to do penance through means such as almsgiving and psalm singing if fasting proves too onerous.[141] Moreover, three of the eight extant Old English homilies for the First Sunday in Lent appear in the Hatton portion of the collection, and two of these connect to *SF*.[142] As Treharne notes, this occasion is an important day for preaching, in which the meaning of Lent as a period of fasting is explained, and as such it involves pragmatic instruction and admonition.[143] The *SF* poet writes within this tradition in the second part of the poem.

138   For these manuscripts, see N. R. Ker, *Catalogue*, 391–99, 412–18; and, more recently, Christine Franzen's descriptions in *Anglo-Saxon Manuscripts in Microfiche Facsimile vol. 6*: Worcester Manuscripts (Tempe, AZ: Medieval and Renaissance Texts and Studies, 1998), 26–43, 56–67.
139   Dobbie edits these as a group in *Anglo-Saxon Minor Poems*, 74–80. The entire text of the OE Benedictine Office is edited and discussed by Ure, *Benedictine Office*. Ure analyzes affinities among the poems, including *SF*, on 55–56.
140   See Sisam, "Seasons of Fasting," 47–48.
141   Robert Spindler, ed., *Das altenglische Bußbuch (sog. Confessionale Pseudo-Egberti)* (Leipzig: Tauchnitz, 1934), I. c., 172–74.
142   Elaine Treharne, "The Life and Times of Old English Homilies for the First Sunday in Lent," *The Power of Words: Anglo-Saxon Studies Presented to Donald G. Scragg on his Seventieth Birthday*, ed. Hugh Magennis and Jonathan Wilcox, Medieval European Studies 8 (Morgantown,: West Virginia University Press, 2006), 210–11.
143   Treharne, "Life and Times," 208–209.

Introduction

The first of the Lenten homilies in the Hatton/Junius collection, Wulfstan's Old English sermon for Lent, preserved uniquely in Hatton 113, fols. 56v–58v, has been called "quite unusual" within the range of homilies for this occasion "because of its essentially pastoral and practical focus," just the kind of approach reflected in *SF*.[144] Wulfstan's work (composed c. 1002) provides instructions for observing the fast until nones that are worded similarly to the directions in *SF*:

> *emb þa nigoþan tyd;   nan is on eorþan,*
> *butan hine unhæl   an geþreatige,*
> *þe mot æt oþþe wæt   ærur þicgan* (*SF*, lines 83–85)
> [at the none hour, no one is on earth, unless illness afflict him, who may consume food or drink earlier]

compared to

> *þæt æfre ænig cristen man ænige dæge ær nontide naðor ne abyrigene ætes ne wætes buton hit for unhæle sy.* (XIV, p. 233, lines 16–18)
> [that no Christian man should ever partake of either food or drink on any day before noontime unless it be for illness.]

These are two rare instances in Old English where the formula *æt . . . wæt* appears in directions for fasting, and the only examples of the formula are in conjunction with *unhæl*.[145] Wulfstan goes on to stress that no matter how lengthy the fast, if it is followed "all too swiftly" by drinking and gluttony, it will be worthless.[146] Given the obvious thematic affinity between Wulfstan's sermon and *SF*, the stylistic links indicate a possible stronger connection between the two works.

---

144   Treharne, "Life and Times," 219–20. For the text, see Dorothy Bethurum, ed., *The Homilies of Wulfstan* (Oxford: Clarendon, 1957), XIV, 233–35. For its dating, see Patrick Wormald, "Archbishop Wulfstan: Eleventh-Century State Builder," in *Wulfstan, Archbishop of York*, ed. Townend, 26–27.
145   Verified in the Concordance.
146   Bethurum, *The Homilies of Wulfstan*, XIV, 234, lines 25–29.

Sources and Influences

Ælfric's First (c. 989) and Second (c. 992) Series homilies for the First Sunday in Lent complete the Lenten selections in the Hatton/Junius collection.[147] The pieces are copied sequentially in Hatton 114 as Ker's items 42 and 43.[148] *SF* has affinities primarily with Ælfric's Second Series version appearing here in an excerpt on the Lenten fast quoted in a composite homily known as Napier 55, in Hatton 114, fols. 49–54.[149] Ælfric's material has undergone certain revisions between the First and Second Series versions that are reflected in the poem. For example, when the poet recounts the history of the Lenten fast in the second part of *SF*, he follows a narrative similar to that in Ælfric2/Napier:

---

147   Peter Clemoes, ed., *Ælfric's Catholic Homilies: The First Series: Text*, EETS s.s. 17 (Oxford: Oxford University Press, 1997), 11, 266–74; and Malcolm Godden, ed., *Ælfric's Catholic Homilies: The Second Series: Text*, EETS s.s. 5 (Oxford: Oxford University Press, 1979), 7, 60–66. For analysis of the body of Ælfric's Lenten works, see Robert K. Upchurch, "Catechetic Homiletics: Ælfric's Preaching and Teaching During Lent," *A Companion to Ælfric*, ed. Hugh Magennis and Mary Swan (Leiden: Brill, 2009), 270–46, esp. 232–33 on the First Sunday in Lent. Dating is provided in Peter Clemoes, "The Chronology of Ælfric's Works," *The Anglo-Saxons: Studies in Some Aspects of Their History and Culture Presented to Bruce Dickins*, ed. P. A. M. Clemoes (London: Bowes and Bowes, 1959), 212–47; repr. in Paul E. Szarmach, ed., with Deborah A. Oosterhouse, *Old English Prose: Basic Readings*, Basic Readings in Anglo-Saxon England 5 (New York and London: Garland, 2000), 56–57.

148   Ælfric's First Series homily is on fols. 42v–49. See Ker, *Catalogue*, 395, and Aaron J. Kleist, "Anglo-Saxon Homiliaries as Designated by Ker," in *The Old English Homily: Precedent, Practice, and Appropriation*, ed. Aaron J. Kleist (Turnhout: Brepols, 2007), 497.

149   Arthur S. Napier, ed. *Wulfstan: Sammlung der ihm zugeschriebenen Homilien nebst Untersuchungen über ihre Echtheit* (Berlin: Weidmann, 1883; repr. with bibliographical appendix by K. Ostheeren, Dublin, 1967), 282–89. Napier 55 is described by D. G. Scragg, "The Corpus of Vernacular Homilies and Saints' Lives before Ælfric," *Anglo-Saxon England* 8 (1979): 223–77; repr. in Szarmach, *Old English Prose*, 103. See also Wilcox, "The Dissemination of Wulfstan's Homilies," 211.

Introduction

> *[Moyses] þæt fæsten heold   feowertig daga*
> *and nyhta samod,   swa he nahtes anbat*
> *ær he þa deoran æ   dryhtnes anfenge. (SF, lines 108–110)*
> [Moses held that fast forty days and nights together, so that he consumed nothing before he received the precious law of the Lord.]

compared to

> *se heretoga Moyses fæste feowertige daga and feowertig nihta tosamne.*
> *To ði þæt he moste godes æ underfon (CH II, 7, lines 11–13; Napier LV, p. 285, lines 15–18)*
> [the army leader Moses fasted forty days and forty nights together so that he might receive God's law]

When he revised the corresponding passage from his First Series homily, Ælfric added the key word *tosamne*, and this change is reflected in *SF* as *samod*.[150] In another revision from the First to the Second Series, Ælfric's original statement that the forty-day fast "was made possible only by divine power, for Moses and Elijah as much as for Christ" was simplified to just the point about Elijah.[151] *SF* follows this revision, presenting Elijah's narrative (from 3 Kings XIX: 4–8) followed by a similar interpretation of his fast:[152]

> *Eft Helias,   eorl se mæra,*
> *him on westene   wiste geþigede,*
> *þær him symbelbread   somod mid wætere*
> *dryhtnes engla sum   dihte togeanes,*
> *and se gestrangud wearð   styþum gyfle*
> *to gefæstenne   feowertig daga*
> *and nihta samod (SF, lines 120–26)*

---

150   Cf. *CH* I, 11, lines 182–83.
151   Cf. *CH* I, 11, lines 184–85. For discussion, see Malcolm Godden, *Ælfric's Catholic Homilies: Introduction, Commentary and Glossary*, EETS s.s. 18 (Oxford: Oxford University Press, 2000), 93. The revised passage in Napier 55 appears on 285, lines 18–20.
152   Napier LV, 285, lines 15–20.

Sources and Influences

> *se mære þegen   mihta ne hæfde*
> *to astigenne   stæppon on ypplen*
> *ær him þæt symbol wearþ   seald fram engle.* (*SF*, lines 129–31)
> [Afterwards, Elijah, the famous leader, received nourishment for himself in the desert, where one of the angels of the Lord set before him feast bread together with water, and he became strengthened by the austere food to fast forty days and nights together. . . . The glorious thane did not have the powers to ascend the steps onto the summit until that feast was given to him from the angel.]

The poet concludes this account by urging his audience to fast from sinful deeds per the example of Elijah, a theme from the liturgy for the Lenten season also expressed in the source homily Ælfric2/Napier.[153]

Yet another link to the Hatton/Junius collection appears in the poet's description of the devil's weapons during the Temptation as Christ fasted for forty days:

> *geseah mærne frean   mannum gelicne*
> *and þa wenan ongann,   wommes gemyndig,*
> *þæt he stræla his   stellan mihte*
> *on þam lichoman* (*SF*, lines 162–65a)
> [He saw the glorious Lord in the likeness of a man and then began to expect, mindful of sin, that he might place his arrows in that body.]

But, as the poet relates, the devil's expectations are thwarted by Christ, who resists him and commits no sin. Wulfstan uses similar images depicting the devil's threats in separate sermons addressed to priests (Bethurum 8b, lines 34–35) and to the laity (Bethurum 8c, lines 65–66) on the efficacy of baptism, one copy of the latter included in Hatton

---

153   Greeson, *Two Old English Observance Poems*, 237. See the commentary to line 140. Ælfric's version of the image appears in *CH* II, 7, lines 35–37 and in Napier 55, 286, lines 12–13. For further discussion of influences on the poet's treatment of Lenten themes, see Richards, "Old Wine," 358–59.

Introduction

113, fols. 16–21. In these examples, the chrism anointed on the chest and shoulders serves as God's shield *þæt deofol ne mæg ænig his ættrenra wæpna him on afæstnian* "so that the devil may not fasten any of his poisonous weapons in him" (Bethurum 8c, lines 65–66). The image of placing or fastening, rather than shooting, a sharp weapon into the body unifies the descriptions in *SF* and the sermons. Coming as it does immediately after stanza XX featuring Christ's baptism, the image in stanza XXI could imply a similar interpretation adopted or recalled from Wulfstan's work.

4.3 Regulatory and Related Texts (lines 184–230a)

The influence of materials from the Hatton/Junius collection continues into the final section of *SF*. Here the poet begins by setting forth certain expectations of priests: that they sing daily Mass, that they exhort their audience to fast properly and make amends for their sins with alms, and that they lead exemplary lives themselves. These aims are congruent with those animating Wulfstan's *Canons of Edgar* (c. 1005–1007), found in Junius 121, fols. 25v–31v.[154] As described by their most recent editor, the *Canons of Edgar* "is a kind of *Pastoral Letter* addressed to the secular clergy, outlining their status, their standards of morality, and their responsibilities towards their flocks."[155] Wulfstan's sources for this work equate to the principal contents of the various manuscripts of the Commonplace Book. Among the sources are Ælfric's three *Pastoral Letters*, two of which appear in Junius 121.[156] Although both the *Canons* and the *Letters* generally reflect the stance of the *SF* poet, we can best

---

154   A thorough description of the manuscript presentation of *Canons* appears in Roger Fowler, ed., *Wulfstan's Canons of Edgar*, EETS o.s. 266 (Oxford: Oxford University Press, 1972), xiii–xiv.
155   Fowler, *Canons*, xlvii.
156   Joyce Hill, "Monastic Reform and the Secular Church: Ælfric's Pastoral Letters in Context," in Hicks, *England in the Eleventh Century*, 117. Some or all of the letters appear in three other versions of the Commonplace Book, including CCCC 190.

Sources and Influences

demonstrate their influence on the poem through a few relevant passages. *Canons* 48, for example, directs all priests to be *anræde* "of one mind" regarding feast and fast days, and to command these in one way, that is, consistently so as not to mislead the people.[157] *Canons* 49 urges that fasts be accompanied with alms, the more to please God.[158] And, most relevant to the last section of *SF*, *Canons* 59 forbids any priest to be an *ealusceop* "ale-poet, one who recites poetry among drinkers" or in any way to *gliwige* "make merry" among the laity.[159]

The *Canons* echo themes in Ælfric's Old English letter to Bishop Wulfsige (fols. 101v–110) and his second Old English letter to Wulfstan (fols. 111–124), likewise found among the texts in Junius 121.[160] The letter to Wulfsige (c. 992–1002) admonishes priests to take their instructional role seriously and urges them to avoid vices, principally drunkenness.[161] The second letter to Wulfstan (c. 1006), less used in the *Canons*, offers directions to priests about fasting before Mass:

> *Seðe aniges þinges onbyrigð, ætes oððe wætes, ostran oþþe ofæt, wines oðð wæteres, ne ræde he pistol ne godspell to mæssan. Gif hit hwa þonne deð, he unawurþaþ God and mid þære dyrstignysse hine sylfne fordeð.* (III, 96, pp. 180–82)
> [He who tastes anything of food and drink, oysters or fruit, wine or water, should not read the epistle or gospel at Mass. If someone does this nevertheless, he dishonors God and with that arrogance destroys himself eternally.]

---

157   Fowler, *Canons*, 13, and his commentary on 36–37.
158   Fowler, *Canons*, 13. His commentary on 37 references Theodulf's *Capitula* XXXVIII.
159   Fowler, *Canons*, 15. Similar commands that may have influenced this pronouncement appear in Ælfric's third *Pastoral Letter* and *Canones Hibernenses* X, both of which were known to Wulfstan, per Fowler, *Canons*, 39.
160   Fehr, Die Hirtenbriefe Ælfrics, Old English Letter to Wulfsige, 1–34; Second Old English Letter to Wulfstan, 146–221. See the revised edition cxxx–cxxxi for updated manuscript information, and cxlv for dating.
161   For additional information on the dates of Ælfric's letters, see Clemoes, "Chronology," 56–57.

Using much the same approach, the *SF* poet criticizes priests who violate the requirement to fast after Mass until the ninth hour:

> sona hie on mergan   mæssan syngað
> and forþegide,   þurste gebæded,
> æfter tæppere   teoþ geond stræta.
> Hwæt! Hi leaslice   leogan ongynnað
> and þone tæppere   tyhtaþ gelome,
> secgaþ þæt he synleas   syllan mote
> ostran to æte   and æpele wyn
> emb morgentyd (*SF*, lines 213–20)

[As soon as they sing Mass in the morning and have consumed (the Eucharist), impelled by thirst, they roam through the streets after the tapster. Alas! They deceitfully begin to lie and urge the tapster repeatedly, say that he may, without sin, give (them) oysters as food and fine wine at morning tide]

These passages, together with *SF* lines 228–29, are the only places in the corpus of Old English wherein *ostran* are mentioned in conjunction with violating the Mass, which again implies more than a casual connection between the works. The poet, however, focuses on the public appearances of the priests after Mass, when their behavior harms the laymen who observe and interact with them. As does Ælfric, the poet condemns such violations of religious law as offensive to God and harmful to the souls of the offenders (*SF*, lines 208–12).

In sum, there are a sufficient number of critical links with the language and themes of Wulfstan-related materials to demonstrate the poet's reliance on a collection such as Hatton/Junius for the second and third parts of *SF* dealing with the Lenten fast and priestly misconduct. But as one conversant with monitory literature, the poet was not limited to these resources. At times he addresses not priests, but *folces mann*, an individual who may be confronted with clergy behaving improperly. In his analysis of a vexed passage from *SF* addressing this issue, Schabram demonstrates that the poet adopted a pair of images

Sources and Influences

from the Old English translation of Gregory's *Regula Pastoralis*.[162] Here the poet instructs his audience not to follow sinning priests and drink the dirty water of iniquity, but to drink the clear water of the teaching of glory, divine truth:

> na þu, folces mann fyrna ne gyme,
> þe gehalgod mann her gefremme,
> ac þu lare scealt lustum fremman
> ryhthicgennde þe he to ræde tæchð,
> drince he him þæt drofe, duge hlutter þe
> wæter of wege, þæt is wuldres lar. (*SF*, lines 202–207)

[don't you, layman, heed the sins that the ordained man may commit here, but you should gladly follow (his) doctrine, thinking what he teaches as counsel is right; let him drink that dirty water (of iniquity), let yourself be availed of the clear water from the (divine) way, that is the teaching of glory.]

The relevant passage from Gregory makes the point more dispassionately:[163]

> Sua ða lareowas hi drincað suiðe hluter wæter, ðonne hi ðone
> godcundan wisdom leorniað, 7 eac ðonne hie hiene læroð; ac hie
> hit gedrefað mid hira agnum unðeawum, ðonne ðæt folc bisenað
> on hira unðeawum, nals on hira lare. (*RP* ch. 2, p. 31, lines 3–6)[164]

---

162   Hans Schabram, "*The Seasons for Fasting* 206f, Mit einem Beitrag zur ae. Metrik," *Britannica: Festschrift für Hermann M. Flasdieck*, ed. Wolfgang Iser and Hans Schabram (Heidelberg: Carl Winter, 1960), 221–40. L. Whitbread first called attention to the link between *SF*, lines 206–207 and the corresponding passage in the Latin version of Gregory's *Regula Pastoralis* in "Four Notes on Old English Poems," *English Studies* 44 (1963): 187–90.

163   Henry Sweet, ed., *King Alfred's West-Saxon Version of Gregory's Pastoral Care*, EETS o.s. 45, 50 (1871; repr., London: Trübner, 2001). The text quoted is that of MS Bodley Hatton 20, completed between 890 and 897 and sent to Worcester by the order of King Alfred. It was annotated in the early eleventh century, possibly by Wulfstan. On these points, see Ker, *Catalogue*, 385–86.

164   Sweet's translation, 30.

Introduction

[Thus the teachers drink very pure water when they learn the divine wisdom, and also when they teach it; but they defile it with their own vices, and set an example to the people by their vices, not by their instruction.]

Once again we see the poet picking up key words from his presumed source—*lare, drince, drofe < gedrefað, hlutter, wæter*—and transforming the images into his own verse message.

The closing lines of *SF* as it survives reflect Alcuin's three-part definition of gluttony, originally in his *Liber de Virtutibus et Vitiis* but also known widely in Anglo-Saxon England.[165] This definition underlies the final outburst in the poet's vigorous complaint that bad priests, by their behavior and example, mislead their congregants to the peril of their souls.[166] First, as we have seen, the miscreants eat and drink too soon:

sona hie on mergan   mæssan syngað (*SF*, line 213)
[as soon as they sing Mass in the morning]

Their thirst drives them through the streets to the tavern. Second, they consume delicacies—*ostran* and *æpele wyn*—even in the morning (*SF*, lines 219–20). And third, they eat and drink too much:

Hi þonne sittende   sadian aginnað,
win seniað,   syllað gelome (*SF*, lines 224–25)

---

165   For details, see the entry on the *Liber de Virtutibus et Vitiis* by Paul E. Szarmach in *Sources of Anglo-Saxon Literary Culture: A Trial Version*, ed. Frederick M. Biggs, Thomas D. Hill, and Paul E. Szarmach (Binghamton: Center for Medieval and Renaissance Studies, SUNY at Binghamton, 1990), 20–21. The analysis presented here is indebted to Hugh Magennis, *Anglo-Saxon Appetites: Food and Drink and Their Consumption in Old English and Related Literature* (Dublin: Four Courts, 1999), 85–92. An especially useful study of Alcuin's work as it was transformed into Old English prose is Paul E. Szarmach, "Vercelli Homily XX," *Mediaeval Studies* 35 (1973): 1–26.

166   See Chadwick B. Hilton, "The Old English *Seasons for Fasting*: Its Place in Vernacular Complaint Tradition," *Neophilologus* 70 (1986): 155–59.

Sources and Influences

[Then, sitting, they begin to become sated, bless the wine, distribute (it) frequently]

As they sate themselves and pour generously, the gluttonous priests bless the wine in seeming Eucharistic parody, betraying the depth of their debauchery.[167]

The array of sources and influences on the *SF* poet indicates that he worked within the didactic and regulatory traditions of the early eleventh century. The relatively straightforward messages of the poem are supported by contemporary Old English prose materials in particular, materials that had an extended life into post-Conquest England. By transforming these approaches and their concerns into poetry, the poet created a new form of vernacular ecclesiastical poetry akin to preaching, whose influence would be felt in the centuries to come.

4.4 SF *and* Menologium

The proper observance of fasts, then, is our poet's subject, and his major topics are three: the English calendar of seasonal fasts, Lenten observances, and priestly conduct, especially fasting after Mass. Each topic entails its own selection of sources, but the materials relate to each other through their authorship (Ælfric and Wulfstan), manuscript associations (the Commonplace Book, Hatton/Junius collection), or authority (Byrhtferth, Gregory, and Alcuin). From the perspective of its sources, *SF* has an integrated three-part structure supported by its lexicon and other aspects of style. The poem has been compared most often to the verse *Menologium*, an Old English metrical calendar describing twenty-eight major Christian feast days within the framework of the seasons and months of the year.[168] Composed in roughly the same

---

167   Magennis, *Anglo-Saxon Appetites*, 92.
168   The most recent editions are by Dobbie in *The Anglo-Saxon Minor Poems*, 49–55; Greeson, *Two Old English Observance Poems*, 179–195; Maria Grimaldi, *Il 'Menologio' poetico anglosassone: introduzione, edizione, traduzione, commento* (Naples:

Introduction

era (first quarter of the eleventh century) and copied into manuscripts containing versions of the Anglo-Saxon Chronicle, the poems share a focus on certain holy days of the liturgical calendar and a nationalistic emphasis on the observances and figures, especially Gregory the Great, important to England.[169] Both poems use Latin names for the months they reference; *SF* does so exclusively, and *Menologium* uses Latin and native terms in tandem.[170] Even their length now is similar (231 lines for *Menologium*), although a portion of *SF* has been lost. But differences between the poems outweigh their common features, to the point that *SF* and *Menologium* are best understood as products of a common tradition of didactic late Old English poetry rather than as works of a single poet.[171]

Menologium appears uniquely on fols. 112–14v in BL Cotton Tiberius B.i, the first of two items prefacing the C version of the Chronicle.[172] *SF*, as we know, was added near the end of a group of miscellaneous texts following a copy (version G) of the Parker Chronicle (version A) in Ot. *SF* was composed and copied in stanzas; *Menologium* was not. Most important, the structure, content, and sources of these works demonstrate the unique aims of each poet. *Menologium* has been well characterized as a catalogue poem, presenting an ordered list of items (in this case, twenty-eight liturgical feasts) amplified by commentary.[173]

Intercontinentalia, 1988); and Katherine O'Brien O'Keeffe, *The Anglo-Saxon Chronicle: A Collaborative Edition*, vol. 5, MS C (Cambridge: D. S. Brewer, 2001), 3–10. Kemp Malone published a translation, "The Old English Calendar Poem," in Studies in Language, Literature, and Culture of the Middle Ages and Later, ed. Bagby Atwood and Archibald A. Hill (Austin: University of Texas Press, 1969), 193–99.

169   Michael Lapidge, "The Saintly Life in Anglo-Saxon England," in *The Cambridge Companion to Old English Literature*, ed. Malcolm Godden and Michael Lapidge (Cambridge: Cambridge University Press, 1991), 249.

170   Earl R. Anderson, "The Seasons of the Year in Old English," *Anglo-Saxon England* 26 (1997): 251.

171   C. L. Wrenn, *A Study of Old English Literature* (New York: Norton, 1967), 160.

172   See Ker, *Catalogue*, 232–33; and O'Brien O'Keeffe, *Anglo-Saxon Chronicle C*, xxv–xcii.

173   Nicholas Howe, *The Old English Catalogue Poems*, Anglistica 23 (Copenhagen: Rosenkilde and Bagger, 1985), 74–86.

Sources and Influences

The poem is organized cyclically, beginning and ending with the Feast of the Nativity of Christ, yet complemented by short, lyrical evocations of the seasons that suggest an Irish influence on the poet.[174] For Easter, the poet quotes three lines from the Old English metrical Psalms.[175] The feasts are covered sequentially, dated by intervals from the preceding event rather than by Roman reckoning. Given its necessarily repetitive format and diction, *Menologium* has been interpreted as a mnemonic for the unlettered to grasp the Christian calendar, but uncertainty remains about its specific purpose or audience.[176]

While there are parallels between the first section of *SF* specifying the English dates for the Ember fasts and *Menologium*, even there lies an important distinction between the two poems. The *SF* poet is arguing for a particular set of dates, not, as the poet in *Menologium*, describing the feasts celebrated generally throughout the country. *Menologium*'s framework of seasonal imagery is absent from *SF*, replaced by the urgency of the poet's message. Moreover, the second and third parts of *SF* do not concern the calendar directly. The introduction to the Lenten fast in the second section defines it as the forty days preceding the Resurrection, and no further reference to computistical matters appears in the remainder of the poem. Rather, *SF* continues with a history of the fast, followed by an attack on non-observant priests.

---

174   See John Hennig, "The Irish Counterparts of the Anglo-Saxon *Menologium*," *Mediaeval Studies* 14 (1952): 98–106; Greeson, *Two Old English Observance Poems*, 87–98; and Elaine Tuttle Hansen, *The Solomon Complex: Reading Wisdom in Old English Poetry*, McMaster Old English Studies and Texts 5 (Toronto: University of Toronto Press, 1988), 98–106.

175   M. J. Toswell, "The Metrical Psalter and *The Menologium*," *Neuphilologische Mitteilungen* 94 (1993): 249–57. Toswell speculates on the motivation for the quotation, 252.

176   Greeson, *Two Old English Observance Poems*, 111–20, and Pauline Head, "Perpetual History in the Old English *Menologium*," in *The Medieval Chronicle: Proceedings of the 1st International Conference on the Medieval Chronicle, Driebergen/Utrecht, 13–16 July, 1996*, ed. Erik Kooper, Costerus n.s. 120 (Amsterdam and Atlanta: Rodopi, 1999), 152–62.

Introduction

Their differences notwithstanding, the didactic elements of *SF* and *Menologium*, supported by repetitive styles and non-poetic vocabulary, offer further evidence for a "prosaic" school of late Old English poetry aimed, at least in part, at an unlettered audience. Many of the poems have an analogue in Old English prose: the prose *Menologium*, the homily on Judgment Day related to *JDay II*, the Lord's Prayer, and the Apostles' Creed, to name the most prominent examples.[177] An earlier tradition saw prose saints' lives inspiring heroic poetic versions, and these often became sophisticated poetry, for example in the work of Cynewulf. Why later writers with non-narrative material chose poetry as their medium remains uncertain, though the poems clearly represent another means of reaching and teaching the unlettered. The differences between *SF* and *Menologium* remind us, however, that poets from the late Anglo-Saxon period could look to a variety of ecclesiastical sources and styles—Latin, English, poetry, and prose—as they shaped their messages.

5. STYLE AND STRUCTURE

5.1 Vocabulary

The vocabulary of *SF* reflects its relatively late date of composition, its poetic affinities, and the types of prose sources that influenced the poet. The word hoard includes several *hapax legomena*, many rare words from the Old English corpus, items from the later Old English poetic lexicon, technical terms from the computus, and numerous words drawn from Old English ecclesiastical prose. Noteworthy examples are

---

177   See E. G. Stanley, "The Prose *Menologium* and the Verse *Menologium*," in *Text and Language in Medieval English Prose: A Festschrift for Tadao Kubouchi*, ed. Akio Oizumi, Jacek Fisiak, and John Scahill, Studies in English Medieval Language and Literature 12 (Frankfurt am Main: Peter Lang, 2005), 255–67. For the relationship between prose and verse in the Vercelli Book and its implications for wider study, see Samantha Zacher, *Preaching the Converted: The Style and Rhetoric of the Vercelli Book Homilies* (Toronto: University of Toronto Press, 2009), 269–78.

Style and Structure

discussed further in the commentary to this edition. For the following cited items, variant spellings have been checked in the Concordance to ensure the accuracy of the descriptions. Line numbers to the citations from *SF* can be located in the glossary.

Words in *SF* otherwise unattested in the surviving corpus of Old English are *ǣlest* "neglect of (religious) law," *forþecgan* "to be consumed by thirst," *herescype* "multitude, troop," *rihthycgan* "to think right," *symbelbrēad* "bread for a feast," *wiglian* in the sense of "to use wiles," and *wulderfrēa* "glorious lord." Four among this group are transparent compounds of the type the poet favors. Caie notes a similar feature in *JDay II* and suggests that the new compounds may arise from that poet's attempts to translate his Latin source closely.[178] *SF* acc. sing. *symbelbread*, translating 3 Kings 19:6 acc. sing. *subcinerius panis* "hearth cake," seems to illustrate such a motive. Caie also points to the addition of prefixes and suffixes, such as *for-* and *-lest* (seen in the examples from *SF* above) as contributing to nonce-word creation.

A larger group of words from *SF* appears rarely in the Anglo-Saxon lexicon. Examples include *ǣnett* "solitude"; *ārwesa* "lord, God"; *atol* as a noun "evil, horror"; *behlǣnan* "to surround"; *dǣdfruma* "doer of deeds, God"; *drōf* "turbid, muddy, dirty"; *ealddagas* "days of old, former days"; *fæstentīd* "time or period appointed for fasting"; *frǣte* "shameful"; *fyrran* "to remove, put something at a distance"; *gebrēfan* "write down briefly"; *gyfl* "food"; *hēowan* "to keep, observe (a fast)"; *higefæst* "firm of mind, resolute"; *hrēmig* in the negative sense "lamenting"; *lengtentīd* "Lent"; *mēþig* "exhausted, weary"; *myrcels* "target"; *nīwian* "renew"; *sadian* "to be sated"; *scryd* "carriage, chariot"; *sēnian* "to bless"; *stæppa* "step"; *styrc* "bullock"; *tæppere* "wine tapster"; *þēodlīce* "as a people"; *unmǣne* "pure"; *wancul* "fickle, unstable"; *wangstede* "place"; and *ypplen* "summit, top."

---

178 Caie, *"Judgement Day II,"* 49. This point is considered further by Michael Lapidge in "Old English Poetic Compounds: A Latin Perspective," in *Intertexts: Studies in Anglo-Saxon Culture Presented to Paul E. Szarmach*, ed. Virginia Blanton and Helene Scheck (Tempe: Arizona Center for Medieval and Renaissance Studies: Turnhout: Brepols, 2008), 17–32, esp. 31.

Introduction

Some of its unusual vocabulary links *SF* to specific ecclesiastical poems drawn from Latin originals. In poetry composed during roughly the same period as *SF* and associated through manuscript context with Archbishop Wulfstan, we find *behlǣnan* "to surround" in *JDay II*, line 115b; *brytta* "bestower" in *JDay II*, lines 117b, 280b; *eorþbugend* "earth dweller, human being" in *Creed*, line 21a, and *JDay II*, line 130b; *gebann* "command, decree" in *JDay II*, line 129a; *gegladian* "appease, propitiate" in *JDay II*, line 222b; *unmǣne* "pure" in *Creed*, line 14a; *uplic* "heavenly" in *Creed*, lines 10a, 32a, 36a, and *JDay II*, lines 46a, 113a, 146a, 300b; and *wlanc* "great" as applied to the Lord in *Creed*, line 48b. There is some overlap between this group of words and those identified by Cronan as having poetic meanings separate from prose usage, but with a twist.[179] For example, the prose use of *brytta* as the base word in a genitive combination, referring to kings, princes, and God, occurs in *SF*: *wuldres bryttan* (line 54b) for God.[180] The secondary meaning—now applied to the devil—found in later poetry, appears in *SF*, line 166b *hearmes brytta*.[181] The metaphoric use of *strǣla* "arrows" in *SF*, line 164a, for the devil's temptations is found primarily in poetry, according to Cronan. The object of the arrows is the body *lichoman* in line 165a, but the poet expands this image further to the devil shooting at a human target *myrcels* in line 172a.[182]

Three technical words found in Byrhtferth's *Enchiridion*, the Old English handbook to the computus, appear in *SF*: *mearce* refers to a "term," that is "a lunar date from which a feast is calculated."[183] The

---

179   Dennis Cronan, "Poetic Meanings in the Old English Poetic Vocabulary," *English Studies* 5 (2003): 397–425.
180   *JDay II*, for example, has *swegles brytta* (line 117b) for the Lord, and *sigores brytta* (line 280b) for Christ.
181   Roberta Frank discusses both aspects of *brytta* in "Poetic Words in Late Old English Prose," in *From Anglo-Saxon to Early Middle English: Studies Presented to E. G. Stanley*, ed. Malcolm Godden, Douglas Gray, and Terry Hoad (Oxford: Clarendon, 1994), 93.
182   Cronan, "Poetic Meanings," 408, 410.
183   Baker and Lapidge, *Enchiridion*, 452. For further information about the poet's use of this work, see "Sources and Influences."

Style and Structure

word *gebrefde,* "written down briefly," refers to directions for determining Leap Year and for the proper conduct of the Passover feast explained in Byrhtferth's work.[184] The vernal equinox, *emniht,* is also referenced in *SF*. These all occur within twenty-five lines in the first part of the poem, *SF,* lines 43–68, where the poet argues for the English dates of the Ember fasts, and indicate how his Old English sources could supply prosaic vocabulary for his text.

The *SF* lexicon includes an abundance of English and Latin borrowings from ecclesiastical prose, a feature it shares with many late Old English poems, including *Maldon*.[185] In addition to *gegladian,* cited previously, *SF* shares *ege* "fear" with *JDay II,* lines 165a and 227b; *gelǣstan* "to carry out, perform, support" with *Maldon,* lines 11b and 15b, and *Creed,* line 40b; *leahtras* "sins" with *JDay II,* line 13, and *Creed,* line 54; *mǣð* "honor" with *Maldon,* line 195b; *sunnandæg* "Sunday" with *Gloria I,* line 25a; *dæghwāmlice* "daily" with *Lord's Prayer II,* line 68; *ābylgan* "to anger, offend" (*SF ǣbylgþ* "offense") with *Lord's Prayer III,* line 22b; and *hluttor* "clear, pure" with *Lord's Prayer III,* line 13a. In fact, Lendinara argues that *SF* contains far more prose words than other contemporary poems.[186] Using her examples and others from *SF,* we find *ælmesdǣd* "almsdeed"; *ǣrfæst* "pious"; *ǣrist* "Easter"; *aginnan* "begin"; *besyrian* "to ensnare"; *brēman* "celebrate, observe, proclaim"; *diht* "speech, voice"; *dihtan* "to establish, place, set"; *dymnis* "evil"; *dyppan* "to dip, immerse,

---

184   Baker and Lapidge, *Enchiridion,* 437. Richards, "Old Wine in a New Bottle," 352.
185   For discussion of many of these examples, see E. G. Stanley, "Studies in the Prosaic Vocabulary of Old English Verse," *Neuphilologische Mitteilungen* 72 (1971): 385–418. He cites *diht* as an example of a Latin loan-word rarely used in poetry, 387. In "Translating Doomsday: *De die iudicii* and its Old English Translation (*Judgement Day II*)," in *Beowulf and Beyond,* ed. Hans Sauer and Renate Bauer, Studies in English Medieval Language and Literature 18 (Frankfurt am Main: Peter Lang, 2007), 33–34, Patrizia Lendinara describes the "exceptional" complement of prose words in *JDay II,* which, however, show little overlap with those in *SF*. This evidence suggests that specific prose sources, rather than late prosaic vocabulary, influenced the lexicon of these poems.
186   Patrizia Lendinara, "La poesia anglosassone alla fine del X secolo e oltre," *AION: Filologia germanica,* n.s. 11 (2001): 12–13.

Introduction

baptize"; *Ēastertīd* "Eastertide"; *forhæfenes* "abstinence"; *fulwiht* "baptism"; *gescead* "power of distinguishing, reason"; *gestrangian* "to strengthen"; *geþicgan* "take, accept, receive"; *geþrēatian* "to afflict"; *gremian* "to offend, provoke"; *gyltan* "to sin"; *gyltig* (as in penitential texts) "culpable, blameworthy"; *heofenware* "inhabitants of heaven"; *lamb* "lamb"; *lēaslīce* (as the adverb) "deceitfully"; *lengten* "Lent"; *lēogan* "lie, deceive"; *mæsse* "Mass"; *nānuht* (< *nānwiht*) "nothing, not at all"; *offrian* "offer, sacrifice"; *pāpa* "Pope"; *Pentecosten* "Pentecost"; *prēost* "priest"; *sacerd* "priest"; *setl* (as the ecclesiastical term) "seat"; *styrc* "bullock"; *synlēas* "sinless, without sin"; *tyhtan* "to urge, persuade"; *þēnung* "ceremonial or ritual service, observance"; *þicgan* "to consume, take"; *þræl* "thrall"; *þwēal* "washing"; *þyngian* "to reconcile with"; *unhǣl* "sickness"; and *wǣt* "drink."

The three-part structure of *SF*, reflected in its content and sources, is reinforced by its vocabulary. In addition to the localized use of technical terms from the computus, the distribution of several basic words, such as those used for "people" and "priest," is instructive. Forms of *leod* appear invariably in parts one and two; *folc* is the operative term in part three. The one exception occurs in line 1b, where *folc* is used in the fourth stressed position for metrical reasons. We find *preost* used in part one, *sacerd* in part three, and no mention of the priesthood in part two. Among the terms for "sin," *womm* appears only in part one and *fyren* in parts two and three. Whereas certain words, such as those pertaining to the Ember fasts, are restricted to portions of the poem dealing with specific topics, the foregoing examples reflect numerous citations and general usage. Given that the overall style of the poem is consistent throughout, and the audience seems to remain constant (see below), the sources for each part must have had a significant influence on the poet's word choices.

5.2 Repetition, Variation, and Doublets

A similar phenomenon is at work in *SF*'s use of poetic devices. As seen in its lexicon, *SF* has close affinities to the Old English poetic

Style and Structure

Creed, part of the Benedictine Office found in Junius 121, and these offer important insights into the poet's methods. Kenneth Sisam first described the shared features in detail: division into eight-line stanzas (the first six stanzas only in *Creed*), similarities in vocabulary, and two identical lines not found elsewhere in Old English poetry.[187] In addition to the words covered previously in the discussion of vocabulary, he cites the use of *mære* "glorious" as a stock adjective in both poems (*SF* eight times in 229 ½ lines, *Creed* three times in 58 lines). To the nearly identical lines quoted by Sisam:

> *heofona heahcyning   her on life* (*SF*, line 4)
> *heofona heahcyning   her for life* (*Creed*, line 51)

and

> *and þone uplican   æþel secað* (*SF*, line 151)
> *þone uplican   eðel secan* (*Creed*, line 37)

I have added the pair

> *geond Romwara   rice nemneð* (*SF*, line 50)
> *under Romwarum   rices and doma* (*Creed*, line 26)[188]

Both poets use the rhyming pairs *fæst* and *gelæst* in the same line, twice in *SF* at lines 71 and 150, and once in *Creed* at line 40. Whitbread identified the phrase *lifes frea*, used in place of the compound *liffrea*, as linking *SF*, lines 3, 19; *JDay II*, line 80; and *Creed*, line 5.[189] Most of these stylistic correspondences with *Creed* occur in part one of *SF*, however, so Sisam's conjecture that the two poems had common authorship, or emanated from the same circle, remains open to question. What we can say is that the first two sections of *SF* were heavily indebted to Latin sources, as was

---

187   Sisam, *Studies*, 47–48.
188   Richards, "Prosaic Poetry," 65–67.
189   Leslie Whitbread, "The OE Poem *Judgment Day II* and Its Latin Source," *Philological Quarterly* 45 (1966): 638.

Creed, and that in conveying his material, the poet drew upon the idiom used by a contemporary for similar didactic purposes.[190]

Aside from the specific links to *Creed* and an extensive prose lexicon, *SF* has many other stylistic features characteristic of late Old English verse. Lendinara has provided a description of such poetry, highlighting doublets and repeated words and phrases as important markers.[191] Doublets in *SF* include *onlyht and gelæred* (line 3a), *earm and dreorig* (line 20b), *leoran and tæcan* (line 114b). Alliterating word pairs such as *wordum and weorcum* (line 74a) and *wordes and weorces* (line 190a) are one type of many repetitions. The formula and alliterative filler, *her on life* (line 4b) is varied by *her for life* (lines 39b and 141b).[192] In addition to *heofona heahcyning* (line 4a), we find *heofena heahcyninges* (line 10a) and *heofona heahcyninges* (line 53a). The *SF* poet creates his own formulae to convey the essentials of the four Ember fasts. For the second fast:

> *on þære wucan   þe æfter cumeð*
> *þam sunnandæge   þe geond sidne wang*
> *Pentecostenes dæg   preostas nemnað,*
> *on þam monþe,   þæs þe me þinceð,*
> *þe man Iunius   gearum nemde. (SF, lines 58–62)*
> [in the week which comes after the Sunday that priests call Pentecost day throughout the wide land, in the month, as it seems to me, that was called Iunius of yore.]

For the third fast:

> *on þære wucan   þe ærur byð*
> *emnihtes dæge   ælda beornum,*
> *on þam monþe,   mine gefræge,*
> *þe man September   [ ] genemneð. (SF, lines 67–70)*

---

190   This conclusion modifies some of the statements in Richards, "Prosaic Poetry."
191   Lendinara, "La poesia," 10–11.
192   See Caie, *"Judgement Day II,"* 55, for a discussion of this usage in *JDay II*.

Style and Structure

[in the week that will be before the day of (the vernal) equinox, for the sons of men, in the month, as I have heard say, which is called September.]

Gregory is designated *gumena pape* in both references to his edict for the English (*SF*, lines 46b and 94b). In stanza XIV, explaining that the Lenten fast was prefigured by Moses, the poet uses this pair of lines:

Eac we feowertig daga   fæsten healden (*SF*, line 103)
he þæt fæsten heold   feowertig daga (*SF*, line 108)

In stanza XVI, the poet echoes lines from stanza XIV while discussing Elijah's fast (*SF*, lines 108b–110a and 125b–127a). Again, in stanza XXIII, lines 177 and 181 are almost identical. Many half-lines are repeated throughout the poem. As these examples indicate, the poet developed stock phrases to communicate his most important doctrinal points and these, together with fillers such as *þæs þe me þinceð* (as it seems to me), line 61b, and *mine gefræge* (as I have heard say), line 69b, indicate his efforts to make a poem out of ecclesiastical materials.[193]

Repetition in *SF* is not limited to the coverage of similar topics. Aside from a reliance on formulaic language, the poet returns to words he has used recently, often for a new sense. At times, this technique could be generously interpreted as word play, but more often it seems to reflect ineptitude. In stanza XII, for example, while attempting to instruct his audience to reject the continental dates for Ember fasts promoted by the Bretons and Franks, he uses an identical phrase in his admonition to follow the dates Gregory gave the English, leading to a confusing directive:

Gif þe þonne secgen   suþan cymene
Brytta oþþe Franca   þæt þu gebann sceole . . . (*SF*, lines 87–88)

---

193   See "Metrical and Linguistic Features" for examples of repetition in metrical patterns and rhyme.

[If Bretons or Franks coming from the south should then say to you that you must (hold to) any (other) decree . . .]

ac þu þæt sylfe heald   þæt þe suþan com
from Romana   rices hyrde (*SF*, lines 92–93).
[but you hold to that (one) yourself, that which came from the south from the guardian of the kingdom of Rome]

In stanza XI, the phrase *boca gerynum* (line 82b), which seems to mean "liturgical books," is echoed by *boca dom* "penitential books" in line 86a, both phrases pertaining to proper observance of the days and hours of the Ember fasts. This could be an example of variation, but the poet may be trying to differentiate between the services for the day found in the *boca gerynum* and the terms of the fast—no food or drink before nones (3 p.m.) except in cases of illness, prescribed in the *boca dom*. In a line such as *SF*, line 121,

him on westene   wiste geþigede
[received nourishment for himself in the desert]

The poet appears to be playing with sound and sense, but we cannot be certain. The same is true for stanza XIX, where we hear of Elijah's *fyren scryd* "fiery chariot" in line 146a but in line 150b are exhorted to atone for our sins (*fyrena gelæstað*) if we hope to follow Elijah and Christ to heaven.

A related device involves phrases that echo each other but convey opposite meanings. The pair *wuldres bryttan* (line 54b) and *hearmes brytta* (line 166b) has already been discussed. In a similar vein, we find *blæda gefylled* "filled with glories" (line 32b) and *atele gefylled* "filled with evil" (line 37b) applied respectively to Christ and the sinner. Christ is called *heofenes weord* "guardian of heaven" in line 153a, whereas his adversary is *susla weard* "guardian of torments" in line 168b. These examples could result from deficient skill, but the relative proximity of some pairs and their similar grammatical structures imply a conscious, if unsubtle, strategy well suited to preaching.

Style and Structure

Among more traditional poetic devices, variation is an important tool for the *SF* poet. Beginning in lines 3b–4a we find *lifes frea* varied by *heofona heahcyning*. In line 33, *heofenwarum ham* is varied by line 34a *eard mid englum*, and so on. There is a nice series of three in lines 45b and 46a and b: *beorn on Rome, Gregorius, gumena papa*. A more sophisticated example appears in the following pair of lines that also displays an instance of metaphor in the poem:

We sint on westene   wuldres blisse,
on þæm ænete   ealra gefeana; (lines 132–33)
[We are in a desert with respect to the bliss of glory, in that solitude (away) from all joys;]

In fact, the second part of *SF*, treating the Lenten fast—as well as fasting more generally—is the primary locus of metaphoric language, the stuff of sermon literature. The image of fasting from sin occurs in lines 140b and 150b. Lines 138–39 equate the Lord's teaching with precious, nourishing food. The poet entreats the audience to ascend the mountain to glory as Elijah did (lines 135, 142–43). The devil's arrows of temptation are alluded to in lines 164–65 and lines 171–72.[194] Further on, a metaphor and a simile appear in the third section of the poem devoted to bad priests: the clear (pure) water of the Lord's teaching contrasts to the dirty water offered by sinful priests in lines 206–7; in lines 221–23, those priests who eat and drink delicacies and fine wine before the appointed hour compare to dogs and wolves unable to restrain their appetites. As the commentary indicates, most of these images are drawn from the Bible or from important ecclesiastical authors such as Ælfric, Gregory, and Alcuin.

---

194   For a full discussion of this image in Old English poetic contexts, see E. G. Stanley, "Old English Poetic Diction and the Interpretation of *The Wanderer, The Seafarer*, and *The Penitent's Prayer*," *Anglia* 73 (1956): 413–66. Repr. in E. G. Stanley, *A Collection of Papers with Emphasis on Old English Literature* (Toronto: Pontifical Institute for Mediaeval Studies, 1987), 234–80. The arrows of the devil are discussed on 238–44 of the latter.

Introduction

Although characteristic of late poetry, features such as doublets, alliterating pairs, and rhyme also demonstrate the influence of ecclesiastical prose, especially that of Archbishop Wulfstan, on *SF*. The poet has a fondness for coordinating verbs such as *onlyht and gelæred* (line 3a), *heold and worhte* (line 18b), and *breman and writan* (line 26b), especially apparent in parts one and two of the poem. He also likes coordinate adjectives, including the doublet *earm and dreorig* (line 20b). Formulae from ecclesiastical prose include *þeoda lareow* (line 96b), *dryhten gremiað* (line 210b), and *mæða bedæled* (line 223b). Beside the alliterating pairs *wordum and weorcum* (line 74a) and *wordes and weorces* (line 190a), we find less traditional examples such as *flæsces oþþe fysca* (line 183a), *folce gynd foldan* (line 187a), and *fisc of flode* (line 230a). He also uses rhyming pairs such as *æt oþþe wæt* (line 85a) along with rhyming half lines: *rincum to ræde* (line 6a) and *sylfum asæde* (line 7a); *her gefremme* (line 203b) and *lustum fremman* (line 204b).[195] In fact, when we compare Andy Orchard's summary of Wulfstan's stylistic elements with those informing *SF*, we can see a remarkable range of similarities.[196] Orchard notes the extent to which Wulfstan employs rhyme, assonance, and alliteration, together with extensive repetition including words, phrases, sentences, themes, and paragraphs, to produce an "oral-traditional" style. He argues that this style transcends prose and poetry—its three important practitioners being Aldhelm, the *Beowulf*-poet, and Wulfstan—but never wins out as the dominant mode of composition. Although the poet of *SF* likely did

---

195   E. G. Stanley, "Rhymes in English Medieval Verse: from Old English to Middle English," *Medieval English Studies Presented to George Kane*, ed. Edward Donald Kennedy, Ronald Waldron, and Joseph S. Wittig (Wolfeboro, NH, and Woodbridge, Suffolk: D. S. Brewer, 1988), 19–54, notes that in Old English, as here in *SF*, "poets used rhyme as an occasional ornament only," and these could be inexact rhymes, 20.

196   A. P. McD. Orchard, "Crying Wolf: Oral Style and the *Sermones Lupi*," *Anglo-Saxon England* 21 (1992): 258–59. More recently, Sara M. Pons-Sanz has provided a detailed analysis of Wulfstan's style in *Norse-Derived Vocabulary in Late Old English Texts*, North-Western European Language Evolution supplement 22 (Odense: University Press of Southern Denmark, 2007), esp. 26–31.

Style and Structure

not know the work of Aldhelm or *Beowulf*, he clearly was influenced by Wulfstan's writings, as his sources and style suggest.

5.3 Voice and Audience

Defining the speaker and audience highlights further connections between *SF* and contemporary sermon literature. According to Sisam, "The censure of lax priests, together with *we bebeodað* 'we command' at line 178, indicates that the [poet] had authority higher than that of an ordinary monk or mass-priest."[197] This is a useful starting point, but there is much within the poem to indicate that, whatever his position, the speaker was a skillful and opinionated preacher. His rhetoric is masterful. On one hand, he invokes the shared Christian heritage of poet and listeners customary in Old English biblical verse. As Renée Trilling points out, this tradition "joins Anglo-Saxon readers to the ancient Hebrews through bonds of commonality and ... holds immediate interest for a relatively broad audience."[198] Using third-person narrative, the *SF* poet recounts Biblical history and exempla germane to his topic. While so doing, he incorporates himself with his audience in phrases such as "we heard," "we learned." Then he applies the lessons with exhortations in the vein of "now we/you must." These techniques are most marked in the first and third sections of the poem, where the material—the dates of the Ember fasts and the problem of bad priests—requires some preparation and explanation before he admonishes the faithful. For example, in part one the poet invokes the authority of written texts in lines 26, 45 (Gregory), 82, and 86 to support his arguments for properly celebrating the Ember fasts. By contrast, the second part of *SF*, dealing with the Lenten fast, moves directly to the familiar figures of Moses and Elijah after three lines of introduction, allowing the Biblical stories to explain the observance. The third and concluding section of the poem

---

197   Sisam, "Seasons of Fasting," 50.
198   Renée R. Trilling, *The Aesthetics of Nostalgia: Historical Representation in Old English Verse* (Toronto: University of Toronto Press, 2009), 233.

Introduction

establishes the duties of priests and the importance of their example before moving to criticism of their shortcomings.

Writing as he does within the tradition of Anglo-Saxon vernacular preaching, the poet seems to be addressing a variety of audiences, both clerical and lay, but none of great sophistication. He assumes little learning beyond the basics of Christian observance. As the sources show, the doctrinal points he makes come primarily from the homilist Ælfric, known for expounding the elements of Christian faith. But, like Wulfstan, he has observed deficiencies in current understanding and practice that he feels compelled to correct. The poet speaks to those who work directly with the laity and those who could be misled if not taught properly.

The poet's construction of his audience thus plays an integral role in shaping the poem and communicating his several messages. An historical prologue of three stanzas opens *SF*, reminiscent of Old English heroic narrative inasmuch as it invokes common knowledge of Moses and the Israelites.[199] Stanza IV introduces the four seasonal (Ember) fasts. Here the poet reminds listeners that *we gehyrdon* about these fasts from teachers, who both spoke and wrote about them. Stanza IV lacks two lines, as noted in the commentary, and in its current state interrupts the story of Christ. Stanza V takes us from Christ's resurrection to the need to follow his example. He promises *us* all a heavenly home if *we* accept his guidance. By stanza VI, the poet gets to the point: *we* are urged to fill our days with charitable deeds and fasting, as Moses advised *us*, and to observe those seasonal fasts that Pope Gregory specified for the English. As a group, these six stanzas establish the importance of teachers, authorities, and role models to all Christians. The poet's rhetoric mirrors the shared commitment he advocates.

The poet uses *we* more sparingly in the next four stanzas, VII–X, which he devotes to each of the four fasts. As we have seen, there is a

---

199 Carol Braun Pasternack discusses this traditional feature in *The Textuality of Old English Poetry*, Cambridge Studies in Anglo-Saxon England 13 (Cambridge: Cambridge University Press, 1995), 151–53.

Style and Structure

formulaic quality to the descriptions of these fasts produced by repetition, stilted constructions, and a limited lexicon. The stanzas explaining the disputed, movable dates of the first and second fasts present special challenges to his poetic skills, since they require greater detail than those describing the fixed fasts. But the poet also needs to convey a sense of the four Ember fasts as a unit, hence he creates a kind of envelope pattern with the opening lines of the first and fourth fasts, whereby he urges the proper observance of these occasions:

We þæt feorme sceolan   fæsten heowan
on þære ærestan   wucan lengtenes (*SF*, lines 47–48)
[We must observe the first fast in the first week of Lent]

and

We þæt feorþe sceolen   fæsten gelæsten
on þære wucan   þe bið ærur full
dryhtnes gebyrde (*SF*, lines 71–73a).
[We must perform that fourth fast in the full week which will be before the birth of the Lord]

The use of structural repetition appears in other ways within these stanzas. In two similar lines for the second (line 61) and third (line 69) fasts (within the envelope), the poet includes a first-person aside in the b verse:

on þam monþe,   þæs þe me þinceð, (*SF*, line 61)
on þam monþe,   mine gefræge, (*SF*, line 69)

Since the poet argues for these dates, the notes of uncertainty ("so it seems to me," "as I have heard") may be nothing more than stock fillers, especially as he repeats line 61b at line 220b. However, the example at line 220b occurs in the midst of his attack on lax priests. It could be

Introduction

more than coincidental that two topics of greatest concern to the poet elicit such personal intrusions. Ward Parks might read these instances as the poet's "half-conscious remembrance of himself engaged in the process of narrating."²⁰⁰ Within these first seventy lines, then, the poet brings both the audience and himself into the poem as recipients and transmitters of Christian teaching, but he does not envision passive listeners. In stanza XII, using the pronouns *þu* and *þe*, he exhorts them to ignore anyone (purposely vague?) who urges the continental dates for the fasts and instead to follow Gregory's dates for the English. Stanza XIII concludes the first section of the poem by stressing the importance of the English dates as established by papal authority and, concomitantly, the obligation of priests to convey the information to laymen.

5.4 Structural Analysis

The central theme of teaching and learning, the true functions of God's messengers on earth and those who would follow Him, can be traced throughout the poem. In stressing the importance of teachers, our poet echoes their cultural leadership as promoted in contemporary sermon literature, especially the works of Ælfric.²⁰¹ In the first section of *SF*, Moses (line 2) and Gregory (line 96) are designated *lareow*, the only instances in the poem. The term *lar* ("doctrine, preaching, teaching") appears five times, at least once in each section. Instruction derives from Moses (line 9), the Lord (line 139), Christ (line 158), and divine doctrine delivered by priests (lines 204, 209). Six variants of the verb *læran* ("teach") occur, divided between the first and second sections; doing the teaching are God (lines 8, 11, 114), priests (line 101),

---

200   Ward Parks, "The Traditional Narrator and the 'I heard' Formulas in Old English Poetry," *Anglo-Saxon England* 16 (1987): 60.
201   Wilhelm G. Busse, *"Swa gað ða lareowas beforan ðæm folce, & ðæt folc æfter.* The Self-Understanding of Reformers as Teachers in Late Tenth-Century England," in *Schriftlichkeit im frühen Mittelalter*, ed. Ursula Schaefer, ScriptOralia 53 (Tübingen: Narr, 1993), 58–106, esp. 63–67.

indeterminate subject (line 118), angels/priests (line 137), and Christ (line 153). Additionally, *tæcan* forms a doublet with *læran* in line 114 and occurs with the priest as subject in line 205. Other words with related meanings, such as *ræd* ("advice, counsel"), appear less frequently but in similar contexts. The many references to teaching reinforce the high responsibility of religious leaders to follow the guidance and example of God and Christ for the benefit of all who need their instruction.[202]

The second section of *SF* offers a more traditional message about the history and proper observance of the Lenten fast but positions the poet and audience in much the same fashion as observed in part one. The opening stanza (XIV) focuses straightforwardly on Moses and his forty-day fast. The first four and one-half lines of stanza XV continue with the Lord's gift of the tablets to Moses and the command to use them for teaching his people. The remaining four and one-half lines (of this unique nine-line stanza) interpret the gift as a sign that, through fasting, *we* may receive peace and an understanding of God's profound mysteries, which we in turn must teach to everyone, if we value this gift. Whereas the first part of *SF* focused on the more procedural aspects of fasting such as dates, times, and rituals, the second section considers the individual experiences of Moses, Elijah, and Christ and their meaning for all mankind. The poet uses repetition to link these figures into one powerful example.[203] Of Moses we learn:

> he þæt fæsten heold   feowertig daga
> and nyhta samod,   swa he nahtes anbat
> ær he þa deoran æ   dryhtnes anfenge. (*SF*, lines 108–110)
> [he held that fast forty days and nights together, so that he consumed nothing before he received the precious law of the Lord.]

---

202   Pons-Sanz stresses Wulfstan's uses of repetition and variation as a means to focus on his message, in *Norse-Derived Vocabulary*, 27.
203   Compare the analysis by Maria Grimaldi in "Il *Mære Lareow* in *The Seasons for Fasting*," *AION: Filologia germanica* 28–29 (1985–86): 241–52, in which she offers symbolic interpretations for these figures.

Introduction

Elijah was so strengthened by bread from the angel that he was able

> *to gefæstenne   feowertig daga*
> *and nihta samod,   swa he nahtes anbat*
> *ær he on Horeb dun   hali ferde.* (*SF*, lines 125–27)
> [to fast for forty days and nights together, so that he
> consumed nothing before he journeyed onto holy Mt. Horeb.]

The treatment of Christ's fast in the wilderness varies a bit as the poet stresses that He had not sinned and that He underwent this privation as an example to all mankind:

> *and he feowertig daga   firude mettas,*
> *eac nihta swa feala   nanuht gyltig,*
> *leodum to lare,   þæt hie on lengten sceolan*
> *efen feowertig daga   fæsten hewan.* (*SF*, lines 156–59)
> [and he removed food for forty days and as many nights, completely
> guiltless, as an example to people that they should adhere to the
> fast in Lent exactly forty days.]

The concluding stanza (XXIII) of this section sums up these portraits:

> *Hæbbe we nu gemearcod   hu þa mæran iu*
> *þæt feowertig daga   fæsten hewdon* (*SF*, lines 176–77)
> [We have now described how those glorious ones formerly observed
> the forty day fast.]

The rhetorical set pieces in the first and second parts of *SF*, foregrounding dates for the Ember fasts and prefiguring the Lenten fast, demonstrate the poet's stylistic tricks in action and suggest that preaching, with its repetition and summing up, informed his poetic efforts.

In part two, the poet devotes four stanzas to Elijah (XVI–XIX), compared to two for Moses. It seems that the ascent of the mountain, the provision of holy nourishment, and the final journey upward to the heavens provided an irresistible paradigm for symbolic interpretation. As the poet relates, the angel's food is the Lord's teaching that sustains us while we fast from sins so that we can ascend to our heavenly home. Within these four stanzas, words such as *wist* "food" (twice), *symbelbread* "feast bread," *gyfle* "food," and *symbel* "feast" develop the idea of heavenly nourishment, the proper reward for fasting. Images of ascent include *to astigenne* "ascend," *ypplen* "summit," *munt* "mountain" (twice), and *uplican* "heavenly." Christ, too, receives four stanzas, wherein the poet focuses on His defeat of the devil, who is armed with the arrows of temptation to sin. The poet infuses these third-person historical narratives with the inclusive *we* and *us* as the beneficiaries of Moses, Elijah, and Christ. However, in the midst of his treatment of Christ, the poet turns to the audience, addressing them with the phrase *synnig man* and directing them to consider how to handle the temptations of the devil themselves. Following Christ's example, he says, will ensure you the help of holy angels. This is the rhetoric of a preacher, and it is a startling intervention in the dispassionate, even scholarly, presentation of Christ. But the personal tone is not sustained, for in the succeeding (and final) stanza XXIII of this section, the poet gives a brief summary of the Lenten fast and its strictures. His didactic purpose once again drives the structure of the poem.

    The third and shortest section of the poem, owing at least partly to its incomplete state, provides two stanzas setting forth the duties and proper conduct of priests before attacking the miscreants and urging listeners to reject the messenger, not the message. But the question of voice and audience is more complex than narrative and general exhortation. Until this third section of the poem, there is little to suggest that such an attack on priests is coming. Recall that in part one, the poet did not specify who might give bad advice about the dates of Ember fasts, just that such advice should be ignored. Stanza XXIV, in fact, opens part three with an ambiguous statement that *sacerdas*, a term used only in this section of the poem, should sing Mass and pray daily *on þam fæstenne* and guide their parishioners to confess and make amends through charitable deeds. Is this a reference to the just-discussed Lenten fast, the Ember fasts, or to fasting more generally? The answer becomes clear; the poet is thinking of all fasting days, because he mentions no specific occasions in the remainder of the text. However, the poet does not proceed with a summation on fasting to conclude the poem; instead, he particularizes the topic and takes it in a new direction. His attention fixes on priests who violate the strictures of observance, especially fasting after Mass.[204] He asserts that sinning priests engender hostility from the Lord and in no way serve Him or their parishioners as they should. In shifting to this final message, he changes his mode of address and rhetorical style.

When the poet enters on strident criticism of lax priests, he separates himself from his audience as well as his (presumably) fellow clergymen. He drops *we* and *us* altogether in the third section of *SF*: he says that *ic* have to tell with sorrow how priests offend the Lord daily by neglecting religious law and providing a bad example to the laity. As he moves from descriptions of offenses he has observed, to the one stanza (XXVI) in which he addresses the laity directly (*na þu folces mann . . . ac þu lare scealt*), and back to more pointed observations about priestly misconduct, the poet seems to envision both clerical and lay audiences for his message.[205] Stanza XXVI counsels the laity to reject the example of sinning clergy and to focus instead on the doctrine they teach. Its message thus culminates those offered earlier in *SF*, which urged listeners (in the second person singular) to accept the proper dates for Ember

---

204   Greeson, *Two Old English Observance Poems*, 63, 63, 85n59, points out, however, that the terms of criticism derive primarily from Lenten homilies.
205   I differ here with Hilton's argument in "The Old English *Seasons for Fasting*: Its Place in the Vernacular Complaint Tradition," 157–58, for solely a lay audience. In a more sustained demonstration of chastising the clergy while admonishing the laity in the audience, see Ælfric's homily for the Second Sunday after Easter (*CH* 1, 17) as elucidated by Robert K. Upchurch in "A Big Dog Barks: Ælfric of Eynsham's Indictment of the English Pastorate and *Witan*," *Speculum* 85 (2010): 505–33, esp. 513–14.

Style and Structure

fasts (stanza XII) and to model themselves after Christ, as portrayed in Lenten observances (stanza XXII).

The movement of the final stanzas offers a rising arc of emotion fueled by a series of base images depicting the sinful behavior of priests. The new rhetorical strategy differs from that of the earlier parts of the poem, where the poet employed repetitive blocks of verses, wordplay, and the like. Beginning with stanza XXV, we encounter a symbolic lord vs. thrall relationship, wherein the thrall, an everyman, having bitterly offended his lord, does not attempt to redeem himself but instead continues to provoke his master. In stanza XXVI, sinning priests, ignorant of proper conduct toward the Lord, are depicted as drinking dirty water from the gutter. In stanza XXVII, continuing to provoke the Lord, these clergymen mislead the faithful by searching out the tapster as soon as they have finished morning Mass. They are not thirsty for doctrine, but for fine wine, as we learn in stanza XXVIII. Their behavior worsens as they lead the tapster into sin through false assurances; they tell him that it is permissible to serve oysters and wine in the morning, in essence to break the fast improperly by serving the priests. To clinch his point, the poet compares such priests to dogs and wolves, who are unable to restrain their appetites. Then in the last stanza XXIX, the poet portrays the priests' blasphemy of the Eucharist as they carouse in taverns, bless the wine, and continue to violate the fast.

In urging his argument, the poet's lexicon becomes ever more riveting as he draws upon an evocative and unusual vocabulary. Warming up in stanza XXV, he refers to priests who *ligegen to fæste on leahtrum hiora* ("remain too fixed in their vices") and refers to a lord who is *bitere onbolgen* ("greatly offended"). In stanza XXVI he uses the rare adjective *drofe* ("muddy, dirty") substantively to depict the type of sustenance preferred by sinning clerics. Emotionally charged words and phrases multiply in the following stanzas. The poet describes priests "renewing strife with" (*sace niwiað*) and "provoking" the Lord (*dryhten gremiað*) as they mislead their followers. As soon as they sing Mass, they head for the tavern *forþegide* ("consumed by thirst") and *þurste gebæded* ("bidden by thirst"), for good

Introduction

measure. He uses *tæppere* ("tapster") twice within three lines (*SF*, lines 215a–217a) to link stanzas XXVII and XXVIII and cement the image of the thirsty, roaming priests and their object. In comparing them to dogs and wolves, the poet observes (stanza XXVII) that they *ne wigliað hwænne hie to mose fon* ("do not use wiles when they take food"). Consumption of delicacies (oysters) and fine wine link stanzas XXVII and XXVIII, as the priests satisfy their appetites and thirst, the very picture of Alcuin's vices. The verbs *sadian* ("to sate") and *seniað* ("bless" the wine) complete the raucous and blasphemous scene of tavern life.[206] Words relating to consumption abound in this part of the poem. In addition to those just cited, we find *drince* (line 206a), *æte* (line 219a), *dreng* (line 227a), *picgan* (line 228b), *etan* (line 229a), and *fisc* (line 230a).

In the third section, the *SF* poet separates himself from both clerical and lay audiences, and speaks with the authority of his role and office. Following a description of their duties, with emphasis on leading by example, he provides the clergy with a graphic evocation of what they are to reject. The poet holds up a mirror for all to view. Meanwhile, he addresses the laity, who must be told how to proceed when faced with errant clergy. Altogether he models the kind of responsibility and behavior he advocates, as the best preachers and teachers do.

5.5 Conclusion

The *SF* poet seems to have known, and possibly worked with, the poets who versified the Benedictine Office. His work also shows influence from the homilists of the late tenth/early eleventh centuries, especially Wulfstan. He drew upon the contemporary vocabulary of vernacular poetry and ecclesiastical prose. As the sources attest, he knew Latin, and his style was influenced by the particular materials he was using. He even followed a three-part structure of the type associated with preaching. But rather than write a traditional sermon, he attempted to render his ideas into poetic communication to an audience of clergy and laity. In

---

[206] See "Sources and Influences" and Magennis, *Anglo-Saxon Appetites*, 91–92.

essence, the style and structure of the poem refine our understanding of its sources and methods while revealing a determination to teach and move the listeners to action.

In a recent study of three anonymous Old English homilies for the First Sunday in Lent, Mary Swan observes that successful preaching "has to be formulaic, has to appeal to and reiterate tradition, but at the same time and by the same means it has to assert a particular set of contemporary ideals which are always defined—whether silently or explicitly—by contrast with competing ones. This combination of dynamism and continuity is central to the performative nature of preaching, which has not only to assert central ideological tenets and identities, but also to keep on reasserting and reconstructing them if they are to be upheld and take effect."[207] The type of movement Swan describes emerges clearly in *SF*. As we have seen, the poet uses formulaic language, drawn from both poetry and prose, to serve his own repetitive, even formulaic, style. He moves from asserting commonly held knowledge and practices to the violation of those, and thus into issues of timeless relevancy. His message is dynamic, "reasserting and reconstructing" the abuses he has observed so that they become imprinted on the consciousness of the audience. For these reasons, the poem is truly a cultural hybrid. Its formal features derive from Old English poetry, but its motivation and effects flow from the Old English sermon tradition.

Scholars have often noted poetic tendencies in the prose of Ælfric and Wulfstan, and to a lesser degree in the work of anonymous homilists and compilers, but the evidence of poetry emulating prose has been focused primarily on vocabulary and formulaic expression until recently.[208] There has been much discussion, for example, about the

---

207 Mary Swan, "Constructing Preacher and Audience in Old English Homilies," in *Constructing the Medieval Sermon*, ed. Roger Andersson (Turnhout: Brepols, 2007), 179–80.

208 See, for example, L. Whitbread, "Notes on the Old English *Exhortation to Christian Living*," *Studia Neophilologica* 23 (1951): 96–102, for a discussion of two poems in MS CCCC 201 and their prose adaptations.

incorporation of a portion of *JDay II* into the homily on Judgment Day known as Napier 29.[209] Eric Stanley argues that the very topic seemed to call forth heightened rhythm, though he also noted a similar relationship between the poem and homily on the Phoenix.[210] Letson writes of the "poetic homily," one that merges the style and structure of poetry, and describes the Vercelli Book as being an organized selection of such works among which "pieces of pure poetry fit comfortably into the overall design."[211] Focusing on one of the poems, *Homiletic Fragment I*, from that same collection, Randle calls the piece a "homiletic poem" possessing an "outward form of traditional vernacular verse" but with inner qualities, including a three-part structure, drawn from the prose homiletic tradition.[212] Randle finds numerous shared features between *Homiletic Fragment I* and *JDay II*, similar to those that inform *SF*. Likewise, the topics covered in *SF*—the controversy over dates for the Ember fasts, the meaning of the Lenten fast, and negligent priests—are not the usual stuff of Old English poetry. Rather, as Chad Hilton has argued, *SF* looks forward to the Middle English tradition of incorporating preaching into verse.[213] *SF* is one of several examples that demonstrate how Old

---

209   The homily, found in Hatton 113, fols. 66–73, was edited by Napier in *Wulfstan: Sammlung der ihm zugeschriebenen Homilien*, 134–43.

210   E. G. Stanley, "*The Judgement of the Damned*, from Corpus Christi College 201 and Other Manuscripts, and the Definition of Old English Verse," in *Learning and Literature in Anglo-Saxon England: Studies Presented to Peter Clemoes on the Occasion of his Sixty-Fifth Birthday*, ed. Michael Lapidge and Helmut Gneuss (Cambridge: Cambridge University Press, 1985), 363–91; repr. in Stanley, *A Collection of Papers*, 353–55.

211   D. R. Letson, "The Poetic Content of the Revival Homily," in *The Old English Homily and Its Backgrounds*, ed. Paul E. Szarmach and Bernard F. Huppé (Albany: SUNY Press, 1978), 139–56, quotations at 140 and 142.

212   Jonathan T. Randle, "The 'Homiletics' of the Vercelli Book Poems: The Case of *Homiletic Fragment I*," in *New Readings in the Vercelli Book*, ed. Samantha Zacher and Andy Orchard (Toronto: University of Toronto Press, 2009), 224. Many of Randle's points about the style (lexicon, repetition, alliteration) and structure of this poem apply as well to those features in *SF*.

213   Hilton, "Vernacular Complaint Tradition," 158.

Principles of This Edition

English poetry began changing its cultural role before the Conquest, a phenomenon that blurred distinctions between poetry and prose, yet affected both genres.[214] It is late poetry, not debased or quasi-poetry. And *SF* is a fully formed poem, more akin to a full sermon than to interludes within ecclesiastical prose or the penitential poetry associated with the Benedictine Revival.[215] These observations tell us that the transition to Middle English writing took multiple routes, many of them associated with spiritual enlightenment. From the time of Caedmon, Old English poetry maintained this connection through the Conquest and beyond. We see in *SF* how the great Anglo-Saxon homilists, who borrowed the rhythms of poetry, inspired it in return to move in new directions.

6. Principles of This Edition

A text with the history of *SF* presents numerous challenges. The poem itself is a relatively late composition from the Anglo-Saxon period transcribed from a faulty copy (Ot) made in the first half of the eleventh century. Elizabethan antiquary Laurence Nowell, the scribe of the extant version of the poem, now in BL Add. 43703, fols. 257–260v (Nw), was not reliably accurate and probably worked in haste, as indicated by the numerous corrections he himself made in his copy. Two relatively short passages from the poem printed by the scholars Abraham Wheelock and Humfrey Wanley, who saw Ot before it burned, provide some helpful readings. But, in the end, an edition of *SF* requires many decisions about emendation.

This editor prefers not to obscure possible evidence of dialect and date by correcting forms that, for example, show variations in unstressed vowels of the endings. Some of these are attributable to Nowell, but

---

214 Anne Savage, "Old and Middle English, Poetry and Prose," *Studies in the Age of Chaucer* 23 (2001): 503–11.

215 See Graham D. Caie, "The Vernacular Poems in MS CCCC 201 as Penitential Literature," in *A Literary Miscellany Presented to Eric Jacobsen*, ed. Graham D. Caie and Holger Nørgaard (Copenhagen: Atheneum, 1988), 72–78.

the general picture reflects the state of lWS found, for example, in the work of Ælfric. On the other hand, when letters are clearly missing, or some other type of identifiable scribal confusion, such as dittography or misinterpretation of minims, is evident, the case for emendation is strong. The pattern of Nowell's copying errors, detailed in "Manuscripts and Editions," together with internal information provided by parallel spellings and constructions within the poem, offer additional bases for editorial intervention. This edition accepts the transcriptions of Wheelock and Wanley, whose work is judged to be more accurate than Nowell's, especially as these scholars were experienced Anglo-Saxonists who copied only short passages from the poem as samples of the text. The insights of previous editors and commentators on *SF* likewise offer guidance for editorial decisions. Justifications for all emendations are provided in the commentary to the poem.

The textual notes offer all of the variant readings in earlier editions of *SF* with the following exceptions. The various proposals to fill perceived lacunae in the text, marked here with empty brackets [ ], are referenced only in the commentary. Grimaldi's edition is not included because it reproduces Dobbie's text. Holthausen's bracketed suggestions, as opposed to his editorial decisions, are omitted because he does not explain their basis nor can they be considered part of his edited text. The present edition also ignores the use of hyphens in Jones's text to indicate compounds and related constructions.

The format and punctuation of the edition are editorial. The poem is printed in eight-line stanzas derived from the Nw format of stanzas (copied as prose) with opening capitals and concluding punctuation. Capitalization and punctuation have been normalized according to modern practice. Decisions regarding punctuation of independent clauses with a period or semi-colon have been determined on the basis of the relationship between the statements. As in modern English, two closely related thoughts, where the second completes the first, are separated by a semicolon. Commas are used to mark phrases, appositives, instances of direct address, and the like. In some cases, commas

Principles of This Edition

also serve to indicate an editorial decision about the interpretation of a passage. Such interpretations are reflected in the translation and the commentary.

Abbreviations found in Nw have been expanded silently, as follows:

7 = *and*; þ = *þæt*; ḡ = *ge-*; a vertical line over the preceding letter = *-m* or *-n*.

Seasons for Fasting

I.

Wæs on ealddagum Israhela folc 1
þurh Moysen, mærne lareow,
onlyht and gelæred, swa hine lifes frea,
heofona heahcyning, her on life
þurh his sylfes word sette for leodum, 5
rincum to ræde, and him runa gescead
sylfum asæde, hu he þone soþan weg
leofum leodscipe læran sceolde.

II.

Þa se leoda fruma larum fyligde
heofena heahcyninges, and þa hæleþ samod, 10
swa hie on leodscipe lærede wæron;
gyf hie wancule weorc ongunnon,
heom þæs of heofonum hearm to leane
asende sigora God, and hie sona to him
fryþa wilnodan and þær fundon raþe, 15
gif hie leahtras heora letan gewyrþan.

---

1. *Israhela*–Wan, Holt, Hil] *Israheala*–Nw, D, G, J   3. *onlyht*–Wan, Hil] *anlyht*–Nw, D, Holt, G, J   *gelæred*–Wan, Holt, Hil] *gelared*–Nw, D, G, J   4. *heofona*–Wan, Hil] *heofna*–Nw, D, Holt, G, J   5. *þurh*–Wan, D, Holt, G, Hilt, J] *þurh þurh*–Nw   8. *sceolde*–D, Holt, G, Hil, J] *sceold*–Nw   9. *Þa*–Nw, D, Holt, G, J] *Ða* Hil   11. *lærede*–Nw, D, G, Hil, J] *lærde*–Holt   12. *leahtras*–Nw, Holt, Hil] *leohtras*–D, G. J   *gyf*–Nw, D, G, Hil, J] *gif*–Holt   *weorc*–D, Holt, G, J] *weorce*–Nw, Hil   *ongunnon*–Nw, D, Holt, G, J] *ongunnan*–Hil   14. *sigora*–D, Holt, G, Hil, J] *sigona*–Nw   *wilnodan*–Nw, D, G, Hil, J] *wilnodon*–Holt   16. *leahtras*–Nw, Holt, Hil] *leohtras*–D, G, J   *gewyrþan*–D, Holt, G, Hil, J] *gewyrpan*–Nw

III.

Feala is mægena   þe sio mære þeod
on þam herescype   heold and worhte,
þendan hie lifes frean   lufian woldon;
ac him se ende wearð   earm and dreorig   20
þa hie besyredon   sylfne dryhten,
on beam setton   and to byrgenne
[ ] gedemdon;   he þær bedigled wæs,
and þy þryddan dæge   þeodum ætywed.

IV.

We þæt gehyrdon   hæleþa mænige   25
on bocstafum   breman and writan,
þæt hie fæstenu   feower heoldon
and þonne offredan   unmæne neat,
þæt is lamb oþþe styrc, leofum to tacne
þe for worulde wæs   womma bedæled.   30

---

18. *herescype*–Nw, D, G, Hil, J] *herescipe*–Holt   19. *þendan*–Nw, D, G, Hil, J] *þenden*–Holt   20. *dreorig*–Holt, G, Hil] *þrealic*–D, J] *þreorig*–Nw   24. *þryddan*–Nw, D, G, Hil, J] *þriddan*–Holt   28. *offredan*–Nw, D, G, Hil, J] *offredon*–Holt   29. *worulde*–D, G, J] *woruld*–Nw, Holt, Hil

Seasons for Fasting

V.

Ac arisan ongan   rices ealdor
of byrgenne,   blæda gefylled,
and mid heofenwarum   ham gesohte,
eard mid englum,   and us eallum
þone hyht gehateð,   gyf we his willaþ   35
þurh rihtne sefan   rædum fyligan.
Nan þær in cumeð   atele gefylled,
womme gewered,   ac scal on wyrd sceacan.

VI.

Nu we herian sceolan   her for life
deorne dædfruman,   and him dogera gerim   40
ælmesdædum   ure gefyllan,
and on fæstenum,   swa se froda iu
Moyses mælde,   and we þa mearce sceolan
heoldan higefæste   [ ] mid Anglum,
swa hie gebrefde us   beorn on Rome,   45
Gregorius,   gumena papa.

---

35. *hyht gehateð*–J] *hyht and gehateð*–Nw, D, G] *hygþ and gehateð*–Holt] *hyht and hateð*–Hil   *gyf*–Nw, D, G, Hil, J] *gif*–Holt   37. *Nan*–G] *Na*–Nw, D, Holt, Hil, J
38. *womme*–D, Holt, G, J] *womo*–Hil] *wommo*–Nw   *gewered*–Holt, G] *gewesed*–Nw, D, Hil, J   39. *for*–D, Holt, G, Hil, J] *fon*–Nw   40. *dogera gerim*–G, J] *geara gerim*–D] *dogra gerim*–Holt] *dogeara gerim*–Hil] *do geara gerim*–Nw   43. *sceolan*–Nw, D, G, Hil, J] *sceolon*–Holt   44. *heoldan* Nw, D, G, Hil, J] *healdan*–Holt   *higefæste*–Nw, D, G, Hil, J] *hygefæste*–Holt   46. *Gregorius*–Nw, D, G, Hil, J] *Gregorious*–Holt

VII.

We þæt forme sceolan   fæsten heowan
on þære ærestan   wucan lengtenes
on þam monþe   þe man Martius
geond Romwara   rice nemneð,   50
and þær twelfe sceolan   torhtum dihte
runa geræden   in þæs rican hofe,
heofona heahcyninges,   herian mid sange,
wlancne weorþian   wuldres bryttan.

VIII.

Ofer þa Eastertid   oþer fæsten   55
ys to bremenne   Brytena leodum
mid gelicum lofe,   þe gelefen hafað,
on þære wucan   þe æfter cumeð
þam sunnandæge   þe geond sidne wang
Pentecostenes dæg   preostas nemnað,   60
on þam monþe,   þæs þe me þinceð,
þe man Iunius   gearum nemde.

---

47. *We*–D, Holt, G, Hil, J] *Þe*–Nw *sceolan*–Nw, D, G, Hil, J] *sceolon*–Holt *heowan*–Nw, D, G, Hil, J] *hegan*–Holt   48. *wucan*–D, Holt, G, Hil, J] *wircan*–Nw   50. *nemneð*–D, Holt, G, J] *nemnað*–Nw, Hil   51. *sceolan*–Nw, D, G, Hil, J] *sceolon*–Holt   56. *ys*–Nw, D, G, Hil, J] *is*–Holt   57. *gelefen*] *gelesen*–Nw, D, G, Hilt] *geleafen*–Holt] *gelesu*–J   58. *þære* D, G, J] *þær*–Nw, Hil] *anr*–Holt *cumeð*–D, Holt, G, J] *cumað*–Nw, Hil   61. *þam*–Nw, D, G, Hil, J] *þæm*–Holt *þinceð*–Nw, D, G, Hil, J] *þynceð* Holt

IX.

Ðonne is þæt þrydde   þinga gehwelces
fæsten on foldan   fyra bearnum
dihte gelicum   on þam deoran hofe   65
to brymenne   beorhtum sange
on þære wucan   þe ærur byð
emnihtes dæge   ælda beornum,
on þam monþe,   mine gefræge,
þe man September   [ ] genemneð.   70

X.

We þæt feorþe sceolen   fæsten gelæstan
on þære wucan   þe bið ærur full
dryhtnes gebyrde,   and we mid deorum scylan
wordum and weorcum   wuldres cyninge
in þa ylcan tid   eallum gemynde   75
þeodne deman   þinga gehwylces,
efne swa swa ærran,   and þone arwesan,
leofne leoda frean,   lifes biddan.

---

63. *þrydde*–Nw, D, G, Hil, J] *þridde*–Holt   64. *fyra*–Nw, D, G, Hil, J] *fira*–Holt
66. *brymenne*–Nw, D, G, Hil, J] *bremenne*–Holt   67. *byð*–Nw, D, G, Hil, J] *bið*–
Holt   68. *beornum*–Nw, D, G, J] *bearnum*–Holt, Hil   71. *sceolen*–Nw, D, G, Hil, J]
sceolon–Holt *fæsten gelæstan*–D, Holt, G, J] *fæste gelæsten*–Nw, Hil   72. *þære*–D, Holt,
G, Hil, J] *þær*–Nw   73. *deorum*–Holt, G] *deornum*–Nw, D, Hil, J   *scylan*–Nw, D, G,
Hil, J] *sculon*–Holt   75. *ylcan*–Nw, D, G, Hil, J] *ilcan*–Holt

XI.

On þissum fæstenum   is se feorþa dæg
and sixta samod   seofoþa getenge   80
to gelæstanne   lifes ealdre
and to bremenne   boca gerynum
emb þa nigoþan tyd;   nan is on eorþan,
butan hine unhæl   an geþreatige,
þe mot æt oþþe wæt   ærur þicgan,   85
þæs þe us boca dom   þeodlic demeð.

XII.

Gif þe þonne secgen   suþan cymene
Brytta oþþe Franca,   þæt þu gebann sceole
her on eorþan   ænig healdan,
þæs þe Moyses iu   mælde to leodum,   90
na þu þæs andfeng   æfre gewyrþe,
ac þu þæt sylfe heald   þæt þe suþan com
from Romana   rices hyrde,
Gregoriæ,   gumena papa.

---

80. *seofoþa*-D, Holt, G, Hil, J] *feoroþa*-Nw *getenge*-Holt] *getinge*-Nw, D, G, Hil, J
83. *tyd*-Nw, D, G, Hil, J] *tid*-Holt   84. *butan*-D, Holt, G, Hil, J] *butan butan*-
Nw   85. *æt*-Holt, G, Hil, J] *hæt*-Nw, D *þicgan*-Holt, G, Hil, J] *þingan*-Nw, D
86. *þeodlic demeð*-Nw, D, G, Hil] *beorhtlic demeð*-Holt] *demeð þeodlic*-J   87. *secgen*-
Whe] *secgan*-Nw, D, Holt, G, Hil, J   88. *Brytta oþþe Franca*] *Brýtt. oþþe Franca*-Whe]
bryttan Franca-D, G] *bryttan oþþe Franca*-Hil] *Bryttan oððe Francan*-J] *brytt Franca*-
Nw, Holt   90. *iu*-Whe, D, Holt, G, Hil, J] *in*-Nw   92. *sylfe*-D, G, J] *sylf*-Nw, Whe,
Holt, Hil   93. *rices*-D, G, Hil, J] *rice*-Nw, Whe, Holt   94. *Gregoriæ*-Nw, Whe, D, G,
Hil, J] *Gregorie*-Holt

XIII.

Þus he gesette   sylf ond dyhte   95
þa þenunga,   þeoda lareow,
fæstentida;   we þam forþ nu gyt
geond Engla land   estum filiað,
swa he æt þæm setle   sylfa gedemde
Sancte Petres.   Preostas syþþan   100
lange lifes tyd   leordun þæt sylfe,
þæt þu oþrum ne scealt   æfre filian.

XIV.

Eac we feowertig daga   fæsten healden
ær þæm æriste   ures dryhtnes,
þæt nu lengtentid   leoda nemnað,   105
and hit ærest ongan   eorl se goda,
mære Moyses,   ær he on munt styge;
he þæt fæsten heold   feowertig daga
and nyhta samod,   swa he nahtes anbat
ær he þa deoran æ   dryhtnes anfenge.   110

---

95. *dyhte*–Nw, D, G, Hil, J] *dihte*–Holt 96. *þeoda lareow*] *þeodlareow*–D, Holt, G, Hil, J] *þeod lareow*–Nw 97. *fæstentida*–Holt] *fæstendtida*–Nw, D, G, Hil, J 98. *geond*–D, Holt, G, Hil, J] *geeond*–Nw *filiað*– D, G, Hil, J] *fyliað*–Holt] *fihað*–Nw 99. gedemde–D, Holt, G, J] *gedemda*–Nw] om. Hil 100. *syþþan*–Nw, D, G, Hil, J] *sippan*–Holt 101. *tyd*–Nw, D, G, Hil, J] *tid*–Holt *leordun*–D, G. Hil, J] *lærdon*–Holt] *leordu*–Nw 102. *filian*–Nw, D, G, Hil, J] *fylian*–Holt 103. *healden*–Nw, D, Holt, G, J] *healdan*–Hil 105. *leoda*–Nw, D, G, Hil, J] *leode*–Holt 107. *styge*–Nw, D, G, Hil, J] *stige*–Holt 109. *nyhta*–Nw, D, G, Hil, J] *nihta*–Holt *anbat*–D, G, J] *onbat*–Holt] *anbate*–Nw, Hil 110. *anfenge*–Nw, D, G, Hil, J] *onfenge*–Holt

XV.

Him þær gesealde   sylfe dryhten
bremne boca cræft,   bæle behlæned,
of his haligan   handa gescrifene,
het hine leodum þone   leoran and tæcan
elda orþancum   eallum to tacne,   115
þæt we mid fæstene magon   freode gewinnan
and þa deopan   dryhtnes gerynu,
þa þe leoran sceolan   leoda gehwylce,
gif us þære duguþe hwæt   dryhten sylleð.

XVI.

Eft Helias,   eorl se mæra,   120
him on westene   wiste geþigede,
þær him symbelbread   somod mid wætere
dryhtnes engla sum   dihte togeanes,
and se gestrangud wearð   styþum gyfle
to gefæstenne   feowertig daga   125
and nihta samod,   swa he nahtes anbat
ær he on Horeb dun   hali ferde.

---

111. *gesealde*–D, Holt, G, Hil, J] *gescealde*–Nw   *sylfe*–Nw, D, G, Hil, J] *sylfa*–Holt   113. *haligan*–Nw, D, G, Hil, J] *halgan*–Holt   114. *leoran*–Nw, D, G, Hil, J] *læran*–Holt   115. *orþancum*–D, Holt, G, Hil, J] *onþancum*–Nw   118. *leoran*–D, Holt, G, Hil, J] *læra*–Holt] *leora*–Nw   *sceolan*–Nw, D, G, Hil, J] *sceolon*–Holt   120. *Helias*–Nw, D, G, Hil, J] *Elias*–Holt   124. *se gestrangud*–D, Holt, G, Hil, J] *ge se strangud*–Nw   *styþum gyfle*–Nw, D, G, Hil, J] *stiþum gifle*–Holt   126. *anbat*–Nw, D, G, Hil, J] *onbat*–Holt

XVII.

Uton þæt gerine   rihte gehicgan,
þæt se mæra þegen   mihta ne hæfde
to astigenne   stæppon on ypplen   130
ær him þæt symbel wearþ   seald fram engle.
We sint on westene   wuldres blisse,
on þæm ænete   ealra gefeana;
nu is helpes tid,   halig dryhten,
hu we munt þinne   mærne gestygan.   135

XVIII.

Sint for englas geteald   eorþbugendum
þa þe dryhtnes word   dædum lærað.
We þa andlifene   ofstum þycgen
and þone deoran wist,   dryhtnes lare;
uton fæstan swa   fyrene dædum   140
on forhæfenesse   her for life,
þæt we þæs muntes mægen   mærþa gestigan
swa se ealda dyde   Elias iu.

---

128. *gerine*–Nw, D, G, Hil, J] *geryne*–Holt   *gehicgan*–Nw, D, G, Hil, J] *gehycgan*–Holt   129. *þegen*–D, Holt, G, Hil, J] *hegen*–Nw   130. *stæppon*–Nw, D, G, Hil, J] *stæppan*–Holt   135. *hu*–D, Holt, G, Hil, J] *hii*–Nw   *gestygan*–Nw, D, G, Hil, J] *gestigan*–Holt   136. *eorþbugendum*–D, Holt, G, J] *eorþburgendum*–Nw, Hilt   138. *andlifene*–D, Holt, G, Hil, J] *and lifene*–Nw   *þycgen*–Nw, D, G, Hil, J] *þicgen*–Holt   140. *fæstan*–D, Holt, G, Hil, J] *sæstan*–Nw   *fyrene*–Nw, D, G, Hil, J] *firene*–Holt   141. *forhæfenesse*–Nw, D, G, Hil, J] *forhæfednesse*–Holt   143. *dyde*–D, Holt, G, J] *dyda*–Nw, Hil

XIX.

Is to hicganne   hu se halga gewat
of þissum wangstede   wuldres neosian;   145
hine fyren scryd   feower mærum
wlangum wicgum   on weg ferede
on neorxnawong,   þær us nergend Crist
gehaten hafað   ham mid blisse,
gif we þæt fæsten her   fyrena gelæstað   150
and þone uplican   æþel secað.

XX.

Nu wæs æt nehstan   þæt us nergend Crist,
halig heofenes weord,   heolp and lærde.
He hine dyppan let   deorum þweale,
fulwihtes baðe,   fyrena bedæled,   155
and he feowertig daga   firude mettas,
eac nihta swa feala   nanuht gyltig,
leodum to lare,   þæt hie on lengten sceolan
efen feowertig daga   fæsten hewan.

---

144. *hicganne*–Nw, D, G, Hil, J] *hycganne*–Holt   145. *neosian*–Nw, D, G, Hil, J] *neosan*–Holt   146. *scryd*–Nw, D, G, Hil, J] *scrid*–Holt   147. *wlangum*–Nw, D, G, Hil, J] *wlancum*–Holt   150. *fyrena*–Nw, D, G, Hil, J] *firena*–Holt   151. *æþel*–Nw, D, G, Hil, J] *eþel*–Holt   153. *weord*–Nw, D, G, Hil, J] *weard*–Holt   *heolp*–Nw, D, G, Hil, J] *healp*–Holt   155. *baðe*] *bæðe*–D, H, G, J] *bað*–Nw, Holt   *fyrena*–Nw, D, G, Hil, J] *firena*–Holt   156. *firude mettas*] *firsude mettas*–D, G, J] *firsude metta*–Hil] *firude metta*–Nw, Holt   158. *sceolan*–Nw, D, G, Hil, J] *sceolon*–Holt   159. *hewan*–Nw, D, G, Hil, J] *hegan*–Holt

XXI.

Hine costude þær   Cristes gewinna   160
on þæm ænete,   eald and fræte;
geseah mærne frean   mannum gelicne
and þa wenan ongann,   wommes gemyndig,
þæt he stræla his   stellan mihte
on þam lichoman.   Næs þæs leahtra nan,   165
ac on hinder gewat   hearmes brytta,
and þær englas hyra   ealdor sohtan.

XXII.

Hige, synnig man,   gyf þe susla weard
costian durre,   þonne he Crist dyde,
wereda wulderfrean,   womma leasne,   170
ne mæg he þæs inne   ahwæt scotian
gif he myrcels næfþ   manes æt egum,
ac he on hinder scriþ,   and þe halig [ ]
englas ærfæste   æghwær helpað,
gif þu dryhtnes her   dædum fylgest.   175

---

164. *stellan*-Nw, D, G, Hil, J] *stelan*-Holt   165. *lichoman*-D, Holt, G, Hil, J] *lichoman an*-Nw   *þæs*-Nw, D, G, Hil, J] *þær*-Holt   167. *hyra*-Nw, D, G, Hil, J] *hira*-Holt   *sohtan*-Nw, D, G, Hil, J] *sohton*-Holt   168. *Hige, synnig*-G, J] *Higesynnig*-Nw, D, Hil] *Synnig*-Holt   *gyf*-Nw, D, G, Hil, J] *gif*-Holt   170. *wereda*-Nw, D, Holt, G, J] *werede*-Hil   *wulderfrean*-Nw, D, G, Hil, J] *wuldorfrean*-Holt   172. *myrcels*-D, Holt, G, Hil, J] *myrcelrs*-Nw   173. *þe*-Nw, D, Holt, G, J] *he*-Hil   174. *ærfæste*-Nw, D, Holt, Hil, J] *arfæste*-Holt] *ærfeste*-G

XXIII.

Hæbbe we nu gemearcod   hu þa mæran iu
þæt feowertig daga   fæsten hewdon,
and we bebeodað   þurh beorn Godes
þæt manna gehwilc   þe ofer moldan wunað
ær þam æreste   ures dryhtnes   180
efen feowertig daga   fæsten hewe
oþ þa nigoþan tid,   and he na bruce
flæsces oþþe fysca,   þæ læs þe he fah wese.

XXIV.

Sceolan sacerdas   singan mæssan,
dæghwamlice   dryhten biddan   185
on þam fæstenne   þæt he freond wese
folce gynd foldan,   and þa fyrna sceolan
þam sacerdan   secgan gehwilce
and þa dymnissa   dædum betan
wordes and weorces,   wuldres ealdor   190
þurh ælmesdæde   eall gegladian.

---

177. *þæt feowertig*–Nw, Hil] *feowertig*–D, Holt, G, J   *hewdon*–Nw, D, G, Hil, J] *hegdon*–Holt   178. *beorn*–Nw, D, G, Hil, J] *bearn*–Holt   179. *ofer*–Holt, G, J] *for*–Nw, D, Hil   180. *æreste*–Nw, D, G, Hil, J] *æriste*–Holt   181. *hewe*–Nw, D, G, Hil, J] *hege*–Holt   183. *fysca*] *fisca*–Holt, G] *fyrna*–Nw, D, Hil, J   *þæ læs þe*–Nw, D, G, Hil, J] *þe læs þe*–Holt   *wese*–D, Holt, G, Hil, J] *were*–Nw   187. *gynd*–Nw, D, G, Hil, J] *gind*–Holt   *fyrna*–Nw, D, G, Hil, J] *firna*–Holt   *sceolan*–Nw, D, G, Hil, J] *sceolon*–Holt   188. *sacerdan*–Nw, D, G, Hil, J] *sacerdum*–Holt   189. *dymnissa*–D, G, Hil, J] *dimnissa*–Holt] *dymnisca*–Nw

XXV.

Þonne is þearf micel   þeoda mænium
þæt þa sacerdos   sylfe ne gyltan,
ne on leahtrum hiora   ligegen to fæste.
Hwa mæg þyngian   þreale hwilcum   195
wiþ his arwesan,   gyf he him ærur hæfð
bitere onbolgen,   and þæs bote ne deð,
ac þa æbyligþe   ealdere wrohte,
dæghwamlice   dædum niwað?

XXVI.

Gyf se sacerd hine   sylfne ne cunne   200
þurh dryhtnes ege   dugeþum healdan,
na þu, folces mann,   fyrna ne gyme
þe gehalgod mann   her gefremme,
ac þu lare scealt   lustum fremman
ryhthicgennde   þe he to ræde tæchð;   205
drince he him þæt drofe,   duge hlutter þe
wæter of wege,   þæt is wuldres lar.

192. *Þonne*–Nw, D, Holt, G, J] *Ðonne*–Hil *þeoda*–Nw, D, Holt, G, J] *þeode*–Hil 193. *sacerdos*–Nw, D, G, Hil, J] *sacerdas*–H *sylfe*–D, Holt, G, J] *sylfne*–Nw, Hil 194. *ne*–Nw, D, Holt, G, J] *no*–Hil *ligegen*–Nw, D, G, Hil, J] *licgen*–Holt 195. *þyngian*–Nw, D, G, Hil, J] *þingian*–Holt *þreale*–Nw, D, Holt, G, J] *þræle*–Holt 196. *gyf*–Nw, D, G, Hil, J] *gif*–Holt 198. *æbyligþe*–Nw, D, G, Hil, J] *æbylgþe*–Holt *ealdere*–Nw, D, G, Hil, J] *ealdre*–Holt 199. *dæghwamlice*–D, Holt, G, Hil, J] *dæg ghamlice*–Nw 200. *Gyf*–Nw, D, G, Hil, J] *Gif*–Holt *sylfne*–D, G, Hil, J] *sylne*–Nw, Holt 202. *na þu*–G, J] *nu þu*–Holt] *nu þa*–Nw, D, Hil *fyrna*–Nw, D, G, Hil, J] *firna*–Holt *ne*–D, Holt, G, J] *ni*–Nw, Hil 203. *gehalgod*–D, Holt, G, J] *gehalgode*–Nw, Hil 204. *fremman*–D, Holt, G, Hil, J] *fremnan*–Nw 205. *ryhthicgennde*–Nw, D, G, Hil, J] *rihthycgende*–Holt *ræde*–D, Holt, G, J] *rædi*–Nw, Hil *tæchð*–Nw, D, G, Hil, J] *tæcð*–Holt 206. *duge hlutter þe*–Nw, Hil, J] *oþþe þæt dæghluttre*–D, Holt] *duge þe hlutter*–G 207. *lar*–Holt, G, J] *lare*–Nw, D, Hil

XXVII.

Ac ic secgan mæg, sorgum hremig,
hu þa sacerdas sace niwiað,
dæghwamlice dryhten gremiað   210
and mid æleste ælcne forlædað
þe him fylian wyle folces manna;
sona hie on mergan mæssan syngað
and forþegide, þurste gebæded,
æfter tæppere teoþ geond stræta.   215

XXVIII.

Hwæt! Hi leaslice leogan ongynnað
and þone tæppere tyhtaþ gelome,
secgaþ þæt he synleas syllan mote
ostran to æte and æþele wyn
emb morgentyd; þæs þe me þingað   220
þæt hund and wulf healdað þa ilcan
wisan on worulde and ne wigliað
hwænne hie to mose fon, mæða bedæled.

---

209. *sace*–Nw, D, G, Hil, J] *sæce*–Holt   211. *æleste*–Nw, G, Hil, J] *æfeste*–D, Holt   212. *wyle*–Nw, D, G, Hil, J] *wile*–Holt   213. *mergan*–Nw, D, G, Hil, J] *mergen*–Holt *syngað*–Nw, D, G, Hil, J] *singað*–Holt   214. *forþegide*–Nw, D, G, Hil, J] *forþiwede*–Holt   216. *ongynnað*–Nw, D, G, Hil, J] *onginnað*–Holt   220. *þæs þe me þingað*–Hil] *þæs þe me þingeð*–D, G, J] *þæ þe me þinceð*–Holt] *þæ þe ø þingað ø me*–Nw   222. *wigliað*–Nw, D, G, Hil] *wicliaþ*–Holt] *wicliað*–J   223. *hwænne*–Nw, G, Hil, J] *hwæne*–D, Holt

XXIX.

Hi þonne sittende   sadian aginnað,
win seniað,   syllað gelome,   225
cweðað Godd life   gumena gehwilcum,
þæt wines dreng   welhwa mote
siþþan he mæssan hafað,   meþig þicgan,
etan ostran eac   and oþerne
fisc of flode.   230

225. *win*–Nw, G, Hil, J] *sinne*–D] *syn*–Holt   *seniað*–Nw, G, Hil, J] *semað*–D, Holt   226. *cweðað*–D, Holt, G, Hil] *cweðað þæt*–J] *cwedað*–Nw   *Godd life*] *goddlife*–Nw, D, G, Hil] *godlice*–Holt] *þæt Godd life*–J   227. *dreng*–Nw, D, G, Hil, J] *drenc*–Holt   *welhwa*–D, Holt, G, Hil, J] *wel wel hwa*–Nw   228. *meþig*–Nw, D, G, Hil, J] *mæþig*–Holt   *þicgan*–Nw, D, Holt, G, J] *þicgen*–Hil   229. *oþerne*–D, Holt, G] *oþerre*–Nw, Hil, J

Seasons for Fasting Translation

Note: This is a literal translation of the poem, tied to the Glossary and scholarly interpretations of difficult passages. Clarifications are included within parentheses as necessary.

I. (ll. 1–8)

In former days the people of Israel were, by Moses the famous teacher, enlightened and taught just as the Lord of Life, high King of the heavens, here in life by his own word placed him before the people as a benefit to men, and to him related himself an understanding of his mysteries, how he (Moses) should show his beloved nation the true way.

II. (ll. 9–16)

Then the ruler of the people (Moses) followed the teachings of the high King of the heavens, and the men did likewise, just as they were taught in the nation. If they began unstable deeds, the God of victories sent harm to them for that, in retribution from heaven, and they at once asked for protection from Him, and found it there quickly if they had cast away their sins.

III. (ll. 17–24)

Many are the powers that the glorious nation possessed and maintained in that troop as long as they would love the Lord of life; but the end for them came to be wretched and sorrowful when they ensnared the Lord himself, set him on a cross and condemned (him) to the grave. He was concealed there, and on the third day revealed to the people.

IV. (ll. 25–30)

We have heard many men proclaim and write in letters that (information), that they observed four fasts and then sacrificed a pure beast, that is a lamb or bullock, as a symbol for the Dear One who was, before the world, free of sins.

V. (ll. 31–38)

But the Prince of the kingdom (Christ) began to arise from the grave, filled with glories, and sought a home with dwellers in heaven, a dwelling with angels, and (he) promises that hope to us all, if we will obey his counsels with an upright spirit. No one filled with evil, covered with sin, will come therein, but (those) must flee into fate.

VI. (ll. 39–46)

Now we must praise here the excellent Doer of deeds (God) for life, and fill a number of days for him with our alms deeds and in fasting, just as the wise Moses said previously, and we must keep those occasions resolutely among the English just as that man in Rome, Gregory, the people's pope, wrote them down briefly for us.

VII. (ll. 47–54)

We must observe the first fast in the first week of Lent, in the month which is called March throughout the kingdom of Romans, and there we must read twelve mysteries with clear speech in the temple of the mighty one, high King of the heavens, praise with song, honor the great Lord of glory.

Translation

VIII. (ll. 55–62)

After Eastertide a second fast is to be observed by the people of Britain with like praise, those who have belief, in the week that comes after the Sunday that priests call Pentecost day throughout the wide land, in the month, as it seems to me, that was called Iunius of yore.

IX. (ll. 63–70)

Then is that third fast by like command prescribed in every respect for the sons of men on earth to celebrate in that precious house with clear song in the week that will be before the day of (the vernal) equinox, in the month, as I have heard say, which is called September.

X. (ll. 71–78)

We must perform the fourth fast in the full week which will be before the birth of the Lord, and we must, with pleasing words and deeds, celebrate the King of glory, the Prince, with all mindfulness in every respect at that same time, just as our ancestors [did], and ask the Lord, dear lord of the people, for life.

XI. (ll. 79–86)

During these fasts, the fourth day, together with the sixth and seventh immediately following, is to be observed for the Lord of life and to be celebrated with mysteries of books at the ninth hour. No one is on earth, unless illness afflict him, who may consume food or drink earlier, as the law of the doom books decrees for us as a people.

XII. (ll. 87–94)

If Bretons or Franks coming from the south should then say to you that you must hold to any (other) decree here on earth, which Moses formerly spoke to the people, let you never value the reception of it, but you hold to that (one) yourself, that which came from the south from the guardian of the kingdom of Rome, Gregory, pope of men.

XIII. (ll. 95–102)

Thus he (Gregory) himself, the people's teacher, set and established the observances of periods of fasting; we still gladly follow those now throughout England, as he himself decreed at the seat of St. Peter. Priests themselves taught that afterwards for a long time, that you never should follow others.

XIV. (ll. 103–110)

Likewise, we hold a forty days' fast prior to Easter, that now people call Lent, and the good leader, glorious Moses, first began it before he ascended on the mountain. He held that fast forty days and nights together, so that he consumed nothing before he received the precious law of the Lord.

XV. (ll. 111–119)

The Lord himself, surrounded by fire, gave to him (Moses) there the celebrated wisdom of books, written from his holy hand, (and) commanded him to instruct and teach that to the people, to all minds of men, as a symbol that we may with fasting attain peace and the profound mysteries of the Lord, which should be taught to each of peoples (everyone), if the Lord gives us the means of salvation.

Translation

XVI. (ll. 120–127)

Afterwards, Elijah, the glorious leader, received nourishment for himself in the desert, where one of the angels of the Lord set before him feast bread together with water, and he became strengthened by the austere food to fast for forty days and nights together, so that he consumed nothing before he journeyed onto holy Mt. Horeb.

XVII. (ll. 128–135)

Let us consider rightly that mystery, that the glorious thane (Elijah) did not have the powers to ascend the steps onto the summit until that feast was given to him from the angel. We are in a desert with respect to the bliss of glory, in that solitude (away) from all joys; now is the time for help, holy Lord, as to how we may ascend your glorious mountain.

XVIII. (ll. 136–143)

Angels are considered as earth-dwellers who teach the word of God by deeds. We should consume the nourishment and the precious food, the Lord's teaching, with haste. Let us fast so from deeds of sin in abstinence here for life, that we may ascend the glories of that mountain as the venerable Elijah did of yore.

XIX. (ll. 144–151)

It must be considered how the holy man (Elijah) departed from this place to seek glory; a fiery chariot carried him away with four horses, proud steeds, into paradise, where Christ the savior has promised us a home amid bliss, if we atone for sins here by fasting and seek the heavenly home land.

XX. (ll. 152–159)

Now at last it came to pass that Christ the savior, holy guardian of heaven, helped and taught us. He had himself baptized with that precious washing, with the immersion of baptism, (although) free from sins, and he removed food for forty days and as many nights, completely guiltless, as an example to people that they should adhere to the fast in Lent exactly forty days.

XXI. (ll. 160–167)

Christ's adversary, old and shameful, tempted him there in the solitude. He saw the glorious Lord in the likeness of a man (*lit.* like to men) and then began to expect, mindful of sin, that he might place his arrows in that body; there was no sin resulting from this, but (on the contrary) the perpetrator of affliction retreated (*lit.* departed back), and there holy angels sought their Prince.

XXII. (ll. 168–175)

Consider, sinning man, if the guardian of torments dare to tempt you, as he did to Christ, glorious Lord of hosts, free of sins, he cannot shoot anything of this within if he does not have a target of evil in sight, but he glides behind, and merciful holy angels will help you in every way, if you will follow here the Lord's example (*lit.* with deeds).

XXIII. (ll. 176–83)

We have now described how those glorious ones formerly observed the forty day fast, and we ordain through the son of God that each man who lives upon earth, before Easter, observe a fast exactly forty days until nones, and he should not eat flesh or fish, lest he be damned.

Translation

XXIV. (ll. 184–91)

Priests must sing Mass, pray to the Lord daily during the fast that he be a friend to people throughout the earth, and everyone must confess the sins to the priests and, to atone for the evils of word and deed by actions, completely appease the Prince of glory through alms deeds.

XXV. (ll. 192–199)

Then (there) is a great need for the multitudes of people that the priests themselves do not sin, nor remain too fixed in their vices. Who can reconcile any thrall with his Lord if he has greatly offended him previously and makes no atonement for it, but daily renews by his actions the annoyance of the old offense?

XXVI. (ll. 200–207)

If the priest does not know how to conduct himself excellently through fear of the Lord, don't you, layman, heed the sins that the ordained man may commit here, but you should gladly follow (his) doctrine, thinking what he teaches as counsel is right; let him drink that dirty water (of iniquity), let yourself be availed of the clear water from the (divine) way, that is the teaching of glory.

XXVII. (ll. 208–215)

But I may say, lamenting in sorrows, how the priests renew strife, daily offend the Lord with (their) neglect of religious law, and mislead each man of the people who will follow them. As soon as they sing Mass in the morning and have consumed (the Eucharist), impelled by thirst, they roam through the streets after the tapster.

XXVIII. (ll. 216–223)

Alas! They deceitfully begin to lie and urge the tapster repeatedly, say that he may, without sin, give (them) oysters as food and fine wine at morning-tide. For this reason it seems to me that a hound and a wolf follow the same practice in the world and don't use wiles when they take food, lacking moderation.

XXIX. (ll. 224–230a)

Then, sitting, they (the priests) begin to be sated, bless the wine, distribute (it) frequently, say God permits (it) to each of men, that everyone weary may partake of a drink of wine after he has Mass, eat oysters as well and other fish from the water.

Commentary

1. *Israhela:* Nw *israheala* This is the first of four readings in lines 1–7a emended to agree with Wanley's transcription of the passage, following the arguments of Sisam, "Seasons of Fasting" (59 and n 1) and Heyworth (358–59) for Wanley's superiority as a copyist. The ultimate source of stanza I is Exodus 3:7–9.

2. *þurh Moysen:* Per Dobbie's note, 194–95, *Moysen* is declined in the Latin acc. sing. The Concordance cites four occurrences of this phrase in the Old English Heptateuch: Exodus 9:35; Leviticus 8:36; and Numbers 1:54, 8:20, plus other examples from ecclesiastical prose, especially the works of Ælfric. *Moyses* is not declined in the Old English poem *Exodus*, however, nor in any other poetry. The references to Moses as a conduit for God's teaching here (stanzas I and II) and later (stanza XV) in *SF* are sufficiently vague to preclude direct links to *Exodus* or to Ælfric. On this point see Edward B. Irving, Jr., *The Old English Exodus*, 67–68.

3. *lifes frea:* L. Whitbread, "The Old English Poem *Judgment Day II* and its Latin Source," 638, cites the late OE usage of the genitive phrase in place of the compound (*liffrea*) as linking *SF*, lines 3 and 19; *JDay II*, line 80; *Creed*, line 5. The Concordance confirms that the phrase appears exclusively in these poems.

5. *þurh:* Correction of dittography, presumably Nowell's.

6. *runa gescead:* "understanding of mysteries." Several forms of $\bar{run}/ger\bar{\imath}ne$ appear elsewhere in *SF* at lines 52a, 82b, 117b, 128a. In each case, the reference seems to be to God's mysteries as embodied in the WORD. Cf. the OE gloss to *Liber Scintillarum* (10.41): *þæt is fullfremed 7 gesceadwislic fæsten, þænne ure mann uttra fæst se inra gebitt; þurh fæsten eac swylce diglu geryna beoð onwrigene 7 godcundes haligdomes diglu beoð geopenude* (Getty, 104–5). In this selection attributed to Isidore, God's mysteries are said to be revealed to those who engage in physical fasting and spiritual prayer: "that is perfect and reasonable

fasting, when our external man fasts (and) the inner (man) prays; through fasting all such secrets of mysteries will be revealed and secrets of the holy sacraments will be manifested."

8. **læran:** "show," hence the dative object *leodum leodscipe*.   **sceolde:** Nw *sceold* is presumably a copying error that violates the expected grammatical form and the rhythm of the verse type A. Cf. *SF*, line 11b *lærede wæron*.

9. **fyligde:** "followed, obeyed," used in this sense primarily in prose prescriptive materials (*DOE fyligian* A.5).

12. **wancule:** "unstable, fickle," modifying either *hie* or *weorc*, the latter option offering a smoother translation. This adjective appears elsewhere twice in the Old English translation of Boethius' *Consolation of Philosophy* (15, line 30; 47, line 20), in neither case applied to a person. See the edition by Walter J. Sedgefield, *King Alfred's Old English Version of Boethius' De consolatione philosophiae*. It is possible that Nw *weorce* was inflected mistakenly to agree with *wancule*, either by the poet or, more probably, Nowell. For grammatical and metrical reasons, the emendation to *weorc* is accepted here.   **ongunnon:** Nowell's copy of the ending is ambiguous: it could be *–an* or *–on*. Since the latter is correct grammatically, it is followed here.

15. **fryþa wilnodan:** "asked for protection," (*DOE friþ* 4.a.ii). See Grimaldi, "The Seasons for Fasting," 81, n 15a. Holthausen, 199, n 15, states that *fryþa* is "gen. Sg. Nach der *u*-Klasse." Cf. *Christ II*, 773: *utan us to fæder   freoþa wilnian* "let us ask (our) father for protection."

16. **leahtras:** It appears that Nowell originally wrote *leohtras* and then corrected to *leahtras*. In his note to to this line, Dobbie comments on the *ea/eo* spelling confusion throughout *SF* but does not offer an explanation for the problem.   **gewyrpan:** < Nw *gewyrpan* Sisam recommends this emendation in "Seasons of Fasting," 53. The translation "cast away" is preferable to "abandon" because it links *gewyrpan* etymologically to *geweorpan*; see Campbell, § 324. Cf. the meaning of *gewyrþe* in *SF*, line 91b: "estimate, value."

17. **feala is mægena:** "many are the powers." According to *DOE fela, feala* "many" can take a singular verb; *mægena* could indicate a copyist's misreading of pl. *mægenu*. Greeson, 180, translates the phrase "many a miracle," but does not provide a corresponding entry in the glossary.

Commentary

18.   *herescype: BTA* "troop," a *hapax legomenon*, possibly echoing *leodscipe* in line 11a.   *heold:* Nowell crossed out a final *e*.

20–24.   See Luke 24:19–21.

20.   *dreorig: DOE* 1a "anguished, sorrowful." All commentators agree that Nw *preoring* is unintelligible and may reflect more problems than a misreading by Nowell. With the exception of Dobbie, 195, n 20, the consensus emendation is to *dreorig*, a term popular with Ælfric, which requires less manipulation than does Dobbie's *prealic* and fits the context well. Cf. *JDay II*, line 35: *ac dreorige hleor   dreccað mid wope* (but [you] torment the sorrowful face with tears), Caie, "*Judgement Day II*", 86–7. See also Meroney, 199.

21.   *besyredon:* "ensnared" < *besyrian*, a verb used most frequently (four examples) in Ælfric's writings; cf. AEHom 3 (Pope I, 255), *Feria VI* for the second week in Lent, line 172, where the infinitive *besyrwan* translates Lat. *tenere*. The passage refers to the scribes and the Pharisees who wish to ensnare Christ but fear to do so on account of the multitude who regard Him as a prophet. Ælfric's source is the pseudo-Haymo homily on Matt. 21:33–46 (*PL* 118, 244–7).

23.   *[ ]:* This is the first of several apparent omissions from the poem. Sisam, "Seasons of Fasting," 60, observes that the proportion of missing words to the entire text is relatively high but he is unsure whether to ascribe the problem to an inept poet, an Anglo-Saxon copyist, or to Nowell. As Sisam indicates, the sense is clear in each case, and the addition of a formulaic filler would correct the defective verse. The question is, which formulaic filler may be missing? Here Dobbie, 195, n 23a, suggests an adverb or adjective alliterating with *d*, such as *deadne, deopne,* or *dierne*. Holthausen, 193, and Sisam support *deadne*, while L. Whitbread, "Notes on The 'Seasons for Fasting'," 250, proposes a noun—*dome* or *dryhtne*, and Meroney, 199, offers *to deaðe*. Despite these suggestions, there is no clear basis upon which to make an emendation.

25–30.   With six rather than the usual eight lines, this is one of three defective stanzas in the poem. Since there are three other stanzas (V, XVII, XXI) that conclude with a two-line independent clause, Nowell, or an Anglo-Saxon copyist, may have omitted the last pair inadvertently. Supporting this idea,

Sisam, "Seasons of Fasting," 47, observes that a reference to the Crucifixion would be the obvious transition between the sacrifice of the lamb or heifer and the Resurrection. Cf. for example, Ælfric's treatment of the topic in *CH* II, 15 (for Easter Sunday), esp. lines 34–49.

26.   **breman:** *DOE* 1b "proclaim (something)."

27.   **fæstenu feower:** Presumably the OE rendering of the Latin *ieiunium quattuor temporum*. The source for *SF*, lines 27–30 is Deuteronomy 16:1–2.

28.   **unmæne:** "pure." A rare adjective used similarly in *Creed*, line 14a: *Ides unmæne*, in reference to the Virgin.

29.   **styrc:** "bullock." Found elsewhere as a simplex only in the writings of Ælfric, per the Concordance.

30.   **for worulde:** Nw *for woruld* Cf. *SF*, line 222a *on worulde*.

31–38.   See Luke 24:46–49.

33.   **heofenwarum:** Nowell corrected a second *o* to *e*.

35.   **hyht gehateð:** It appears that Nowell first wrote *7* and then corrected to *3* but neglected to cross out *7*. See Sisam, 33–34. Greeson, 219–20, interprets *hyht* as a 3rd sing. pres. indic. contracted form of *hyhtan* "to hope," which would be the unique attestation of the form as a finite verb. The present edition interprets *hyht* as an asm noun modified by *þone*. *SF*, line 35b seemingly alliterates on *his* (type C), a possible indication of the poet's metrical carelessness according to Greeson, 219.

37.   **Nan:** The emendation from Nw *na* assumes that the final *n* (or, more probably, nasal abbreviation) was omitted by a copyist. Given the singular verbs *cumeð* (cf. *SF*, line 58b) and *scal*, which otherwise lack a subject, together with the awkwardness of *na* and the presumption of two additional copying errors in the following line of this independent clause, the case for intervention is strong. Omission of final *–n* occurs three other times in the poem: *fæste[n]* in line 71; *leordu[n]* in line 101; *leora[n]* in line 118.

38.   **womme:** "with sin." Emended from Nw *wommo* by all editors. Nowell himself corrects a number of similar copying errors involving unstressed vowels. In line 33, for example, he corrects *heofona* to *heofena*, and in line 43 he changes *mælda* to *mælde*.   **gewered:** Nw *gewesed* "covered." See Greeson 220, n 38 for analysis. This is an example of scribal confusion of long *r* with

Commentary

long *s*, of which there are three further examples in the poem at lines 172 (*myrcels* < *myrcelrs*) and 183 (*fysca* < *fyrna*), (*wese* > *were*). Neither form, *gewered* < *gewerian* nor *gewesed* < *gewēsan*, occurs in the corpus of OE with an abstract concept like "sin." *Gewered*, in the sense used here, normally refers to garments, but these can be the clothes of angels; *gewesed* "soaked," on the other hand, refers to a liquid such as vinegar, wine, or water. Since the description of being covered in sin as opposed to, hypothetically, angels' garments, or glory, better fits those barred from the heavenly home depicted in the stanza, *gewered* is preferable as the metaphoric form.   **scal:** An unusual form of *sceal*, possibly a copying error, not found elsewhere in the poem; cf. *scealt*, lines 102 and 204. Although most examples of *scal* occur in prose, it appears in *Gen. A,B*, line 663. See Campbell §156.   **on wyrd:** Sisam 54 proposes emending to *forwyrd* per the example of *Andreas*, line 1594b: *in forwyrd sceacan*. However, since the latter is not a formula, there is no compelling reason to emend.

39.   **her for life:** Nw *fon* A copyist, probably Nowell, has confused *r* and *n*. There is similar confusion evident in lines 115 (*orþancum* < *onþancum*) and 229 (*oþerne* < *oþerre*). Nowell corrects himself in line 122 (*wætere* < *wætene*). Line 39b is a formula that appears as well in *SF*, line 141b and *Creed*, line 51b, but nowhere else in the corpus of OE. *SF*, line 4b has the variant *her on life*.

40.   **dædfruman:** "doer of deeds, God." DOE *dædfruma* lists seven occurrences of the word, all in poetry; the example in *Andreas*, line 72, also refers to God. **dogera:** Nw *do geara* An unusual form that clearly means *dogera* "days." The separation of the first two syllables may reflect uncertainty in Nowell or his exemplar about the word and hence have led to the addition of *a* to form *geara* "years" following *do*. For discussion, see Whitbread, "Notes," 250; Sisam, "Seasons of Fasting," 51; Meroney 199; and Leslie 555. Alternatively, Nowell may have anticipated the final *a* as he did in producing *Israheala* in *SF*, line 1. The phrase *dogera gerim* is a variant of the poetic formula found in *Beowulf*, lines 823a (*dogor gerimes*) and 2728a (*dogera dægrim*) and elsewhere in the corpus. A contemporary example appears in *Menologium*, line 96a *dogera rimes*, cited by Whitbread, "Notes," 250.

43.   **mælde:** Nowell corrected final *a* to *e*.

44. **higefæste:** "resolutely," one of two occurrences of this word recorded in the Concordance. Although *B-T*, Greeson 182, and Jones 159 interpret this as an adjective, the construction is ambiguous, as it is in the Exeter Book *Riddle 40*, in *The Old English Riddles of the "Exeter Book"*, ed. Craig Williamson, 95, line 14: *hygefæste heold*. In this edition both examples are interpreted as adverbs, per *DOE fæste*.   [ ]: Holthausen 193, Whitbread, "Notes," 250, Sisam, "Seasons of Fasting," 60, n 1, and Jones 158 propose *hēr* to fill the seeming lacuna in the b verse with an alliterating long monosyllable of the type found in *SF*, lines. 4b, 39b, 141b, and 203b.

45.   **hie:** Queried by Greeson 222 as a possible mistake for *he*, but clearly acc. pl.

47.   **We:** Nw *Þe* The capital shows confusion between thorn and wynn. The emendation to *We* is per the parallel construction in *SF*, line 71a.   **fæsten heowan:** "celebrate...fast." Nowell corrected *fæstan* to *fæsten*. This is a formulaic expression in *SF*, also appearing in lines 159b, 176b, and 181b. In all instances the on-verse alliterates on the number, *forme* here, *feowertig* elsewhere. The origin of *hēowan* is uncertain. Dobbie 195 suggests *hēgan* < *gehēgan* "do, perform, hold" and notes that the alternation of intervocalic *g* and *w* occurs elsewhere in OE, as in *hīwan/hīgan* "family." The history of this development, together with vocalization leading to forms such as dat. pl. *hēowum*, appears in Campbell §412, 619.5. The usage of *hēowan* "to observe a fast" is said to be unique to *SF* in *BTA*, but the Concordance cites a possible parallel *heweð fif feste*, quoted by Wanley 233 from *HomM 15*, 8.1. Although Wanley gives only the incipit and explicit from this homily, which is otherwise unidentified, its language is clearly very late Old English.

48.   **wucan:** Corrected from Nw *wircan* on the basis of comparable examples in *SF*, lines 58a, 67a, and 72a.   **lengtenes:** This is the first of the disputed dates for Ember fasts, inasmuch as it depends upon the moveable date of Easter. *SF* has the only poetic uses of the word, per the Concordance.

50.   **nemneð:** Nw *nemnað* Cf. *SF*, lines 62b and 70b where *man* takes the singular form of this same verb, whereas a plural subject precedes *nemnað* in *SF*, lines 60b and 105b. The line echoes *Creed*, line 26: *under Romwarum   rices and doma*.

Commentary

51–52.   *twelfe sceolan....torhtum dihte/runa gerædan:* A probable reference to the liturgy for the day, the lessons for the Saturday of Ember week, according to Dobbie 195. This edition follows Greeson 226, who interprets *dihte* here as instr. sing. and in line 65 as a dat. sing. noun referring to the reading of the lessons in order; see *DOE dihte* 3.d: "utterance, speech, voice." Two instances of the pret. 3 sing. verb *dihte* < *dihtan* "establish, place set" occur in *SF*, lines 95b and 123b.

54.   *wlancne:* Sisam, "Seasons of Fasting," 48 points out that *Creed*, line 48 also applies the adjective *wlanc* to the Divinity; this is the only other such example found in the Concordance.   *wuldres bryttan:* DOE *brytta* b.iii "Lord of glory."

57.   *gelefen:* "belief." Nowell made a false start after the prefix that, although excised, appears to be *lufe*; he then wrote *lesen*. Given his propensity to confuse *f* and long *s*, and the fact that *gelefen* makes sense, whereas *gelesen* is an unknown word, emendation is a reasonable choice here. Jones 403–404 argues for *gelesu* "readings" modifying the previous half-line and clarifying the liturgical practice referenced there, but the proposal is unconvincing.

58–62.   *on þære wucan:* The second disputed date for an Ember fast, this time located in June and again dependent upon the date of Easter. Nw *þær* is emended to the dat. sing. fem. per the identical constructions in lines 47 and 67. Nw *cumað* is emended to the sing. *cumeð* per the parallel construction in l. 37a.

59.   *sunnandæge:* A rare poetic usage of this word, which otherwise appears only in *Gloria I*, l. 25. See E. G. Stanley, "Studies in the Prosaic Vocabulary of Old English Verse," 389.

65–66.   *gelicum:* Sisam, "Seasons of Fasting," 54, proposes reading *gelicum* as parallel with *beorhtum*, "with the like clear song," but it modifies *dihte* when the latter is read as a dat. sing. noun per Greeson as above, lines 51–52. As Greeson observes (226), the context refers once more to the reading of the lections.

66.   *brymenne:* Nowell first wrote *dry*, then crossed through the false start and began the correct word.

69.   *mine gefræge:* A poetic formula "as I have heard say," per *DOE gefræge*.

Commentary

70.   *[ ]:* Holthausen 200, followed by Jones 160, proposes the emendation *side* to fill the lacuna, citing *sidne* (*SF*, l. 59b) as a parallel instance of an alliterating *s* in the b half-line. The example of *SF*, line 62b is instructive, where the relatively meaningless *gearum* precedes *nemde* to alliterate with the name of the month *Iunius*. Here *side*, the type of word occasionally omitted by Nowell, would fill the same function for *September*, though it should be noted that the word appears otherwise only as an adjective (line 59) in the poem. For less persuasive suggestions, see Whitbread, "Notes," 250.

71.   *fæsten gelæstan:* Emended from Nw by analogy with the parallel construction in *SF*, line 47b *fæsten hēowan*.

72.   *þære:* Nw *þær* Emended on analogy with the same constructions in *SF*, lines 48a and 67a, as per the emendation in l. 58a.   *bið:* The *i* is written above a crossed-out *y*.   *full:* As Sisam, "Seasons of Fasting," 53 points out, the poet here provides an awkward translation of the ordinance attributed to Gregory which specifies *in plena hebdomada*.

73.   *deorum:* Nw *deornum* "secret" makes no sense within the context here of public observances of the fast, as Greeson observes, 227. Cf. line 65b, where *deoran* is used in reference to the observance of the third fast. There are no instances of *deorn* in *SF*, whereas all five examples of *deor* reflect the divine meaning proposed here. Following Sisam, 54, the emendation should be understood as "pleasing (to God)."

76.   *deman:* "celebrate" takes dative of person in *SF*, per *DOE deman* II.F. Hence the objects *cyninge* (line 74b) and *þeodne* (line 76a). The verb (as *demeð*) is used in another sense ("decrees") in line 86b, per *DOE* II.D.   *gehwylces:* Nowell made another false start by omitting the *h* and then correcting the mistake.

77.   *arwesan:* "revered, honored one, the Lord." This noun, also found in line 196a, appears elsewhere only in the Winteney version of the Benedictine Rule, 63.115.20, per *DOE arwesa*.

80.   *seofoþa:* This emendation from Nw *feoroþa* is required for the sense of the passage that has already covered fasting on the fourth (Wednesday) and sixth (Friday) days of the week. A copyist, possibly Nowell, must have confused long *s*, *f*, and long *r* to produce this reading. See notes to *SF*, lines

Commentary

38 and 57 above, and Greeson 228–29.   ***getenge:*** < Nw *getinge* Greeson 229 keeps the Nw reading and interprets it as modifying *dæg*, but thereby strains the meaning of the inflected infinitives: "...are eloquent in the service [*to gelæstanne*] of the Prince of Life and for honoring him [*to bremenne*] by the mysteries of the missals at the ninth hour" (185). Dobbie's note (196) offers "eloquent to serve and to celebrate." His translation captures the infinitives but also accepts *getinge* "eloquent", which normally is applied to persons or speech, according to *BT* and *BTS*. Better is the emendation to the adverb *getenge* "near to, close to, immediately following," which more nearly fits the sense of the passage. See Sisam, "Seasons of Fasting," 59 and n 2. Jones 160–61 keeps *getinge* but translates it as *getenge*. Two other instances of *i/e* confusion appear in *SF*, lines 202 (*ne* < *ni*) and 205 (*ræde* < *rædi*).

82.   ***gerynum:*** Nowell corrected an *i* with a *y* above it.

83.   ***þa nigoþan tyd:*** Nowell again corrected an *i* to *y* in *tyd*. The phrase is a reference to nones. Frederick J. Tupper, as cited by Dobbie 196, n 83b–86, explains this passage in "Anglo-Saxon *Dæg-mæl*," 174–75.

84.   ***butan:*** Nw *butan butan* The dittography is actually a misplaced catchword, coming at the end of Nw p. 258 and the first word on p. 259. The phrase *butan...an* means "except only" per *DOE an* A.4.c.vii.

85.   ***æt oþþe wæt ærur picgan:*** Two emendations are required to make sense of this line. The first, Nw *hæt* to *æt*, restores the widely-used prose formula, a correction made by Dorothy Whitelock in "Old English," 32, and referenced by Sisam, "Seasons of Fasting," 54, n 1. For a related use of *æt*, see, *SF*, line 219a. A similar problem with initial *h* before a vowel, which Nowell corrects, occurs in *SF*, line 119a (*hus* > *us*). The second emendation required in this line, Nw *þingan* to *picgan*, per Whitbread, "Notes," 250, provides the necessary verb of consumption.

86.   ***boca dom:*** "law of the doom books." Possibly a reference to the laws of Æthelred, specifically V. 15 and VI. 23 on the observance of fasts, though this phrase can refer more broadly to penitential books, per *DOE dom* 6.6.a. See Liebermann, *Die Gesetze*, 1:240, 252 for V and VI Æthelred. The rare phrase *boca dom* is distinct from the compound *domboc*, which most often refers to the laws of Alfred and Ine.   ***þeodlic:*** "as a people." Sisam, "Seasons of Fasting,"

51 and Greeson 310 interpret this rarity as an adjective "national." Given its ambiguous syntactical position, however, it works better as an adverb. Since final *e* is not required metrically and, according to Campbell §668 and n 1, *peodlic* as an adverb is an acceptable form, emendation is unnecessary. The translation "national" also implies a legal interpretation of *boca dom* that may be inaccurate, as in Greeson's translation (185): "because the national ordinance of the books decrees it for us." Hilton, "An Edition and Study," 64 offers an attractive interpretation derived from OE *gepeodlic*: "as the judgment of books deems proper for us." The difficulty lies in the translation of *gepeodlic*, meaning "social" according to *BTS* and *BTA*. Without more evidence, the passage must be translated literally while its significance remains obscure.   Line 86 is the only line in *SF* that does not alliterate. Sisam 51 proposes reversing the words in the b verse to achieve alliteration, and Jones 162 follows suit. Sisam also conjectures that the awkward phrasing here could result from translating a Latin source. Since there are no instructive parallels in Nowell's copies of poetry, including *SF*, this edition follows Nw.

87–94.   This is the stanza transcribed from Ot and published by Wheelock 96. Since Wheelock there gives specific page and line references that do not fit Nowell's transcript, but do reflect what we know of Ot, we can assume that he copied directly from it. This edition follows Wheelock's readings because he is the more accurate transcriber. However, comparison of Nw and Whe indicates that the text in Ot was defective in places; see the notes to specific words below.

87.   **secgen:** Nw *secgan* Wheelock prints *secgen*, the plural subjunctive form.

88.   **Brytta oþþe Franca:** Nw is defective here: *brytt Franca* Wheelock prints *Brýtt. oþþe Franca*. The dot following *Brýtt.* may indicate an abbreviation though, if accurate, it would be the only recorded instance of this usage in the poem. Regardless, *Brytt* needs an ending when, as here, it is interpreted as the noun "Breton." Following Grant, "A Note," 304, the emendation is to the nom. pl. *Brytta*, in coordination with *Franca*. Per the Concordance, the paired terms *Brytt-* and *Franc-* first appeared in the Anglo-Saxon Chronicle entries for 890 (MS D, the "Worcester Chronicle," MS Cotton Tiberius B. iv) and 891 (MS C, the "Abingdon Chronicle," MS Cotton Tiberius B. i).

Commentary

90.   *iu:* Wheelock's reading is superior to Nw *in*; Nowell may have had doubts about the final letter since he does not finish the second stroke of *n* as he does elsewhere.

91.   *andfeng:* Based upon the general sense of this line, namely, advice to the listener not to accept the continental dates for Ember fasts in place of those mandated for the English by Gregory, this edition accepts the interpretation offered by Dobbie 196 and *DOE andfeng* 1.c. "never value the reception of it." *SF,* line 110b employs the 3 sing. subj. verb *anfenge* < *anfon* in a related but positive sense, with reference to Moses receiving the law of the Lord.

92.   *sylfe:* The emendation is necessary for grammar and meter, though *sylf* appears in both Nw and Whe. The three other examples of the nom. sing. reflex. form (at lines 95b, 99b, 111b) are grammatically and metrically correct.

93.   *rices:* Both Nw and Whe have *rice,* which needs correction to make sense. Cf. line 31b *rices ealdor.* Grant, "A Note," 304 interprets this example as further evidence that Ot had a corrupt copy of the poem. Final *s* is also omitted from line 156b *mettas* and line 220b *þæs.*

95.   *dyhte:* Here, as cited in *DOE dihtan* 4b in conjunction with *gesettan:* "establish, institute, appoint." The verb is used differently in *SF,* line 123b *dihte,* as *DOE* 7 "to set, place, put, lay before."

96.   *þeoda lareow:* Nw *þeod lareow* is metrically faulty. Emendation here follows Sisam 50 and the genitive plural of *SF,* line 192b *þeoda mænium.*

97.   *fæstentida:* Nw *fæstend tida* Two mistakes typical of Nowell seem to lie behind this word: uncertain division of compounds and what Greeson 232 terms "dittographic anticipation." Per the *DOE, fæstentida* otherwise occurs primarily in works associated with Wulfstan.   *forþ nu gyt:* Translated following *DOE forþ* A.3a.vii "still."

98.   *geond:* Nw *geeond* Corrects a copying error (dittography).   *filiað:* Emended from Nw *fihað* as parallel in meaning with *filian,* line 102b. A copyist seemingly misinterpreted *li* as *h.*

99–100.   The present edition follows Holthausen 195 but differs from Dobbie and Greeson in the punctuation of these lines, construing the dependent clause (*swa he...*) to refer back to the pronoun *þam,* which in turn refers to the periods of fasting established by Pope Gregory for the English. The phrase *æt þæm setle* alludes to the See of St. Peter.

99. **gedemde:** Nw *gedemda* is emended to the pret. 3 sing. Nowell struggled with this word, having corrected the second *e* from *a*.

100. **Sancte:** The gen. sing. masc. form is a development of Latin *sancti*; see Greeson, 232.

101. **leordun:** "taught" < *læran*. It appears that Nowell had difficulty with the form in Ot and, having copied all of the letters, added a nasal sign over the *u*, then crossed out the sign. This is the first instance of *læran/gelæran* with an *eo* spelling in *SF*. Per the Concordance, the alternation (5 *æ* vs. 3 *eo*) within one work may be unique. It suggests confusion between *læran* (to teach) and *leornian* (to learn), possibly attributable to Nowell.

103. **healden:** Nowell has corrected the unstressed vowel of the ending from *a* to *e*.

106. **eorl :** Here in reference to Moses and in *SF*, line 120b to Elijah, the poet follows the practice of referring to Old Testament figures with the epithet found, for example, in the poems *Gen A,B*.

107–110. Deuteronomy 9:9.

109. **anbat:** A variant of the verb *onbitan*, emended from Nw *anbate*, per the identical construction in *SF*, line 126b.

110. **dryhten:** Nowell corrected this word by inserting *y* above the line.

111. **gesealde:** Nw *gescealde* The sense of the passage, reinforced by the similar phrasing of *SF*, line 119b at the close of the stanza, supports emendation here. The correct spelling is reflected in the past participle *SF*, line 131b *seald*.

111–112. Exodus 19:18.

114. **þone:** Refers to *SF*, line 112a *bremne boca cræft*, as Dobbie notes 197.

115. **orþancum:** "minds." Emended from Nw *on þancū*. Cf. line 122b *wætere*, where it appears that Nowell first wrote *n* for *r*, further evidence of his tendency to confuse these letters.

116. Another possible echo of *Creed*, line 40.

117. **deopan:** Sisam 50 points out that the meter and the meaning of this line would be preserved by *deoplican*. Since the poet employs numerous other

Commentary

short A3 verses in the first half line, however, there is insufficient evidence for emendation.

118.   ***leoran:*** Nw *leora* Emended on analogy with *SF,* line 114b.

119.   The (extra) ninth line of the stanza contributes little meaning to the unit, leading Sisam 47 to propose that it is a later addition. If so, the addition was made by someone familiar with the poet's idiom, since it echoes *SF,* line 111 which opens the stanza.   ***gif:*** *DOE gif* 1 provides a means for interpretation. Here *gif* introduces a conditional clause describing a conceded condition "in which the condition is…accepted as being fulfilled and applying to the matter in question." The referent is the gifts of the Lord, the focus of the stanza and its "envelope."   ***us:*** Nowell began with an *h* and then crossed it out.   ***duguþe hwæt:*** "the means of salvation." This unique phrase has been translated "something of value/benefit" and "some portion of virtue," but tools such as the Concordance, the *DOE*, and the *MED* offer some new ideas that make better sense here. In association with *dryhten, dugup* often is defined as "salvation"; see *DOE dugup* 3.b. And, used as a pronoun, the neuter form of OE *hwa, hwæt* has a range of interpretations that persist into ME, including "the means"; see *MED what* 1.c. Since the phrase sets the meaning of line 119, the more specific translation proposed here, linked to contemporary usage, better conveys its sense.

120.   ***Helias:*** 3 Kings 19:4–9.

122.   ***symbelbread:*** a *hapax legomenon.*   ***wætere:*** Nowell first wrote *n* and then corrected to *r.*

124.   ***se gestrangud:*** Nw *gesestran gud* Nowell's confusion here began with the interchange of initial *s* and *g* and continued with *–an,* which he seems to have interpreted as an infinitive ending. Greeson 234 points out that Dobbie's emendation of an obvious copying error is supported by the Biblical allusion: *…comedit et bibit, et ambulavit in fortudine cibi illius…* in 3 Kings 19:8. The unstressed *u* (for *o*) of the weak 2 past participle is retained here.   ***gyfle:*** "food" per *DOE gyfl,* a rare word used similarly only in *Guthlac B,* line 1300.

127.   ***hali:*** "holy" acc. sing. masc. modifying *munt* per 3 Kings 19:8 *…ad montem Dei Horeb.*

129. *þegen:* Another emendation to correct a probable copying error. The masc. noun *hege* "hedge" is meaningless here.

130. *ypplen:* "summit." As shown in the Concordance, this word is known otherwise only from glosses.

133. *ænete:* "solitude." Used identically here and in *SF*, line 161a, the rare feminine noun is modified by dsm or n *þæm* in both instances.

135. *hu:* Nw *hii* A probable copying error owing to minim confusion.

136–38. **Sint for englas geteald:** Schabram, "Zur Interpretation der 18. Strophe," analyzes stanza XVIII closely and accepts Holthausen's view that Malachi 2:7 has influenced this phrase. Citing *BT* and three examples from OE prose, he interprets *geteald* as the past participle of *DOE tellan* III (b): "with an object and prepositional phrase, *to consider as (to, for, on)*." Thus Schabram translates these lines, "Angels are considered as earth-dwellers who teach the word of God by deeds."

136. *eorþbugendum:* Nw *eorþ burgendum* "earth dwellers, human beings." Emended (by eliminating the intrusive *r*) to the usual form found, for example, in the writings of Ælfric and in late OE poetry such as *Creed*, line 21a, and *JDay II*, line 130b. The word *eorþburg* refers to an earthwork, rather than a person, as the context here requires.

138. *andlifene:* Nw *and lifene* The poet here develops the metaphor of proper, strengthening nourishment being the Lord's teaching. See *DOE andleofen* 1.c figurative: "spiritual sustenance, nourishment."

140. *fæstan:* Nw *sæstan* The Nw form is corrected for another *s/f* confusion in the transmission of the text. Here, as in *SF*, line 150, listeners are exhorted to fast not from food and drink but from sinful deeds. The ultimate source likely is Isaiah 58:5–6, but the phrase "to fast from sins" occurs in the liturgy for Lent. As Greeson 237 points out, this can be found in the Latin hymn attributed to Gregory the Great, *Audi, benigne conditor*, sung at Vespers during Lent. A similar phrase appears in the collect of the second Monday of Lent, *sectando justiciam, a culpa jejunet*. And St. Leo expresses the same thought at the end of the sixth lesson of Matins for the first Sunday of Lent. In short, the image is common to Lenten observances. Moreover, it also occurs in more general treatments

Commentary

of fasting such as chapter 10 of the *Liber Scintillarum*, (ed. Getty) attributed to Isidore.

142. Schabram, "Zur Interpretation der 18. Strophe," 300, n 24, argues that Grimaldi's interpretation of these lines in her edition 89 is correct: "that we may ascend the glories of that mountain." Mitchell, *OE Syntax*, §2846, reads the clause as expressing an intended result.

143. **se ealda...Elias:** follows the normal order for preceding a name cited in *DOE eald* I.A.1.a.i, but here as elsewhere in *SF* the referent name is separated from the adjective phrase and appears in the b verse. **dyde:** Nowell corrected *dæda* to *dyda*, but final *a* is emended to *e* to render the pret. 3 sing. "did," as in *SF*, line 169b.

145. **wangstede:** "place." A poetic word found as spelled here in *Andreas*, line 987 and *Elene*, lines 792 and 1095, per the Concordance. It appears as *wongstede* elsewhere.

146. **fyren scryd:** See 2 Kings 2:11.

147. **wlangum:** Although the usual spelling appears in line 54a, this is the first of three examples in the third and last part of the poem (the others being line 220b *þingað* and line 227a *dreng*) with –*ng* spellings for the expected –*nc*. Since –*ng* could reflect the poet's idiom, given that he seems to be speaking with his own voice here, and is possibly relevant to questions of dialect and date, the forms are retained.

150. **fæsten her fyrena gelæstað:** "atone for sins here by fasting" per *DOE fæsten* 2, 1.c.ii. figurative.

152. **wæs:** "came to pass" per B-T *wesan* I.6.

154–57. Matthew 4:1–4. These two statements about the purpose of Christ allowing himself to be baptized (when he was sinless) and to undertake a forty-day fast (while guiltless)—namely, to provide an example to his sinful and guilty followers—echo the orthodox rationale offered by Ælfric in his Second Series homily on the Epiphany, ed. Godden (*CH* II, 3, 198). See also Greeson's discussion, 239.

155. **fulwihtes baðe:** Nw *bað* A formula: *DOE fulluht, fulwiht* 6 "the immersion of baptism." There are examples of *bað* in Old English texts, so no change of the stem vowel is required. However, given Nowell's inconsistency with

Commentary

final *e* and the apposition of *bað* with *þweale*, this emendation to the dat. sing. ending is accepted for grammatical reasons. Metrically, final *–e* also provides a resolved stress for the type E half-line.   **fyrena bedæled:** *DOE bedælan* 2 "freed from sin."

156.   **firude mettas:** "removed food." The form *firude* < *DOE fyrran* 1.a "remove" is retained here because, although a rarer word than *firsude* < *fyrsian*, it has the same meaning. In the OE translation of the Confessional of pseudo-Egbert, the section on fasting, including Ember fasts, ed. Spindler in *Das ae Bussbuch*, has the phrases *forgang hwit* (170, line 15) "abstain from dairy foods, eggs, fish" and *forgange flæsc and win* (173, line 59) "abstain from meat and wine." This would be the expected usage but for the need to alliterate *feowertig*. Given problems with final *s* in Nw, the object *mettas* is emended to the strong masc. acc. pl. ending.

160–67.   The images and vocabulary of this stanza echo those found in *Christ II*, lines 763b–780a, which speak of the protection Christ offers from the devil, lest the *wrohtbora/ in folc godes....forð onsendeð/ of his brægdbogan.... biterne stræl* (lines 763b–765b); lest "the accuser send forth into God's people a sharp arrow from his deceitful bow." The devil's weapons are covered as well in some of Wulfstan's sermons, the ultimate source being Ephesians 6:14–17. E. G. Stanley discusses this image in "Old English Poetic Diction and the Interpretation of *The Wanderer, The Seafarer,* and *The Penitent's Prayer.*"

161.   **fræte:** Nowell made a false start omitting the *r*, crossed out *fæ*, and began again. According to the *DOE* the meaning is "wanton, shameful, or foul," not "proud" as Greeson argues 239–40. Jones 167 translates *fræte* as "perverse."

163.   **gemyndig:** The *i* has been written over *y* in Nw.

164.   Greeson 240 analyzes this passage in the context of the Old English prose *Guthlac*, where the term *stræl* is used as a metaphor describing the devil's temptations. See also Peter Dendle's discussion of the Vercelli Book and the devil's arrows in *Satan Unbound: The Devil in Old English Narrative Literature*, 33–35.   **stræla:** Nowell added the *r* above the line.

165.   **lichoman:** Nw *lichoman an*, a seeming case of dittography.   **þæs:** Here and in line 171a the poet employs the genitive of respect. Greeson 241–42

Commentary

reads these examples as adverbs of time "afterwards," but his interpretation works much better in line 165b than in line 171a. Both could reflect a copyist's confusion of long *s* and *r*, and therefore be read as *þær*. Since, however, there is no compelling reason to emend, the Nw readings stand. **leahtra:** Although Holthausen 200 translates this as "injuries," the poet's usage at lines 16a and 194a, "sins" or "vices," works here as well.

166. **hearmes brytta:** *DOE brytta* c.ii "perpetrator of affliction."

168. **Hige:** "consider." Following Sisam, "Seasons of Fasting," 51, the first element of what is written as the compound *Higesynnig* in Nw works better when interpreted as the imperative singular of *hicgan*, a verb used with similar meaning in *SF*, lines 128b and 144a. The emendation also supports the alliteration. Mitchell, *OE Syntax*, §3564, points to the subjunctive [*durre*] in the *gyf* clause as requiring an imperative [*Hige*] in the "Then-clause."

170. **wereda:** Nowell corrected final *e* to *a*.   **wulderfrean:** a *hapax legomenon*, although the related (in meaning) *wuldorcyning* appears frequently in the corpus of OE.   **womma leasne:** Nowell crossed out *po* before writing *womma*, having misread the wynn as *p*. The formula, discussed by Peter Orton in *The Transmission of Old English Poetry*, 117, occurs with slight variation seven times in Old English verse. It is applied similarly to Christ in *Christ III*, line 1451.

172. **myrcels:** Nw *myrcelrs* "target." This is a rare word (five instances) found most often in saints' lives, according to the Concordance. Nowell apparently corrected his misreading of *r* for *s* but neglected to cross out the *r*.   **egum:** Dobbie 197 interprets this as a variant of *eagum*, confirmed by *DOE eage* 1.c.ix.d. Campbell §312 describes the form in the context of lWS smoothing (131).

173. **scrip:** A contracted form, metrically correct. See Fulk, *A History of Old English Meter*, §331.   [ ]**:** Whitbread's suggestion ("Notes," 250) of *þegnas* to fill the lacuna in the b verse is appealing because the term has been applied previously in *SF*, line 129 to Elijah, *se mæra þegen*. Sisam, "Seasons of Fasting," 60 proposes *werod*, while Holthausen 201 offers *þreat* (also Jones, 168) or *scolu*, neither of which occurs otherwise in the poem. Since there are no appositives for *englas* elsewhere in *SF* and the requirements of alliteration are covered by *halig*, we lack conclusive guidance to identify the missing noun.

Commentary

175.   *dryhtnes:* Whitbread, "Notes," 251 and Sisam, "Seasons of Fasting," 56 counter Dobbie's suggestion (197) that *dryhtne* would be an improvement, noting that *fylgan* takes a dative object here (*dædum*) as in line 36b. The correct translation, then, is "follow the Lord's example."   **her:** Nowell first wrote *ærd* and then crossed it out.

176.   On the use of the inverted form *hæbbe we*, see H. M. Flasdieck, "Untersuchungen über die germanischen schwachen Verben III. Klasse (unter besonderer Berücksichtigung des Altenglischen)," *Anglia* 59 (1935): §17 gamma, 25, and Campbell §762. This inversion is found in homiletic prose, where it can occur as a subjunctive form or, as here, in construction with a past participle.   **gemearcod:** "described." This is another term used frequently in Byrhtferth's *Enchiridion*, but one that also appears in a variety of other Old English texts. It does not carry the technical sense that *mearc* bears in the *Enchiridion* and *SF*.

178.   *we bebeodað:* From this phrase, Sisam, "Seasons of Fasting," 50 concludes that the poet had greater authority than an ordinary monk or mass-priest.

179.   Since this line seems to reflect the formula *men ofer moldan* "men upon earth," as found, for example, in *Dream of the Rood*, lines 12 and 180 and *Prayer*, line 32a, Nw *for* is emended to *ofer* following Sisam, "Seasons of Fasting," 56.

180.   *æreste ures dryhtnes:* "Easter" per *DOE æriste* B.2.a. Nowell crossed out a final *t* on *ures*.

182.   *bruce:* < *brūcan* As used in penitential texts in reference to partaking of food or drink; see *DOE* sense 1.A.i.

183.   *fysca:* Nw *fyrna* At lines 140b and 150b the poet uses *fyrena* in the expression "fast from sins," but to couple this term with meat, especially as the objects of *brucan*, is at odds with the conventional objects of this direction found in penitential texts. Both flesh and fish are prohibited, for example, in chapter 40 of the OE translation of Theodulf's *Capitula*, ed. Sauer, 391, A. As Greeson points out on 243, the *SF* reference is to the normal injunction against taking food until the ninth hour on fast days. The poet returns to the issue of eating fish prematurely at lines 219–220a and 229–230a. Under the

Commentary

circumstances, it seems that one or more copyists, possibly including Nowell, confused *s* and *r* again and then corrected to a word familiar in the poem (lines 140b, 150b, 155b, 187b, 202b).   *fah:* "damned," per *DOE fah* 1.e, poetic use.   *wese:* Nw *were* Presumably another example of *s/r* confusion. Cf. *SF*, line 186b *freond wese.*

185.   *dæghwamlice:* "daily." This is one of two instances of the adverb *dæghwamlice* in *SF*, a word normally found in homiletic and religious prose. It appears as an adjective in *Lord's Prayer II*, at l. 69a, in the context of "daily bread."

186.   *wese:* Nw *we se* Nowell left a space between the two syllables that implies two words; this confusion, following another problem with the same form in line 183b, may indicate that he was simply unfamiliar with it.

187.   *gynd:* For the history of this development of *geond*, see Campbell §177. The form is not useful for determining dialectal influence. Since, however, this is the only instance among five examples in *SF* where such a spelling of *geond* occurs, it could be the result of scribal interference.

188.   *sacerdan:* For the dat. pl. ending in lW-S, see Campbell §378. *gehwilce:* "everyone." Used infrequently as a stand-alone pronoun, this form, when it has an *e* ending, seems to be in the nominative plural; cf. Ælfric, *CH* I, 2, line 71: *Gehwilce...cendon* "all...declared." The singular form appears in *JDay II*, line 121a: *þæt gehwylc underfo* "so that each will receive" (Caie, 90–91).

189.   *dymnissa:* Nw *dymnisca* "evils," per *DOE dymnis* 1.g, the feminine accusative plural object of *betan* "atone for," per *DOE betan* B.1. A copying mistake seems to lie behind the form in Nw.

191.   *eall:* Modifies the following verb. Nowell first wrote *ealle* and then crossed out the final *e*.

192.   *mænium:* "multitudes." Probably a lW-S form, per Campbell §267.

193.   *sacerdos:* This form is unique to *SF* in the poetical corpus, but used with sing. and pl. meanings in OE prose, per the Concordance.   *sylfe:* Nw *sylfne* Emended to the nominative plural form to agree with *þa sacerdos.* Compare *SF*, line 200 *se sacerd hine sylfne ne cunne...healdan*, where *hine sylfne* functions as the sing. direct object of *healdan* "to conduct."

Commentary

194. ***ligegen to fæste:*** Meroney 200 observes that this could be a poetic formula; if so, it would be a variant of *wunian to fæste* with a similar meaning (*DOE fæste* 1.a. "remain too fixedly") perhaps coined to alliterate with *leahtrum*. *SF*, line 16a has a similar example (*gif hie leahtras heora*) followed by an awkward *letan* carrying the alliteration in the b verse.

195. ***þyngian:*** "reconcile with" per *B-T* II.6. Nowell corrected *i* with *y*.   ***þreale:*** A Norse borrowing found prominently in the writings of Archbishop Wulfstan. See Greeson 19; Richard Dance, "Sound, Fury, and Signifiers;" 51–53; and the Concordance, *þræll* and *þreal*.

196. ***arwesan:*** A substantival adjective "Lord." Greeson's translation of this passage 193, lines 195–97, represents the text most accurately: "Who can reconcile any thrall with his Lord if he (the priest) has bitterly offended him before, and makes no amends for it?" The same form *arwesan* is used in apposition with *frean* in *SF*, lines 77b–78a. Elsewhere in the corpus of Old English it appears as a respectful epithet for religious personnel. In *DOE arwesa* the present instance of the term is assigned a general meaning "lord." But because in this stanza the poet addresses the role of priest as intercessor, the reference to the divinity can be assumed. *SF*, lines 209–10 returns to this theme of priests renewing strife with and thereby provoking the Lord through their sinful behavior.   ***ærur:*** The double comparative form allows the Sievers type B metrical pattern.

197. ***onbolgen:*** < *abolgen* See *DOE abelgan* 2.a. "to anger or offend God," which takes a dative or accusative of the one offended (*him*, line 196b).

198–99. ***æbyligþe:*** Nowell wrote *y* over *i* in the second syllable.   By construing *ealdere wrohte* as gen. sing. fem., Sisam, "Seasons of Fasting," 56 offers the best translation: "but daily renews by his actions the injury of the old offense." Note the implied comparison of neglectful priests with the work of the devil found, for example, in a homily for the fourth or sixth Sunday after Epiphany printed in Assmann 14 (164–69), at lines 102–114. In the previous stanza XXIV, the *SF* poet has reviewed the duties of priests to sing Mass, pray for the souls of the faithful, and exhort their listeners to turn away from evil ways to a better life of almsgiving. Now, the poet addresses the role of the priest as intercessor and reminds him that he must be free from sin if he is to gain God's mercy for others.

Commentary

199. **dæghwamlice:** After *dæg*, Nowell crossed out *hw* and wrote *ghamlice*. He writes the form correctly in *SF*, lines 185a and 210 a.

200–207. There is an unusually high number of obvious copying errors in stanza XXVI, some evident in Nowell's own corrections and others requiring emendation. Perhaps this portion of Ot was corrupt or fatigue had set in by the time Nowell reached this stage in the copying. Especially odd are two instances of *i* appearing in place of the expected *e* (see below).

200. **sylfne:** Nw *sylne* Cf. line 21b *sylfne dryhten*.

201. **dugeþum:** "excellently." See *DOE dugup* 1a for the adverbial usage. **healdan:** Nowell crossed out a redundant nasal abbreviation over the second *a*.

202. **na þu:** Emended from Nw *Nu þa*, per the analyses of Sisam, "Seasons of Fasting," 56 and Greeson 246. The same phrase appears in *SF*, line 91a in the poet's instruction to his audience not to heed false teaching about the dates of Ember fasts. Here, similarly, he warns the laity not to be misled by the possible wrongdoing of priests; see Mitchell's interpretation of this passage, *OE Syntax*, II, §2395. Given that it follows a dependent clause, Nowell's capital *N* does not signal the beginning of a new sentence. **folces mann:** *DOE folc* 6.a "member of the laity, layman." **ne:** Nw *ni* See note to l. 80.

203. **gehalgod:** Nw *gehalgode* Beginning with Dobbie 104, all editors have excised the final *e* on grammatical grounds, but it is also a problem for Sievers type B, as compared, for example, with line 201a. **her:** Nowell inserted *h* above the line. **gefremme:** See *DOE gefremman* 3.a.i. (after *firene*) "commit a sin." Bruce Mitchell, "Adjective Clauses," 320, provides an interpretation of the poet's use of the subjunctive here: the speaker expresses "doubt or uncertainty about the priest's sins—'whatever they may be' is the implication."

204. **fremman:** Nw *fremnan* Emended to correct another minim misreading.

205. **ryhthicgennde:** Another *hapax legomenon*; Greeson 194 translates this line "thinking what he teaches as counsel is right." **ræde:** Nw *rædi* See note to line 80.

206–207. Schabram, "206f," argues against emendation on the grounds that the meaning is clear, further supported by *DOE deag* A.2 "avails, is helpful to" with a dative object (2nd pers. acc. sing. *þē*). Greeson 246–50 offers an analysis of earlier interpretations of these lines. See also Whitbread,

"Four Notes," 189–90, and Leslie 557–58. The latter states that line 206b is a metrical type E, but actually it is a type D2.   *lar:* Nw *lare* The extraneous *e* is incorrect both grammatically and metrically. *SF,* lines 139b and 204a use *lare* correctly as an acc. sing.; there are no other instances of the nom. in the poem. Given Nowell's problems with final *e* (he corrects himself in lines 18b *heold* < *heolde* and 191b *eall* < *ealle*), this edition follows Sisam,"Seasons of Fasting," 56–57 and Greeson 194 and emends to *lar.*

208.   Magennis 88–92 offers a full analysis of the remainder of the poem in the context of an attack on undisciplined and irreligious clergy. He builds upon Hilton's characterization of *SF* as a complaint poem. The closing stanzas comprise a mix of homiletic formulae and rare vocabulary.   **sorgum hremig:** "lamenting in sorrow." The poetic formula is used similarly in *Soul and Body I geohþu hremig,* line 9, and *II gehþu hremig,* line 9 "lamenting in sorrow."

210.   *dryhten gremiað:* "provokes the Lord." A formulaic phrase from homiletic prose, also occurring as *God gremian*; see *DOE gremian* 1a.

211.   *æleste:* According to the *DOE,* a *hapax legomenon* < *ælyst,* meaning "neglect of (religious) law." For analysis of this word, see Sisam,"Seasons of Fasting," 57. Jones 401 translates the form as "irreligion."   *forlædað:* "mislead." As Magennis notes (91), the *Laws of the Northumbrian Priests* 11 specifies punishment for priests who lead people astray regarding the proper observance of festivals or fasts. See Liebermann, *Die Gesteze* I: 381 for the text.

213–215.   These lines introduce the first of Alcuin's three-part definition of gluttony, namely that the bad priests eat and drink too soon after Mass, and opens the parody of their behavior. Roberta Frank, "Old English *Æræt,*" 299–302 treats the importance of "early eating" to the Anglo-Saxons. See also Magennis 93–94.

214.   *forþegide:* < *forðecgan DOE* "consumed." See Sisam's discussion of the verb and its meaning, 57, which indicates that this form of *þecgan* is unique, confirmed by the *DOE. Christ,* line 1509a has the phrase *þurste geþegede,* but here in *SF* the direct object is *mæssan.* Stanley (private communication) points out the satirical violence of the poet, who portrays the elements of the Eucharist serving as "mere stimulants to crapulosity" for the lax priests, making them long for food and drink.

Commentary

215.   *tæppere:* Used here and in line 217a, this word is known otherwise only as a gloss for Latin *tabernarius* and *caupo*, both meaning "shop keeper" or "innkeeper."

219–220.   The second element of gluttony, namely, the consumption of delicacies, is described here.

220–223.   Regarding the third element of gluttony, eating and drinking excessively, the poet draws a comparison to the untimely and immoderate eating habits of animals, similar to one made in Ælfric's *Sermo de Memoria Sanctorum* (Skeat I: 359, lines 315–20), as noted by Sisam, "Seasons of Fasting," 58, n 1.

220.   *emb:* Nowell wrote *e* over an indecipherable letter.   *morgentyd:* Nowell wrote *y* over *i*.   *þæs þe me þingað:* Nw *þæ þe þingað me* Nowell used insertion marks to indicate that *me* should precede the verb. The missing *s* probably results from eyeskip. The plural ending on *þingað* is retained here although the phrase appears with variant orthography and inflection in *SF*, line 61b. The ending may represent a copying mistake, uncertainty in the unstressed vowel, or even confusion about the subject. Furthermore, since this is the second of three examples (the others being line 147 *wlangum* and line 227 *dreng*) of *–ng* for *–nc* in the last section of the poem, the spelling *þing-* is left unchanged. Mitchell discusses possible interpretations of the *þæs þe* clause in *OE Syntax* II, §2874.

222.   *wigliað:* Meroney 200 proposes this as a form of *wiclian* "hesitate, waver, dally," consistent with scribal substitutions of *g* for *c* elsewhere in this portion of the poem (line 220b *þingað*, line 227a *dreng*). He interprets its use as an example of litotes. But, as Magennis 90 points out, there are no attestations of *wiclian* in Old English. Ælfric uses *wīglian* as a verb once (*CH* I, 6, line 162), meaning to prognosticate auguries, while condemning the practice. Nominal forms such as *wīglere* "diviner, soothsayer, sorcerer" and *wīglung* "divination, sorcery" appear in OE homiletic references to pagan customs. However, a related noun *wīgle* may provide an essential hint for the usage in *SF*. Used as the devil's *wīgeles* "tricks, sorcery" in late OE and early ME, *wīgel* is related to "wile" and may be a reflex of ON *véla* "to defraud or betray." For further information, see *BT* and *BTS wīgel*, *MED wigelen*, *OED*

133

wiggle, wile. The sense of this passage is that dogs and wolves never *wigliað* "use wiles" when it comes to eating, putting aside their expected behavior and rushing voraciously to their food. Their habits are compared to those of priests who do not wait the proper interval for consumption after Mass, as appropriate to their office, and instead respond to their physical appetites. The metaphor is strained, but the meaning is clear. See Sisam, "Seasons of Fasting," 58 and Hilton, "Edition and Study," 34 for alternate interpretations of the passage.

223.   *fon:* Following this word, Nowell made a false start on the next word and crossed it out.   *mæða bedæled:* "lacking in moderation." See *DOE bedælan* 1 "bereft of" and Ælfric's use of *mæþ* "degree, measure" cited by Godden in *CH* glossary, 740.

224–230.   The third element of gluttony pursued by bad priests, eating and drinking too much.

224.   *sadian:* "to sate." Otherwise attested only with reference to ravens feeding their young in the OE version of the *Enlarged Rule of Chrodegang of Metz*, ch. 81 (96, line 7) *sadað*, pres. ind. pl. This verb choice links well to the gluttony depicted in the previous stanza.

225.   *seniað:* Nw *semað* "bless." Leslie 558 confirms the problem with minims as typical of the confusion resulting from Nowell's habits of transcription. See also Sisam, "Seasons of Fasting," 58 and Magennis 89, n 16 on issues related to Nw here. Magennis 92 points out the Eucharistic parody involved in priests blessing the forbidden wine. This is especially true given that the verb *senian* normally is used to bless the Eucharist or to make the sign of the cross or the Holy Trinity.

226.   *cweðað:* Nw *cwedað* There is only one other instance of *cweðað* (*cwedaþ*) cited in the Concordance, a gloss to the Gallican Psalter in BL MS Arundel 60 (c. 1073 according to Gneuss 60, no. 304). Both examples may reflect copying errors.   *Godd life:* The form *Godd* appears frequently in Wulfstan's homilies. Jones's interpretation (406) of line 206—"say that God would allow to every man"—is persuasive, although his insertion of *þæt* following *cweðað* is unnecessary grammatically or metrically. See *DOE cweþan* A 24 (with indirect speech without *þæt*). Adding *þæt* obscures the series of pres.

Commentary

ind. pl. verbs—*aginnað, seniað, syllað, cweðað*—in four succeeding half-lines, whose cumulative effect is to portray the outrageous behavior of the erring priests. Hilton's proposal in *An Edition and Study*, 80, that a toast *Goddlife* is intended by the phrase, also has merit. Magennis 91 cites the criticism in Assman homily 12, lines 69–73, of those who drink excessively while toasting the health of comrades and become drunk in the process. The case for Jones's reading is stronger. however, for the stylistic reasons cited above.

227. **welhwa:** Nw *wel.wel hwa* Dittography followed by Nowell's false start with a wynn before *h* which he then crossed out before completing the word.

228. **meþig:** < *meðe* "weary, exhausted" (with labor, hunger, disease, etc.) according to *B-T*, surely used with irony here.

229. **operne:** Nw *operre* See note to line 39.

230. Following the on-verse, the title of a charm, part of the next text, fills out the line in Nw. The hand is Nowell's, but the title seems to have been added some time after he completed the poem, perhaps as a means for insuring the correct assembly of the pages. This would be in keeping with his practice of using catchwords elsewhere.

Preface to Glossary

The glossary presents an alphabetized list comprising every occurrence of each word in *Seasons for Fasting*. Headwords indicate the nominative singular form of most nouns, exceptions being those nouns found only in plural form. Verbs are listed by the infinitive form. Pronouns are grouped under the nominative singular form for each person, demonstrative, or definite article. Adjectives are in the nominative singular masculine form. Words beginning with the digraph *æ* are incorporated under *a* and follow those beginning with *ad*; words beginning with *þ* follow those beginning with *t*. Words with the prefix *ge-* are listed together alphabetically since they comprise a substantial component of the poet's lexicon and there usually is no alternate form without the prefix in the poem's corpus. Long vowels are indicated as required.

Each headword is followed by a designation of its part of speech. The gender of each noun is specified. Verbs are marked strong or weak accompanied by a class number. One or more translations is given, depending upon the usage within the poem. The *Dictionary of Old English A–G* (*DOE*) and *An Anglo-Saxon Dictionary*, ed. Joseph Bosworth and T. Northcote Toller, *Supplement* by Toller, with *Addenda and Corrigenda* by Alistair Campbell (*B–T, B–TS*, and *B–TA* respectively) provide the bulk of the definitions. A smaller number are drawn from previous editions and analyses, with references provided in the Commentary .

Following the definition, the specific citations appear. Where no oblique form of a word is given before a citation, the headword stands. Unless stated otherwise, the indicative mood of the verb is assumed. Forms of nouns, verbs, adjectives, and pronouns are separated by semicolons. Variant spellings of a given form are separated by commas. For abbreviations, please refer to the list following.

List of Abbreviations in Glossary

a	accusative	poss.	possessive
adj.	adjective	prep.	preposition
adv.	adverb	pres.	present
anom. vb.	anomalous verb	pres. ptc.	present participle
conj.	conjunction	pret.	preterite
d	dative	pret. pres. vb.	preterite present verb
def. art.	definite article		
demonstr.	demonstrative	pron.	pronoun
f	feminine	quasi-subst.	quasi-substantive
g	genitive	refl.	reflexive
imper.	imperative	rel. part.	relative particle
impers.	impersonal	s, sg.	singular
indecl.	indeclinable	subj.	subjunctive
inf.	infinitive	vb 1–7	strong verb
infl. inf.	inflected infinitive	vb I–III	weak verb
		1	first person
i	instrumental	2	second person
interj.	interjection	3	third person
inter. pron.	interrogative pronoun		
m	masculine		
neg.	negative		
n	neuter		
nom.	nominative		
num.	number		
pp.	past participle		
pers.	person		
p, pl	plural		

Seasons for Fasting Glossary

ac	conj. "but" 20, 31, 38, 92, 166, 173, 198, 204, 208.
ǣ	f. "law" as 110.
ǣbylgþ	f "offense" ds *ǣbyligþe*, 198.
ǣfre	adv. "ever" 91, 102.
æfter	prep. "after" 58, 215.
ǣghwǣr	adv. "everywhere" 174.
ǣlc	pron. "each one" asm *ǣlcne*, 211.
ælde	mp "men" gp *ælda*, 68, *elda*, 115.
ǣlest	f "neglect of (religious) law" ds *ǣleste*, 211.
ælmesdǣd	f "almsdeed" ap *ælmesdǣde*, 191; dp *ælmesdǣdum*, 41.
ǣnett	f "solitude" ds *ǣnete*, 133, 161.
ǣnig	adj. "any" asn 89.
ǣr	prep. "before" 104, 107, 110, 127, 180.
ǣr	adv. "until" 131.
ǣrest	adj. "first" dsf *ǣrestan*, 48.
ǣrest	adv. "first" 106.
ǣrfæst	adj. "pious" np *ǣrfæste*, 174.
ǣrist	m "resurrection, Easter" ds *ǣriste*, 104, *ǣreste*, 180.
ǣrra	p "ancestors, forebears" npm *ǣrran*, 77.
ǣrur	prep. "before, previously, earlier" 67, 72, 85, 196.
æt	prep. "at, in" 99, 152, 172.
ǣt	m "food" as 85; ds *ǣte*, 219.
ætȳwan	vb I "reveal" pp *ætȳwed*, 24.
æþele	adj. "fine" asn 219.
aginnan	vb 1 "begin" pres. 3 pl. *aginnað*, 224.
āhwæt	pron. "anything" 171.
ān	adj. "only" nsm 84.

Glossary

anbītan < onbītan	vb 1 "consume, taste" pret. 3 sing *anbāt*, 109, 126.
and	conj. "and" 3, 6, 10, 14, 15, 18, 20, 22, 24, 26, 28, 33, 34, 40, 42, 43, 51, 73, 74, 77, 80, 82, *ond* 95, 106, 109, 114, 117, 124, 126, 139, 151, 153, 156, 161, 163, 167, 173, 178, 182, 187, 189, 190, 197, 211, 214, 217, 219, 221, 222, 229.
andfeng	m "reception" as *andfeng*, 91.
andleofen	f "spiritual sustenance, nourishment" as *andlifene*, 138.
anfōn <onfōn	vb 7 "receive, take" pret. subj. sg. *anfenge*, 110.
Angle	mp "English people" dp *Anglum*, 44.
ārīsan	vb 1 "arise" inf. 31.
ārwesa	m "lord" as *ārwesan*, 77, 196.
āsecgan	vb III "tell, narrate, relate" pret. 3 sg. *asæde*, 7.
asendan	vb I "inflict, send, visit upon" pret. 3 sg. *asende*, 14.
āstīgan	vb 1 "ascend, climb" infl. inf. *āstīgenne*, 130.
atol	n "evil, horror" ds *atele*, 37.
bǣl	n "fire, flame" ds *bǣle*, 112.
bæþ	n "immersion" ds *baðe*, 155.
bēam	m "cross" as 22.
bearn	n "child, son" as *beorn*, 178; dp *bearnum*, 64, *beornum* 68.
bebēodan	vb 2 "command, ordain" pres. 1 pl. *bebēodað*, 178.
bedǣlan	vb I "(be) devoid of, deprived of" pp *bedǣled*, 30, 155, 223.
bedīglan	vb I "conceal, cover, hide" pp *bedīgled*, 23.
behlǣnan	vb I "surround" pp *behlǣned*, 112.
bēon	anom vb "to be" pres. 3 sg. *byð*, 67, *is* 17, 29, 63, 79, 83, 134, 144, 192, 207, *ys* 56; 1, 3 pres. pl. *sint*, 132, 136; pret. 3 sg. *wæs*, 1, 23, 30, 152, *næs* (neg.) 165; pret. 3 pl. *wæron*, 11; pret. subj. sg. *wese*, 183, 186.

140

Glossary

beorht	adj. "clear" dsm *beorhtum*, 66.
beorn	m "man" ns 45; as 179.
besyrian	vb II "ensnare" pret. 3 pl. *besyredon*, 21.
bētan	vb I "atone for" inf. 189.
biddan	vb 5 "ask, pray" inf. 78, 185.
bitere	adv. "greatly" 197.
blǣd	m "glory" gp *blǣda*, 32.
bliss	f "bliss" gs *blisse*, 132; ds 149.
bōc	f "book" gp *bōca*, 82, 86, 112.
bōcstæf	m "letter" dp *bōcstafum*, 26.
bōt	f "atonement" as *bōte*, 197.
brēman	vb I "celebrate, observe, proclaim" inf. 26; infl. inf. *brēmenne*, 56, 82, *brȳmenne* 66.
brēme	adj. "celebrated" asm *brēmne*, 112.
brūcan	vb 2 "partake of" pres. subj. sg. *brūce*, 182.
Bryten	f "Britain" gs *Brytena*, 56.
brytta	m "lord, perpetrator" ns 166; as *bryttan*, 54.
Brytta	mp "Bretons" n 88.
būtan	conj. "except, unless" 84.
byrgenn	f "grave, tomb" ds *byrgenne*, 22, 32.
costian	vb II "tempt, try" inf. 169; pret. 3 sg. *costude*, 160.
cræft	m "wisdom" as 112.
Crist	m "Christ" ns 148, 152; as 169; gs *Cristes*, 160.
cuman	vb 4 "come" pres. 3 sg. *cumeð*, 37, 58; pret. 3 sg. *com*, 92; pp npm *cymene*, 87.
cunnan	pret. pres. vb "know how (to)" pres. subj. sg. *cunne*, 200.
cweðan	vb 5 "say" pres. 3 pl. *cweðað*, 226.
cyning	m "king" ds *cyninge*, 74.
dǣd	f "deed" dp *dǣdum*, 137, 140, 175, 189, 199.
dǣdfruma	m "doer of deeds, God" as *dǣdfruman*, 40.
dæg	m "day" ns 79; as 60; ds *dæge*, 68; instr. sg. 24 *dæge*; gp *daga*, 103, 108, 125, 156, 159, 177, 181.

Glossary

dæghwāmlīce	adv. "daily, every day" 185, 199, 210.
dēag	pret. pres. vb. "avail, benefit" pres. subj. sg. *duge*, 206.
dēman	vb I "celebrate" inf. 76; pres. 3 sg. *dēmeð*, 86.
dēop	adj. "deep, profound" apn *dēopan*, 117.
dēore	adj. "dear, excellent, pleasing, precious" asf *dēoran*, 110; asm *dēorne*, 40, 139; dsn *dēoran*, 65, *dēorum*, 154; dpn *dēorum*, 73.
diht	m.n. "speech, voice" ds *dihte*, 51, 65.
dihtan	vb I "establish, place, set" pret. 3 sg. *dyhte*, 95, *dihte*, 123.
dōgor	n "day" gp *dōgera*, 40.
dōm	m "decree" ns 86.
dōn	anom vb "do" pres. 3 sg. *dēð*, 197; pret. 3 sg. *dyde*, 143, 169.
drenc	m "drink" as *dreng*, 227.
drēorig	adj. "anguished, sorrowful" nsm 20.
drincan	vb 3 "drink" pres. subj. sg. *drince* 206.
drōf	adj. "turbid, muddy, dirty" asn *drōfe*, 206.
dryhten	m "lord" ns 111, 119, 134; as 21, 185, 210; gs *dryhtnes*, 73, 104, 110, 123, 137, 139, 175, 180, 201.
dugeþum	adv. "excellently" 201.
duguþ	f "benefit, value, salvation" gs *duguþe*, 119.
dūn	m "mountain" as 127.
durran	pret. pres. vb "dare" pres. subj. sg. *durre*, 169.
dymnis	f "evil" ap *dymnissa*, 189.
dyppan	vb I "dip, immerse, baptize" inf. 154.
ēac	adv. "also" 103, 157, 229.
eald	adj. "old, venerable" nsm 161, *ealda*, 143; gsf *ealdere*, 198.
ealddagas	mp "days of old, former days" dp *ealddagum*, 1.
ealdor	m "prince" ns 31, as 167, 190; ds *ealdre*, 81.
eall	adv. "completely, entirely" 191.

Glossary

eall	adj. "all" gpm *ealra*, 133; dp *eallum*, 34; dsm 75; dpm 115.
eard	m "dwelling place, heavenly home" as 34.
earm	adj. "wretched" nsm 20.
Ēastertīd	f "Eastertide" as 55.
efen	adv. "exactly" 159, 181.
efne swā swā	adv. "just as" 77.
eft	adv. "afterwards, again, in turn" 120.
ege	m "fear" as 201.
ēage	n "eye, sight" dp *ēgum*, 172.
Ēlias	m "Elias, Elijah" ns *Hēlias*, 120; *Ēlias*, 143.
emb	adv. "at, about" 83, 220.
emniht	n "vernal equinox" gs *emnihtes*, 68.
ende	m "end" ns 20.
engel	m "angel" ds *engle*, 131; np *englas*, 136, 167, 174; gp *engla*, 123; dp *englum*, 34.
Engla land	n "England" as 98.
eorl	m "leader, man" ns 106, 120.
eorþbugend	m "earth dweller, human being" dp *eorþbugendum*, 136.
eorþe	f "earth" ds *eorþan*, 83, 89.
ēstum	adv. "gladly" 98.
etan	vb 5 "eat" inf. 229.
ēþel	m "homeland, heaven" as *ǣþel*, 151.
fæstan	vb I "fast" inf. 140.
fæste	adv. "fixed" 194.
fæsten	n "fast, fasting" ns 55, 64; as 47, 71, 103, 108, 150, 159, 177, 181; ds *fæstene*, 116, *fæstenne* 186; ap *fæstenu*, 27; dp *fæstenum*, 42, 79.
fæstentīd	m "time or period appointed for fasting" gp *fæstentīda*, 97.
fāh	adj. "damned" nsm 183.
fela	indecl. "many" *feala*, 17, 157.

fēorþa	adj. "fourth" nsm 79; asn *fēorþe*, 71.
fēower	num. "four" 27, 146.
fēowertig	num. "forty" 103, 108, 125, 156, 159, 177, 181.
fēran	vb I "go, journey" pret. 3 sg. *fērde*, 127.
ferian	vb I "carry" pret. 3 sg. *ferede*, 147.
findan	vb 3 "find" pret. 3 pl. fundon, 15.
fisc	m "fish" as 230; gp *fysca*, 183.
flǣsc	n "flesh, meat" gs *flǣsces*, 183.
flōd	*m* "water" ds *flōde*, 230.
folc	n "folk, people" ns 1; gs *folces*, 202, 212; ds *folce*, 187.
folde	f "earth" as *foldan*, 187, ds 64.
fōn	vb 7 "seize, take, eat" inf. 223.
for	prep. "before, in front of, for the sake of, as" 5, 30, 39, 136, 141.
forhǣfenes	f "abstinence" ds *forhǣfenesse*, 141.
forlǣdan	vb I "mislead" pres. 3 pl. *forlǣdað*, 211.
forma	adj. "first" asn *forme*, 47.
forþ	adv. "still" 97.
forþecgan	vb I "be consumed by thirst" pp np *forþegide*, 214.
frǣte	adj. "shameful" nsm 161.
fram	prep. "from" *from* 93, *fram* 131.
Franca	m "Franks" np 88.
frēa	m "lord" ns 3; as *frēan*, 19, 78, 162.
fremman	vb I "follow, perform" inf. 204.
frēod	f "peace" as *frēode*, 116.
frēond	m "friend" ns 186.
friþu	f "peace protection" gs *fryþa* 15.
frōd	adj. "wise" nsm *frōda*, 42.
fruma	m "chief, ruler, prince" ns 9.
full	adj. "full" dsf 72.
fulwiht	n "baptism" gs *fulwihtes*, 155.

Glossary

fyligian	vb I, II "follow, obey" inf. *fyligan* 36, *filian* 102, *fylian* 212; pres. 2 sg. *fylgest*, 175; pres. 1 pl. *filiað*, 98; pret. 3 sg. *fyligde*, 9.
fīras	mp "men, people" gp *fȳra*, 64.
fyren	f "sin" gs *fyrene*, 140; ap *fyrna*, 187; gp *fyrena*, 150, 155, *fyrna* 202.
fȳren	adj. "fiery" nsn 146.
fyrran	vb I "remove" pret. 3 sg. *firude*, 156.
gēarum	adv. "of yore" 62.
gebǣdan	vb I "force, impel" pp np *gebǣded*, 214.
gebann	n "decree" as 88.
gebrēfan	vb I "write down briefly" pret. 3 sg. *gebrēfde*, 45.
gebyrd	f "birth" ds *gebyrde*, 73.
gedēman	vb I "judge, decree" pret. 3 sg. *gedēmde*, 99; pret. 3 pl. *gedēmdon*, 23.
gefæstan	vb I "fast" infl. inf. *gefæstenne*, 125.
gefēa	m "spiritual joy" gp *gefēana*, 133.
gefrǣge	n "knowledge" instr. sg. 69.
gefremman	vb I "commit" pres. subj. sg. *gefremme*, 203.
gefyllan	vb I "fill, spend" inf. 41; pp *gefylled*, 32, 37.
gegladian	vb II "appease, propitiate" inf. 191.
gehālgian	vb II "consecrate, ordain" pp nsm *gehālgod*, 203.
gehātan	vb 7 "promise" pres. 3 sg. *gehāteð*, 35; pp *gehāten*, 149.
gehicgan	vb III "consider" inf. 128.
gehwilc	pron. "each, every" ns 179; np *gehwilce*, 188; gsn *gehwelces*, 63, *gehwylces* 76; ds *gehwylce*, 118; dsm *gehwylcum*, 226.
gehȳran	vb I "hear" pret. 1 pl. *gehȳrdon*, 25.
gelǣran	vb I "teach" pp *gelǣred*, 3.
gelǣstan	vb I "carry out, perform" inf. 71; infl. inf. *gelǣstenne*, 81; pres. 1 pl. *gelǣstað*, 150.

Glossary

gelēafa	m "belief" as *gelēfen*, 57.
gelīc	adj. "like" asm *gelīcne*, 162; dsm *gelīcum*, 65; dsn *gelīcum*, 57.
gelōme	adv. "frequently" 127, 225.
gemearcian	vb II "describe, point out" pp *gemearcod*, 176.
gemynd	f "mind, remembrance" ds *gemynde*, 75.
gemyndig	adj. "mindful" nsm 163.
genemnan	vb I "call" pres. 3 sg. *genemneð*, 70.
geond	prep. "throughout" 50, 59, 98, 215; *gynd* 187.
gerǣdan	vb I "read" inf. 52.
gerīm	n "number" as 40.
gerīne	n "mystery" as 128; ap *gerȳnu*, 117; dp *gerȳnum*, 82.
gescēad	n "power of distinguishing, reason" as 6.
gescrīfan	vb 1 "write" pp asm *gescrifene*, 113.
gesēcan	anom vb "seek" pret. 3 sg. *gesohte*, 33.
gesellan	vb I "give" pret. 3 sg. *gesealde*, 111.
gesēon	vb 5 "see" pret. 3 sg. *geseah*, 162.
gesettan	vb I "set, confirm" pret 3 sg. *gesette*, 95.
gestīgan	vb 1 "ascend, mount" pres. subj. pl. *gestȳgan*, 135.
gestrangian	vb 2 "strengthen" pp *gestrangud*, 124.
getellan	vb I "tell, number, reckon, esteem, consider" pp *geteald*, 136.
getenge	adv. "close to, near to, immediately following" 80.
geþicgan	vb I "take, accept, receive" pret. 3 sg. *geþigede*, 121.
geþrēatian	vb II "afflict" pres. subj. sg. *geþrēatige*, 84.
gewerian	vb II "cover" pp *gewered*, 38.
gewinna	m "adversary" ns 160.
gewinnan	vb 3 "gain, win" inf. 116.
gewītan	vb 1 "depart" pret. 3 sg. *gewāt*, 144, 166.
gewyrpan	vb I "cast away" *inf.* 16.
gewyrþan	vb I "estimate, value" imp. sg. *gewyrþe*, 91.
gif, gyf	conj. "if" 12, 16, 35, 87, 119, 150, 168, 172, 175, 196, 200.

Glossary

God	m "God" ns 14, *Godd* 226; gs *Godes*, 178.
gōd	adj. "good" nsm *gōda*, 106.
Gregorius	m "Gregory" ns 46; ds *Gregoriae*, 94.
gremian	vb II "offend, provoke" pres. 3 pl. *gremiað*, 210.
guma	m "man" *gumena*, 46, 94, 226.
gyfl	n "food" ds *gyfle*, 124.
gyltan	vb I "sin" pres. subj. pl. 193.
gyltig	adj. "culpable, blameworthy" nsm 157.
gȳman	vb I "heed" pres. subj. sg. *gȳme*, 202.
gyt	adv. "yet" 97.
habban	vb III "have" pres. 3 sg. *hafað*, 57, 149, 228, *hæfð* 196, *næfþ* (neg.) 172; pres. 1 pl. *hæbbe*, 176; pret. 3 sg. *hæfde*, 129.
hæleþ	m "hero, man, warrior" np 10; gp *hæleþa*, 25.
hālga	m "saint" ns 144.
hālig	adj. "holy" nsm 134, 153, npm 173; asm *hali*, 127; dsf *haligan*, 113.
hām	m "home" as 33, 149.
hand	f "hand" ds *handa*, 113.
hātan	vb 7 "command" pret. 3 sg. *hēt*, 114.
hē	pers. pron. "he" ns *hē*, 7, 23, 95, 99, 107, 108, 109, 110, 126, 127, 154, 156, 164, 169, 171, 172, 173, 182, 183, 186, 196, 205, 206, 218, 228; as *hine*, 3, 84, 114, 146, 154, 160, 200; gs *his*, 5, 35, 113, 164, 196; ds *him*, 6, 14, 20, 40, 111, 121, 122, 131, 196, 206; np *hie*, 11, 12, 14, 16, 19, 21, 27, 158, 213, 223, *hi* 216, 224; ap *hie*, 45; gp *heora*, 16, *hyra* 167, *hiora* 194; dp *heom*, 13, *him* 212.
hēahcyning	m "high king" ns 4; gs *hēahcyninges*, 10, 53.
healdan	vb 7 "hold, keep, possess" inf. *heoldan*, 44, *healdan*, 89, 201; pres. 3 pl. *healdað*, 221; imper. sg. *heald*, 92; pres. subj. pl. *healden*, 103; pret. 3 sg. *heold*, 18, 108; pret. 3 pl. *heoldon*, 27.

Glossary

hearm	m "affliction, harm, injury" as 13; gs *hearmes*, 166.
help	m "help" gs *helpes*, 134.
helpan	vb 3 "help" pres. 3 pl. *helpað*, 174; pret. 3 sg. *heolp*, 153.
heofen	m "heaven" gs *heofenes*, 153; gp *heofona*, 4, *heofena* 10, 53; dp *heofonum*, 13.
heofenwaru	fp "inhabitants of heaven" dp *heofenwarum*, 33.
hēowan	vb I "keep, observe" inf. 47, *hewan* 159; pret. 3 pl. *hewdon*, 177; pres. subj. sg. *hewe*, 181.
hēr	adv. "here" 4, 39, 89, 141, 150, 175, 203.
herescype	m "troop" ds 18.
herian	vb II "praise" inf. 39, 53.
hicgan	vb III "consider" infl. inf. *hicganne*, 144; imper. sg. *hige*, 168.
higefæst	adj. "firm of mind, resolute" *higefæste*, adv. 44.
hinder	adv. "back, behind" 166, 173.
hit	pers. pron. "it" as 106.
hluttor	adj. "clear, pure" *hlutter*, asn 206.
hof	n "dwelling, temple" ds *hofe*, 52, 65.
Horeb	m "Horeb" as 127.
hrēmig	adj. "lamenting" ns 208.
hū	adv. "how" 7, 135, 144, 176, 209.
hund	m "hound" ns 221.
hwā	pron. "who" interrog. nsm 195; indef. asn *hwæt*, 119.
hwænne	conj. "when" 223.
hwæt	interj. "what" 216.
hwilc	adj. "any" dsm 195.
hyht	m "hope" asm 35.
hyrde	m "guardian" ds 93.
ic	pers. pron. "I" ns 208; ds *me*, 61, 220.
ilca	adj. "same" asf *ylcan*, 75; apf *ilcan*, 221.
in	prep. "in" 37, 52, 75.

Glossary

inne	adv. "within" 171.
Israhele	mp "Israelites" gp *Israhela*, 1.
iū	adv. "formerly, once" 42, 90, 143, 176.
Iunius	m "June" as 62.
lǣran	vb I "teach" inf. 8, *lēoran*, 114, 118; pres. 3 pl. *lǣrað*, 137; pret. 3 sg. *lǣrde*, 153; pret. 3 pl. *lēordun*, 101; pp npm *lǣrede*, 11.
lǣtan	vb 7 "cause to, have" pret. 3 sg. *lēt*, 154; pret. subj. pl. *lētan* 16.
lamb	n "lamb" ns 29.
lang	adj. "long" asf *lange*, 101.
lār	f "doctrine, preaching, teaching" ns 207; as *lāre*, 139, 204; ds *lāre* 158; dp *lārum*, 9.
lārēow	m "teacher" ns 96; as 2.
leahter	m "sin, vice" ap *leahtras*, 16; gp *leahtra*, 165; dp *leahtrum*, 194.
lēan	n "recompense, reward" ds *lēane*, 13.
lēas	adj. "free" asm *lēasne*, 170.
lēaslice	adv. "deceitfully" 216.
lengten	m "Lent" as 158; gs *lengtenes*, 48.
lengtentīd	f "Lent" as 105.
lēode	mp "people" np *lēoda*, 105; gp *lēoda*, 9, 78, 118; dp *lēodum*, 5, 56, 90, 114, 158.
lēodscipe	m "nation, people" ds 8, 11.
lēof	adj. "beloved, dear" asm *lēofne*, 78; dsm *lēofum*, 8, 29.
lēogan	vb 2 "lie" inf. 216.
licgan	vb 5 "lie, remain" pres. subj. pl. *ligegen*, 194.
līchoma	m "body" ds *līchoman*, 165.
līf	n "life" gs *līfes*, 3, 19, 78, 81, 101; ds *līfe*, 4, 39, 141.
līfan	vb I "permit, allow" pres. subj. sg. *līfe*, 226.
lof	n "praise" ds *lofe*, 57.
lufian	vb II "love" inf. 19.

Glossary

lustum	adv. "gladly, willingly" 204.
mægen	n "might, power, strength" np *mægena*, 17.
mǣlan	vb I "say, speak" pret. 3 sg. *mǣlde*, 43, 90.
mænig	adj. "many" apm *mænige*, 25.
menigu	f "multitude" dp *mænium*, 192.
mǣre	adj. "famous, glorious" nsm 107, *mǣra* 120, 129; nsf *mǣre*, 17; asm *mǣrne*, 2, 135, 162; npm *mǣran*, 176.
mǣrþu	f "glory" gp *mǣrþa*, 142.
mæsse	f "Mass" as *mæssan*, 184, 213, 228.
mǣð	f "degree, measure" gp *mǣða*, 223.
magan	pret. pres vb. "may" pres. 3 sg. *mæg*, 171, 195, 208; pres. 1 pl. *magon*, 116; pres. subj. pl. *mægen*, 142; pret. 3 sg. *mihte*, 164.
man	m "people, one" ns 49, 62, 70.
mān	n "evil" gs *mānes*, 172.
mann	m "man" ns 168, 202, 203; gp *manna*, 179, 212; dp *mannum*, 162.
Martius	m "March" as 49.
mearc	f "occasion, term (of time)" ap *mearce*, 43.
mearh	m "horse" dp *mǣrum*, 146.
mergen	m "morning" as *mergan*, 213.
mete	m "food" ap *mettas*, 156.
mēþig	adj. "weary, exhausted" nsm 228.
micel	adj. "great" ns 192.
mid	prep. "amidst, among, with" 33, 34, 44, 53, 57, 73, 116, 122, 149, 211.
miht	f "power" ap *mihta*, 129.
mīn	poss. pron. "mine, my" isn *mīne*, 69.
molde	f "earth" ds *moldan*, 179.
mōnaþ	m "month" ds *mōnþe*, 49, 61, 69.
morgentȳd	f "morning-tide, morning" as 220.
mōs	n "food" ds *mōse*, 223.
mōtan	pret. pres. vb. "be allowed, permitted" pres. 3 sg. *mōt*, 85; pres. subj. sg. *mōte*, 218, 227.

Glossary

Moyses	m "Moses" ns 43, 90, 107; as *Moysen*, 2.
munt	m "mount, mountain" as 107, 135; gs *muntes*, 142.
myrcels	m "target" as 172.
nā	adv. "not" 91, 182, 202.
nāht	n "nothing" gs *nāhtes*, 109, 126.
nān	pron. "no one, no" ns 37, 83, 165.
nānwiht	adv. "nothing, not at all" *nānuht*, 157.
ne	adv. "not, nor" 102, 129, 171, 193, 194, 197, 200, 202, 222.
nēat	n "beast" as *nēat*, 28.
nēhst	adj. "last, latest" dsn *nēhstan*, 152.
nemnan	vb I "call, name" pres. 3 sg. *nemneð*, 50; pres. 3 pl. *nemnað*, 60, 105; pret. 3 sg. *nemde*, 62.
neorxnawong	m "paradise" as 148.
nēosian	vb II "seek" inf. 145.
nergend	m "savior" ns 148, 152.
nigoþa	num. "ninth" asf *nigoþan*, 83, 182.
niht	f "night" gp *nihta*, *nyhta* 109, 126, 157.
nīwian	vb II "renew" pres. 3 sg. *nīwað*, 199; pres. 3. pl. *nīwiað*, 209.
nū	adv. "now" 97, 105, 134, 176; conj. 39, 152.
of	prep. "from, of, out of" 13, 32, 113, 145, 207, 230.
ofer	prep. "after, upon" 55, 179.
offrian	vb II "offer, sacrifice" pret. 3 pl. *offredan*, 28.
ōfstum	adv. "with haste, speedily" 138.
on	prep. "on, onto, in, during" 1, 4, 11, 18, 22, 26, 38, 42, 45, 48, 49, 58, 61, 64, 65, 67, 69, 72, 79, 83, 89, 107, 121, 127, 130, 132, 133, 141, 147, 148, 158, 161, 165, 166, 173, 186, 194, 213, 222.
onbelgan	vb 3 "offend, make angry" pp *onbolgen*, 197.
onginnan	vb 3 "begin" pres. 3 pl. *ongynnað*, 126; pret. 3 sg. *ongan*, 31, 106, *ongann* 163; pret. 3 pl. *ongunnon*, 12.
onlīhtan	vb I "enlighten" pp *onlyht*, 3.

Glossary

orþanc	m "mind" dp *orþancum*, 115.
ostre	f "oyster" ap *ostran*, 219, 229.
ōþ	conj. "until" 182.
ōþer	adj. "other, second" nsn 55; asm *ōþerne*, 229; dpf *ōþrum*, 102.
oþþe	conj. "or" 29, 85, 88, 183.
pāpa	m "Pope" ns 46, 94.
Pentecosten	m "Pentecost" gs *Pentecostes*, 60.
Petrus	m "Peter" gs *Petres*, 100.
prēost	m "priest" np *prēostas*, 60, 100.
rǣd	m "benefit, counsel" ds *rǣde*, 6, 205; dp *rǣdum*, 36.
raþe	adv. "quickly" 15.
rīce	adj. "mighty, powerful" gsm *rīcan*, 52.
rīce	n "kingdom" as 50; gs *rīces*, 31, 93.
riht	adj. "upright" asm *rihtne*, 36.
rihte	adv. "rightly" 128.
rihthycgan	vb III "think right" pres. ptc. nsm *ryhthicgennde*, 205.
rinc	m "man" dp *rincum*, 6.
Rōm	f "Rome" ds *Rōme*, 45.
Rōmāne	mp "Romans" gp *Rōmāna*, 93.
Rōmware	mp "the people of Rome, Romans" gp *Rōmwara*, 50.
rūn	f "mystery" gp *rūna*, 6, 52.
sācerd	m "priest" ns 200; np *sācerdas*, 184, 209, *sācerdos* 193; dp *sācerdan*, 188.
sacu	f "strife" as *sace*, 209.
sadian	vb II "be sated" inf. 224.
samod	adv. "also, together" 10, 80, 109, 126, *somod* 122.
sanct	m "saint" gs *sancte*, 100.
sang	m "singing, song" ds *sange*, 53, 66.
sceacan	vb 6 "flee, hurry off" inf. 38.
scotian	vb II "shoot" inf. 171.

Glossary

scrīpan	vb 1 "creep" pres. 3 sg, *scrīp*, 173.
scryd	n "chariot" ns 146.
sculan	pret. pres. vb "must, ought, shall" pres. 2 sg. *scealt*, 102, 204; pres. 3 sg. *scal*, 38; pres. subj. sg. *sceole*, 88; pres. subj. pl, *sceolan*, 39, 43, 47, 51, *sceolen* 71, *scylan* 73, 118, 158, 184, 187; pret. 3 sg. *sceolde*, 8.
sē	m dem. and rel. pron. "the, who, he" ns 9. 20, 42, 79, 106, 120, 124, 129, 143, 144, 200; as *þone*, 7, 35, 77, 114, 139, 151, 217; gs *þæs*, 52, 142; ds *þām*, 18, 49, 59, 61, 165, 180, *þǣm* 104, 188; is *þȳ*, 24; np *þā*, 10, 176, 193, 209; dp *þām*, 97, 188.
sē þe	rel. pron. "which, who" npm *þā þe*, 137; apn 118.
sēcan	vb I pres. 3 pl. *sēcað*, 151; pret. 3 pl. *sōhtan*, 167.
secgan	vb III "say" inf. 188, 208; pres. 3 sg. *secgað*, 218; pres. subj. pl. *secgen*, 87.
sefa	m "spirit" as *sefan*, 36.
sellan	vb I "give" inf. *syllan*, 218; pres. 3 sg. *sylleð*, 119; pres. 3 pl. *syllað*, 225; pp *seald*, 131.
sēnian	vb II "bless" pres. 3 pl. *sēniað*, 225.
sēo	f dem. and rel. pron. ns *sīo*, 17; as *þā*, 55, 75, 83, 110, 138, 182, 198; gs *þǣre*, 119; ds *þǣre* 48, 58, 67, 72; ap *þā*, 43, 96, 117, 187, 189, 221.
seofoþa	num. "seventh" nsm 80.
September	m "September" as 70.
setl	n "seat, as an ecclesiastical term" da *setle*, 99.
settan	vb I "set, place" pret. 3 sg. *sette*, 5; pret. 3 pl. *setton*, 22.
sīd	adj. "wide" asm *sīdne*, 59.
sigor	m "victory" gp *sigora*, 14.
singan	vb 3 "sing" inf. 184; pres. 3 pl. *syngað*, 213.
sittan	vb 5 "sit" pres. ptc. np *sittende*, 224.
siþþan, syþþan	adv. "after, afterwards" 100, 228.
sixta	num. "sixth" nsm 80.

Glossary

sōna	adv. "at once, immediately, as soon as" 14, 213.
sorg	f "sorrow" dp *sorgum*, 208.
sōþ	adj. "true" asm *sōþan*, 7.
stæppa	m "step" ap *stæppon*, 130.
stellan	vb I "place, set" inf. 164.
stīgan	vb 1 "ascend" pret. subj. sg. *stȳge*, 107.
strǣl	f "arrow" ap *strǣla*, 164.
strǣt	f "street" ap *strǣta*, 215.
styrc	n "bullock" ns 29.
styþ	adj. "austere" dsn *styþum*, 124.
sum	pron. "one" ns 123.
sunnandæg	m "Sunday" ds *sunnandæge*, 59.
sūsl	n "evil" gp *sūsla*, 168.
sūþan	adv. "from the south" 87, 92.
swā	adv. "as, since, so that" 3, 11, 42, 45, 99, 109, 126, 140, 143, 157.
sylf	pron. "own, same, self, very" ns *sylf, sylfe, sylfa*, refl. 92, 95, 99, 111; asm *sylfne*, 21, 200; gsm *sylfes*, 5; dsm *sylfum*, 7; np refl. *sylfe*, 101, 193.
symbel	n "feast" ns 131.
symbelbrēad	n "feast bread" as 122.
synlēas	adj. "sinless, without sin" nsm 218.
synnig	adj. "sinful" nsm 168.
tācn	n "symbol" ds *tacne*, 29, 115.
tǣcan	vb I "teach" inf. 114; pres, 3 sg. *tǣchð*, 205.
tæppere	m "tapster" as 215, 217.
tēon	vb 2 "journey, roam" pres. 3 pl. *tēoþ*, 215.
tīd	f "time" ns 134; as 75, 182, *tȳd*, 83, 101.
tō	prep. "as, for, from, to" 6, 13 14, 22, 29, 56, 66, 81, 82, 90, 115, 125, 130, 144, 158, 205, 219, 223.
tō	adv. "too" 194.
tōgēanes	prep. "before" 123.
torht	adj. "bright, clear" dsm *torhtum*, 51.
twelf	num. "twelve" ap *twelfe*, 51.

Glossary

tyhtan	vb I "urge, persuade" pres. 3 pl. *tyhtaþ*, 217.
þā	adv. "then, when" 9, 21, 163.
þǣr	adv. "there, where" 15, 23, 37, 51, 111, 122, 148, 160, 167.
þæs þe	adv. "as, since, for this reason" 61, 86, 90, 220.
þæt	pron. "that" ns 25, 29, 63, 131, 207; as *þæt*, 47, 71, 92, 101, 105, 108, 128, 150, 177, 206; gs *þæs*, 13, 91, 165, 171, 197; ds *þām*, 65, 69, 186, *þǣm*, 99, 133, 161.
þæt	conj. "that" 27, 88, 92, 102, 116, 129, 142, 152, 158, 164, 179, 186, 193, 218, 221, 227.
þe	rel. part. "which, who" 17, 30, 49, 57, 58, 59, 62, 67, 70, 72, 85, 118, 137, 179, 203, 205, 212.
þæ læs þe	adv. "lest" 183.
þearf	f "need" ns 192.
þegen	m "servant, thane" ns 129.
þendan	adv. "as long as, while" 19.
þēnung	f "ceremonial or ritual service, observance" ap *þēnunga*, 96.
þēod	f "nation" ns 17; gp *þēoda*, 96, 192; dp *þēodum*, 24.
þēoden	m "prince" as *þēodne*, 76.
þēodlīce	adv. "as a people" 86.
þicgan	vb 5 "consume, take" inf. 85, 228; pres. subj. pl. *þycgen*, 138.
þincan	vb impers. "appear, seem" pres. 3 sg. *þinceð*, 61; pres. 3 pl. *þingað* 220.
þing	n "respect, way" gp *þinga*, 63, 76.
þis	dem. pron. "this" dsm *þissum*, 145; dp 79.
þonne	"as, then" 27, *Ðonne* 63, 87, 169, 192, 224.
þrǣl	m "thrall" ds *þrēale*, 195.
þrydda	num. "third" ism *þryddan*, 24; nsn *þrydde*, 63.
þū	pers. pron. "you" ns 88, 91, 92, 102, 175, 202, 204; as *þē*, 168, 173, ds 87, 92, 206; gs asm *þīnne*, 135.
þurh	prep. "by, through, with" 2, 5, 36, 178, 191, 201.

Glossary

þurst	m "thirst" ds *þurste*, 214.
þus	adv. "thus" 95.
þwēal	n "washing" ds *þwēale*, 154.
þyngian	vb II "reconcile with" inf. 195.
unhǣl	f "sickness" ns 84.
unmǣne	adj. "pure" asn *unmǣne*, 28.
uplīc	adj. "heavenly" asm *uplīcan*, 151.
ūre	poss. pron. "our" gsm *ūres*, 104, 180; dpf *ūre*, 41.
uton	anom. vb "let us" subj. pl. 128, 140.
wǣt	n "drink" as 85.
wæter	n "water" as 207; ds *wætere*, 122.
wancul	adj. "fickle, unstable" apn *wancule*, 12.
wang	m "land" as 59.
wangstede	m "place" ds 145.
wē	pers. pron. "we" np 25, 35, 39, 43, 47, 71, 73, 97, 103, 116, 132, 135, 138, 142, 150, 176, 178; dp *ūs*, 34, 45, 86, 119, 148, 152.
weard	m "guardian, keeper" ns *weord* 153, 168.
weg	m "way" as 7, 147; ds *wege*, 207.
welhwā	pron. "everyone" ns 227.
wēnan	vb I "expect, hope" inf. 163.
weorc	n "action, deed, work" gs *weorces*, 190; ap *weorc*, 12; dp *weorcum*, 74.
weorþan	vb 3 "become, come about" pret. 3 sg. *wearð*, 20, 124, 131.
weorþian	vb II "honor" inf. 54.
wered	n "host, band" gp *wereda*, 170.
wēsten	m "desert, wilderness" ds *wēstene*, 121, 132.
wicg	n "steed" dp *wicgum*, 147.
wiglian	vb II "pull tricks, use wiles" pres. 3 pl. *wigliað*, 222.
willan	anom. vb "will, be willing" pres. 1 pl. *willaþ*, 35; pres. 3 sg. *wyle*, 212; pret. 3 pl. *woldon*, 19.
wilnian	vb II "ask for" pret. 3 pl. *wilnodan*, 15.

Glossary

wīn	n "wine" as *wȳn*, 219, *wīn* 225; gs *wīnes*, 227.
wīse	f "way, manner" ap *wīsan*, 222.
wist	m,f "food, sustenance" asf *wiste*, 121; asm *wist*, 139.
wiþ	prep. "with" 196.
wlanc	adj. "great, proud" asm *wlancne*, 54; dpn *wlangum*, 147.
womm	m "evil, sin" gs *wommes*, 163; ds *womme*, 38; gp *womma*, 30, 170.
word	n "word" as 5, 137; gs *wordes*, 190; dp *wordum*, 74.
woruld	f "world" ds *worulde*, 30, 222.
wrītan	vb 1 "write" inf. 26.
wrōht	f "offense" gs *wrōhte*, 198.
wucu	f "week" ds *wucan*, 48, 58, 67, 72.
wulderfrēa	m "glorious lord" as *wulderfrēan*, 170.
wuldor	n "glory" gs *wuldres*, 54, 74, 132, 145, 190, 207.
wulf	m "wolf" ns 221.
wunian	vb II "dwell, live" pres. 3 sg. *wunað*, 179.
wyrcan	vb I "attain, bring about" pret. 3 sg. *worhte*, 18.
wyrd	n "fate" as 38.
ypplen	n "summit, top" as 130.

Bibliography

I. Editions of *Seasons for Fasting*

Dobbie, Elliott Van Kirk, ed. *The Anglo-Saxon Minor Poems.* 98–104. The Anglo-Saxon Poetic Records 6. New York: Columbia University Press. 1942.
Greeson, Hoyt St. Clair, Jr. "Two Old English Observance Poems: 'Seasons for Fasting' and 'The Menologium'—an Edition." Ph.D. dissertation. University of Oregon, 1970.
Grimaldi, Maria, ed. and trans. "*The Seasons for Fasting.*" *Annali Istituto Universitario Orientale Napoli: Filologia germanica* 24 (1981): 71–92.
Hilton, Chadwick B., Jr. "An Edition and Study of the Old English 'Seasons for Fasting'." Ph.D. dissertation. University of Tennessee, 1983.
Holthausen, Ferdinand. "Ein altenglisches Gedicht über die Fastenzeiten." *Anglia* 71 (1952–53): 191–201.
Jones, Christopher A., ed. and trans. *Old English Shorter Poems*, 1: Religious and Didactic. 156–73. Dumbarton Oaks Medieval Library 15. Cambridge: Harvard University Press, 2012.
Puckett, Anita M. "The Old English *Seasons for Fasting*: A Translation." M.A. thesis. University of North Carolina, 1973.
Robinson, Fred C., and Eric Gerald Stanley, eds. *Old English Verse Texts from Many Sources.* Item 33. Early English Manuscripts in Facsimile, 23. Copenhagen: Rosenkilde and Bagger, 1991.

II. Manuscripts, Textual Notes, Commentaries on *SF*

Berkhout, Carl T. "Laurence Nowell (1530–ca. 1570)." *Medieval Scholarship: Biographical Studies on the Formation of a Discipline*, vol. 2: Literature and Philosophy, ed. Helen Damico, with Donald Fennema and Karmen Lenz. 3–17. New York and London: Garland, 1998.

Bibliography

Brackmann, Rebecca. *The Elizabethan Invention of Anglo-Saxon England: Laurence Nowell, William Lambarde, and the Study of Old English*. Studies in Renaissance Literature 30. Cambridge: D. S. Brewer, 2012.

British Museum, *Catalogue of Additions to the Manuscripts 1931–35*. London: British Museum, 1967.

Dammery, Richard J. "The Law Code of King Alfred the Great: A Study, Edition and Translation." Doctoral thesis. Cambridge University, 1991.

Downey, Sarah. "Too Much of Too Little: Guthlac and the Temptation of Excessive Fasting." *Traditio* 63 (2008): 89–127.

Flower, Robin. "Laurence Nowell and a Recovered Anglo-Saxon Poem." *British Museum Quarterly* 8 (1934): 130–32.

Flower, Robin. "The Text of the Burghal Hidage." *London Medieval Studies* 1 (1937): 60–64.

Grant, Raymond J. S. "Laurence Nowell's Transcript of BM Cotton Otho B. xi." *Anglo-Saxon England* 3 (1974): 111–24.

Grant, Raymond J. S. "A Note on 'The Seasons for Fasting'." *Review of English Studies* 23 (1972): 302–304.

Grant, Raymond J. S. *Laurence Nowell, William Lambarde, and the Laws of the Anglo-Saxons*. Costerus New Series 108. Amsterdam and Atlanta: Rodopi, 1996.

Grimaldi, Maria. " Il *Mære Lareow* in *The Seasons for Fasting*." *Annali Istituto Universitario Orientale Napoli: Filologia germanica* 28–29 (1985–86): 241–52.

Heyworth, P. L. "The Old English 'Seasons of Fasting'." *Mediaeval Studies* 26 (1964): 358–59.

Hilton, Chadwick B., Jr. "The Old English *Seasons for Fasting*: Its Place in the Vernacular Complaint Tradition." *Neophilologus* 70 (1986): 155–59.

Ker, Neil R. *Catalogue of Manuscripts Containing Anglo-Saxon*. Oxford: Clarendon, 1957. Second ed. with supplements, 1990.

Ker, Neil R. "Membra Disiecta, Second Series." *British Museum Quarterly* 14.4 (1940): 81–82.

Leslie, Roy F. "Textual Notes on *The Seasons for Fasting*." *JEGP* 52 (1953): 555–58.

Bibliography

Lutz, Angelika. *Die Version G der Angelsächsischen Chronik, Rekonstruktion und Edition.* Texte und Untersuchungen zur englischen Philologie 11. Munich: Fink, 1981.

Meaney, Audrey L. "London, British Library Ms. 43703." *Old English Newsletter* 19:1 (Fall, 1985): 34– 35.

Meaney, Audrey L. "Variant Versions of Old English Medical Remedies and the Compilation of Bald's Leechbook." *Anglo-Saxon England* 13 (1984): 235–68.

Meroney, Howard. "Review of *ASPR 6*." *Modern Philology* 41 (1943–44): 198–200.

Plumer, Danielle Cunniff. "The Construction of Structure in the Earliest Editions of Old English Poetry." *The Recovery of Old English: Anglo-Saxon Studies in the Sixteenth and Seventeenth Centuries*, ed. Timothy Graham. 243–79. Kalamazoo: Medieval Institute, Western Michigan University, 2000.

Prescott, Andrew. "Robin Flower and Laurence Nowell." *Old English Scholarship and Bibliography: Essays in Honor of Carl T. Berkhout*, ed. Jonathan Wilcox. 41–61. Old English Newsletter Subsidia 32. Kalamazoo: Medieval Institute, Western Michigan University, 2004.

Prescott, Andrew. "'Their Present Miserable State of Cremation': the Restoration of the Cotton Library." *Sir Robert Cotton as Collector*, ed. C. J. Wright. 391–454. London: British Library, 1997.

Schabram, Hans. "*The Seasons for Fasting* 206f. Mit einem Beitrag zur ae. Metrik." *Britannica: Festschrift für Hermann M. Flasdieck*, ed. Wolfgang Iser and Hans Schabram. 221–40. Heidelberg: Winter, 1960.

Schabram, Hans. "Zur Interpretation der 18. Strophe des altenglischen Gedichts *The Seasons for Fasting*." *Anglia* 110 (1992): 296–306.

Scragg, Donald. *A Conspectus of Scribal Hands Writing English, 960–1100.* Publications of the Manchester Centre for Anglo-Saxon Studies 11. Cambridge: D. S. Brewer, 2012.

Sisam, Kenneth. "Humfrey Wanley." *Studies in the History of Old English Literature.* 259–77. Oxford: Clarendon, 1953.

Sisam, Kenneth. "Seasons of Fasting." *Studies in the History of Old English Literature.* 45–60. Oxford: Clarendon, 1953.

Smith, Thomas. *Catalogue of the Manuscripts in the Cottonian Library 1696*, ed. C. G. C. Tite. Cambridge: D. S. Brewer, 1984.

Tite, Colin G. C. *The Early Records of Sir Robert Cotton's Library: Formation, Cataloguing, Use.* London: British Library, 2003.

Tite, Colin G. C. *The Manuscript Library of Sir Robert Cotton.* The Panizzi Lectures 1993. London: British Library, 1994.

Torkar, Roland. "Zu den ae. Medizinaltexten in Otho B. xi and Royal 12 D. xvii. Mit einer Edition der Unica (Ker, No. 180 art. 11 a–d)." *Anglia* 94 (1976): 319–38.

Torkar, Roland. *Eine altenglische Übersetzung von Alcuins De Virtutibus et Vitiis, Kap 20. Untersuchungen und Textausgabe.* Texte und Untersuchungen zur englischen Philologie 7. Munich: Fink, 1981.

Wanley, Humfrey. *Librorum Veterum Sepentrionalium, qui in Angliae Bibliothecis extant, nec non multorum Veterum Codicum Septentrionalium alibi extantium Catalogus Historico-Criticus, cum totius Thesauri Linguarum Septentrionalium sex Indicibus.* In George Hickes, *Linguarum Veterum Septentrionalium Thesaurus,* 2. (Oxford, 1705).

Warnicke, Retha M. "The Laurence Nowell Manuscripts in the British Library." *British Library Journal* 5 (1979): 201–02.

Wheelock, Abraham. *Historiae Ecclesiasticae Gentis Anglorum Libri V. a Venerabili Beda Presbytero scripti...* Cambridge, 1643; reissued 1644.

Whitbread, L. "Four Notes on Old English Poems." *English Studies* 44 (1963): 187–90.

Whitbread, Leslie. "Notes on the 'Seasons for Fasting'." *Notes and Queries* 191 (1946): 249–52.

Whitelock, Dorothy. "Old English." *Year's Work in English Studies* 23 (1944): 32.

Wormald, Patrick. "BL, Cotton MS. Otho B. xi: A Supplementary Note." *The Defense of Wessex: The Burghal Hidage and Anglo-Saxon Fortifications,* ed. David Hill and Alexander R. Rumble. 59– 68. Manchester and New York: Manchester University Press, 1996.

Wormald, Patrick. "The Lambarde Problem: Eighty Years On." *Alfred the Wise: Studies in Honour of Janet Bately,* eds. Jane Roberts, Janet L. Nelson, and Malcolm Godden. 237–75. Woodbridge, UK: D. S. Brewer, 1997; rpr. in Patrick Wormald, *Legal Culture in the Early Medieval West.* 140–78. London: Hambledon, 1999.

Bibliography

III. Editions of Related Texts

Ælfric's Catholic Homilies: The First Series, ed. Peter Clemoes. Early English Text Society s.s. 17. Oxford: Oxford University Press, 1997.

Ælfric's Catholic Homilies: The Second Series: Text, ed. Malcolm Godden. Early English Text Society s.s. 5. Oxford: Oxford University Press, 1979.

Ælfric's Catholic Homilies: Introduction, Commentary and Glossary, by Malcolm Godden. Early English Text Society s.s. 18. Oxford: Oxford University Press, 2000.

Ælfric's De Temporibus Anni, ed. Martin Blake. Anglo-Saxon Texts 6. Cambridge: D. S. Brewer, 2009.

Ælfric's Lives of Saints, ed. W. W. Skeat. Early English Text Society o.s. 76, 82, 94, 114. London, 1881– 1900; rpr. in two vols. 1966.

Ælfwine's Prayerbook, ed. Beate Günzel. Henry Bradshaw Society 108. London: Boydell, 1993.

Die altenglische Bußbuch (sog. Confessionale Pseudo-Egberti), ed. Robert Spindler. Leipzig: Tauchnitz, 1934.

Die altenglische Version des Halitgar'schen Bußbuches, ed. Josef Raith. Bibliothek der angelsächsischen Prosa 13. Hamburg: H. Grand, 1933; rpr. Darmstadt: Wissenschaftliche Buchgesellschaft, 1964.

Amalarii Episcopi Opera Liturgica Omnia, ed. J. M. Hanssens. Studi e testi 138–40. Three vols. Città del Vaticano: Biblioteca apostolica vaticana, 1948–50.

Das angelsächsiche Prosa-Leben des hl. Guthlac, ed. Paul Gonser. Anglistische Forschungen 27. Heidelberg: Winter, 1909; rpr. Amsterdam: Swets and Zeitlinger, 1966.

Anglo-Saxon Prognostics: An Edition and Translation of Texts from London, British Library, MS Cotton Tiberius A.iii, ed. R. M. Liuzza. Cambridge: D. S. Brewer, 2011.

The Anglo-Saxon Chronicle: A Collaborative Edition, vol. 5, MS C, ed. Katherine O'Brien O'Keeffe. Cambridge: D. S. Brewer, 2001.

Assmann, B. *Angelsächsische Homilien und Heiligenleben*. Bib. ags. Prosa 3. Kassel, 1889. Rpr. with intro. by Peter Clemoes, Darmstadt: Wissenschaftliche Buchgesellschaft, 1964.

The Battle of Brunanburh, ed. Alistair Campbell. London: W. Heinemann, 1938.
The Battle of Maldon, ed. D. G. Scragg. Manchester: Manchester University Press, 1981.
The Benedictine Office, ed. James M. Ure. Edinburgh: Edinburgh University Press, 1957.
Biblia Sacra Latina ex Biblia Sacra Vulgatæ Editionis. Sixti V. et Clementis VIII. London: Bagster, 1977.
Byrhtferth's Enchiridion, ed. Peter S. Baker and Michael Lapidge. Early English Text Society s.s. 15. Oxford: Oxford University Press, 1995.
Cross, J. E. "A Newly Identified Manuscript of Wulfstan's 'Commonplace Book', Rouen Bibliothèque Municipale, MS 1382 (U. 109), fols. 173r–198v." *Journal of Medieval Latin* 2 (1992): 63–83.
Dobbie, Elliott Van Kirk, ed. *The Anglo-Saxon Minor Poems*. The Anglo-Saxon Poetic Records 6. *The Menologium*, 49–55; *The Judgment Day II*, 58–67; *The Lord's Prayer II*, 70–74; *The Gloria I*, 74–77; *The Lord's Prayer III*, 77–78; *The Creed*, 78–80; *A Prayer*, 94–96. New York: Columbia University Press, 1942.
Ecgberht, *Dialogus ecclesiasticae institutionis. Councils and Ecclesiastical Documents Relating to Great Britain and Ireland*, ed. A. W. Haddan and W. Stubbs. Three vols. Oxford, 1871; rpr. Oxford: Clarendon, 1964. 3: 411.
Eight Old English Poems, ed. John C. Pope. Third ed. rev. by R. D. Fulk. New York: Norton, 2001.
The Old English Version of the Enlarged Rule of Chrodegang together with the Latin Original, an Old English Version of the Capitula of Theodulf together with the Latin Original, an Interlinear Old English Rendering of the Epitome of Benedict of Aniane, ed. Arthur S. Napier. Early English Text Society o.s. 150. London: Oxford University Press, 1916.
Die Gesetze der Angelsachsen, ed. Felix Liebermann. Three vols. Halle: Niemeyer, 1903; 1906/12; 1916; rpr. Aalen: Scientia, 1960.
Getty, S. S. "An Edition with Commentary of the Latin/Anglo-Saxon *Liber scintillarum*." Ph.D. dissertation. University of Pennsylvania, 1969.
Hall, Thomas N. "Wulfstan's Latin Sermons." *Wulfstan, Archbishop of York*, ed. Townend. 93–139.

Bibliography

Die Hirtenbriefe Ælfrics in altenglischer und lateinischer Fassung, ed. Bernhard Fehr. Bibliothek der angelsächsischen Prosa 9. Hamburg: Henri Grand, 1914. Rpr. with a supplement by Peter Clemoes. Darmstadt: Wissenschaftlice Buchgesellschaft, 1966.

Homilies of Ælfric: A Supplementary Collection, ed. John C. Pope. Two vols. Early English Text Society o.s. 259, 260. Oxford: Oxford University Press, 1967–68.

The Homilies of Wulfstan, ed. Dorothy Bethurum. Oxford: Clarendon, 1957.

King Alfred's Old English Version of Boethius' De consolatione philosophiae, ed. Walter J. Sedgefield. Oxford: Clarendon, 1899; rpr. Darmstadt: Wissenschaftlice Buchgesellschaft, 1968.

King Alfred's West Saxon Version of Gregory's Pastoral Care, ed. Henry Sweet. Early English Text Society o.s. 45, 50. London: Trübner, 1871; rpr. Oxford: Oxford University Press, 2001.

Klaeber's Beowulf and the Fight at Finnsburg, ed. R. D. Fulk, Robert E. Bjork, and John D. Niles. Fourth ed. Toronto: University of Toronto Press, 2009.

Krapp, George P., and Elliott Van Kirk Dobbie, eds. *The Exeter Book*. The Anglo-Saxon Poetic Records 3. *Christ I*, 3–15; *Christ III*, 27–49; *Guthlac A, B*, 49–88; *Soul and Body II*, 174–78. New York: Columbia University Press, 1936.

Krapp, George P., ed. *The Junius Manuscript*. The Anglo-Saxon Poetic Records 1. *Genesis A, B*, 1–87. New York: Columbia University Press, 1931.

Krapp, George P., ed. *The Vercelli Book*. The Anglo-Saxon Poetic Records 2. *Andreas*, 3–51; *Soul and Body I*, 54–59; *Homiletic Fragment I*. 59–60; *Dream of the Rood*, 61–65. New York: Columbia University Press, 1932.

Leechdoms, Wortcunning, and Starcraft, ed. Oswald Cockayne. Three vols. Rolls Series 35. London: Longman, Green, 1864–66.

The Leofric Missal, vol. 1, ed. Nicholas Orchard. Henry Bradshaw Society 113. London: Boydell, 2002.

Il 'Menologio' poetico anglosassone: introduzione, edizione, traduzione, commento, ed. Maria Grimaldi. Naples: Intercontinentalia, 1988.

"The Old English Calendar Poem," trans. Kemp Malone. *Studies in Language, Literature, and Culture of the Middle Ages and Later*, ed. Bagby

Atwood and Archibald A. Hill. 193–99. Austin: University of Texas Press, 1969.

The Old English Exodus, ed. Edward B. Irving, Jr. Yale Studies in English 122. New Haven: Yale University Press, 1953; rpr. Hamden, CT: Archon, 1970.

The Old English Poem "Judgement Day II", ed. Graham D. Caie. Anglo-Saxon Texts 2. Cambridge: D. S. Brewer, 2000.

The Old English Riddles of the "Exeter Book", ed. Craig Williamson. Chapel Hill: University of North Carolina Press, 1977.

Old English Liturgical Verse, ed. Sarah Larratt Keefer. Peterborough, ON: Broadview, 2010.

The Old English Riming Poem, ed. O. D. Macrae-Gibson. Cambridge: D. S. Brewer, 1983.

The Parker Chronicle and Laws (Corpus Christi College, Cambridge 173), facsimile ed. Robin Flower and Hugh Smith. Early English Text Society o.s. 208. London: Oxford University Press, 1941 for 1937; rpr. 1973.

Patrologia Latina, ed. J.-P. Migne. Paris: Garnieri, 1844–55.

Theodulfi Capitula in England, ed. Hans Sauer. Münchener Universitäts-Schriften, Institut für Englische Philologie, Texte und Untersuchungen zur Englischen Philologie 8. Munich: Wilhelm Fink, 1978.

Die Winteney-Version der Regula s. Benedicti, ed. A. Schröer. Halle, 1888. Rpr. with an appendix by Mechthild Gretsch. Tübingen: Max Niemeyer, 1978.

Wulfstan's Canons of Edgar, ed. R. Fowler. Early English Text Society o.s. 266. Oxford: Oxford University Press, 1972.

A Wulfstan Manuscript Containing Institutes, Laws and Homilies: British Museum Cotton Nero A. I, ed. H. R. Loyn. Early English Manuscripts in Facsimile 17. Copenhagen: Rosenkilde and Bagger, 1971.

Wulfstan: Sammlung der ihm zugeschriebenen Homilien nebst Untersuchungen über ihre Echtheit, ed. Arthur S. Napier. Berlin: Weidmann, 1883. Rpr. with bibliographical appendix by K. Ostheeren. Dublin, 1967.

Bibliography

IV. LANGUAGE AND METER

Beechy, Tiffany. *The Poetics of Old English*. Farnham, UK: Ashgate, 2010.

Bliss, A. J. *The Metre of Beowulf*. Oxford: Blackwell, 1958; rev. ed. 1967.

Bredehoft, Thomas A. *Authors, Audiences, and Old English Verse*. Toronto: University of Toronto Press, 2009.

Bredehoft, Thomas A. "Ælfric and Late Old English Verse." *Anglo-Saxon England* 33 (2004): 77–107.

Bosworth, Joseph, ed. *An Anglo-Saxon Dictionary*, ed. and enlarged by T. Northcote Toller. Oxford: Oxford University Press, 1898. *Supplement*, ed. Toller, 1921. *Enlarged Addenda and Corrigenda to the Supplement*, ed. Alistair Campbell. Oxford: Clarendon, 1972.

Brunner, Karl. *Altenglische Grammatik, nach der Angelsächsische Grammatik von Eduard Sievers*. Tübingen: Niemeyer, 1965.

Cable, Thomas. *The English Alliterative Tradition*. Philadelphia: University of Pennsylvania, 1991.

Cable, Thomas. "Metrical Style as Evidence for the Date of *Beowulf*." *The Dating of Beowulf*, ed. Colin Chase. 77–82. Toronto Studies in Old English 6. Toronto: University of Toronto Press, 1981; rpr. 1997.

Caie, Graham D. "Text and Context in Editing Old English: The Case of the Poetry in Cambridge, Corpus Christi College 201." *The Editing of Old English*, ed. Scragg and Szarmach. 155–62.

Campbell, A. *Old English Grammar*. Oxford: Clarendon, 1959.

Cronan, Dennis. "Poetic Meanings in the Old English Poetic Vocabulary." *English Studies* 5 (2003): 397–425.

Dance, Richard. "'*Þær wearð hream ahafen*': A Note on Old English Spelling and the Sound of *The Battle of Maldon*." *The Power of Words: Anglo-Saxon Studies Presented to Donald G. Scragg on His Seventieth Birthday*, ed. Jonathan Wilcox and Hugh Magennis. 278–317. Medieval European Studies 8. Morgantown: West Virginia University Press, 2006.

Dance, Richard. "Sound, Fury, and Signifiers; or Wulfstan's Language." *Wulfstan, Archbishop of York*, ed. Townend. 29–61.

Dictionary of Old English: A to G on CD-ROM, ed. Angus Cameron, Ashley Crandell Amos, and Antonette diPaolo Healey. Toronto: Centre for Medieval Studies, 2008.

Flasdieck, H. M. "Untersuchungen über der germanischen schwachen Verben III. Klasse (unter besonderer Berücksichtigung des Altenglischen)." *Anglia* 59 (1935): 1–192.

Frank, Roberta. "Poetic Words in Late Old English Prose." *From Anglo-Saxon to Early Middle English: Studies Presented to E. G. Stanley*, ed. Malcolm Godden, Douglas Gray, and Terry Hoad. 87–107. Oxford: Clarendon, 1994.

Fulk, R. D. *A History of Old English Meter*. Philadelphia: University of Pennsylvania Press, 1992.

Griffith, M. S. "Alliterative Licence and the Rhetorical Use of Proper Names in *The Battle of Maldon*." *Prosody and Poetics in the Early Middle Ages: Essays in Honour of C. B. Hieatt*, ed. M. J. Toswell. 60–79. Toronto: University of Toronto Press, 1995.

Griffith, M. S. "Poetic Language and the Paris Psalter: the Decay of the Old English Tradition." *Anglo-Saxon England* 20 (1991): 167–86.

Hutcheson, B. R. *Old English Poetic Metre*. Cambridge: D. S. Brewer, 1995.

Lapidge, Michael. "Old English Poetic Compounds: A Latin Perspective." *Intertexts: Studies in Anglo-Saxon Culture Presented to Paul E. Szarmach*, ed. Virginia Blanton and Helene Scheck. 17–32. Tempe: Arizona Center for Medieval and Renaissance Studies; Turnhout: Brepols, 2008.

Lapidge, Michael. "On the Emendation of Old English Texts." *The Editing of Old English*, ed. Scragg and Szarmach. 53–67.

Lass, Roger, and John Anderson, eds. *Old English Phonology*. Cambridge: Cambridge University Press, 1975.

Lendinara, Patrizia. "La poesia anglosassone alla fine del X secolo e oltre." *Annali Istituto Universitario Orientale Napoli: Filologia germanica* n.s. 11 (2001), 7–46.

Lendinara, Patrizia. "Translating Doomsday: *De die iudicii* and its Old English Translation (*Judgement Day II*)." *Beowulf and Beyond*, ed. Hans Sauer and Renate Bauer. 17–67. Studies in Medieval Language and Literature 18. Frankfurt am Main: Peter Lang, 2007.

Bibliography

Logsdon, Gay Marie. "*Maldon, Brunanburh, Finnsburh Fragment,* and Finnsburh Episode: An Inquiry into Tradition and Alternative Styles in Old English Poetry." Ph.D. dissertation. Univ. of Texas at Austin, 1989.

Luick, Karl. *Historische Grammatik der englischen Sprache.* Two vols. I: Leipzig: Tauchnitz, 1921; II: suppl. by Friedrich Wild and Herbert Kozol. Leipzig: Tauchnitz, 1940.

Malone, Kemp. "When Did Middle English Begin?" *Curme Volume of Linguistic Studies,* ed. J. T. Hatfield, W. Leopold, and A. J. F. Zieglschmid. Language Monographs 7. (Baltimore: Waverly, 1930): 110–17.

Marckwardt, Albert H. "Verb Inflections in Late Old English." *Philologica: The Malone Anniversary Studies,* ed. Thomas A. Kirby and Henry Bosley Woolf. 79–88. Baltimore: Johns Hopkins University Press, 1949.

McIntosh, Angus. "Wulfstan's Prose." *British Academy Papers on Anglo-Saxon England,* ed. E. G. Stanley. 111–44. Oxford: Oxford University Press, 1990.

Middle English Dictionary, ed. Hans Kurath, Sherman A. Kuhn, John Reidy, and Robert E. Lewis. Ann Arbor: University of Michigan, 1952–2001.

A Microfiche Concordance to Old English, ed. Antonette diPaolo Healey and Richard L. Venezky. Toronto: Centre for Medieval Studies, 1980.

Minkova, Donka. *Alliteration and Sound Change in Early English.* Cambridge: Cambridge University Press, 2003.

Mitchell, Bruce. "Adjective Clauses in Old English Poetry." *Anglia* 81 (1963): 298–322.

Mitchell, Bruce. *Old English Syntax.* Two vols. Oxford: Oxford University Press, 1985.

Momma, Haruko. *The Composition of Old English Poetry.* Cambridge Studies in Anglo-Saxon England 20. Cambridge: Cambridge University Press, 1997.

Momma, Haruko. "Rhythm and Alliteration: Styles of Ælfric's Prose up to the *Lives of Saints.*" *Anglo- Saxon Styles,* ed. Catherine E. Karkov and George Hardin Brown. 253–69. Albany : State University of New York Press, 2003.

Ogawa, Hiroshi. *Language and Style in Old English Composite Homilies.* Medieval and Renaissance Texts and Studies 361. Tempe : Arizona Center for Medieval and Renaissance Studies, 2010.

O'Keeffe, Katherine O'Brien. "Deaths and Transformations: Thinking through the 'End' of Old English Verse." *New Directions in Oral Theory*, ed. Mark C. Amodio. 149–78. Medieval and Renaissance Texts and Studies 287. Tempe : Arizona Center for Medieval and Renaissance Studies, 2005.

Orchard, A. P. McD. "Crying Wolf: Oral Style and the *Sermones Lupi.*" *Anglo-Saxon England* 21 (1992): 239–64.

Orton, Peter. *The Transmission of Old English Poetry*. Westfield Publication in Medieval and Renaissance Studies 12. Turnhout: Brepols, 2000.

Pons-Sanz, Sara M. *Norse-Derived Vocabulary in Late Old English Texts: Wulfstan's Works, a Case Study*. Northwestern European Language Evolution supplement 22. Odense: University Press of Southern Denmark, 2007.

Richards, Mary P. "Prosaic Poetry: Late Old English Poetic Composition." *Old English and New: Studies in Language and Linguistics in Honor of Frederic G. Cassidy*, ed. Joan H. Hall, A. N. Doane, and Dick Ringler. 63–75. New York and London: Garland, 1992.

Russom, Geoffrey. "Dating Criteria for Old English Poems." *Studies in the History of the English Language*, ed. Donka Minkova and Robert Stockwell. 245–65. Berlin/New York: Mouton de Gruyter, 2002.

Scragg, D. G., and Paul E. Szarmach, eds. *The Editing of Old English*. Cambridge: D. S. Brewer, 1994.

Sievers, Eduard. *Altgermanische Metrik*. Halle: Niemeyer, 1893.

Stanley, E. G. *In the Foreground: Beowulf.* Cambridge: D. S. Brewer, 1994.

Stanley, E. G. "*The Judgement of the Damned*, from Corpus Christi College 201 and Other Manuscripts, and the Definition of Old English Verse." *Learning and Literature in Anglo-Saxon England: Studies Presented to Peter Clemoes on the Occasion of His Sixty-Fifth Birthday*, ed. Michael Lapidge and Helmut Gneuss. 363–91. Cambridge: Cambridge University Press, 1985. Rev. and rpr. Eric Gerald Stanley. *A Collection of Papers with Emphasis on Old English Literature*. 352–83. Toronto: Pontifical Institute of Mediaeval Studies, 1987.

Stanley, E. G. "Old English Poetic Vocabulary: 'The Formal Word Precise but Not Pedantic.'" *Essays on Old, Middle, Modern English and Old Icelandic*

Bibliography

in Honor of Raymond P. Tripp, Jr., ed. Loren C. Gruber, Meredith Crellen Gruber, and Gregory K. Jember. 177–200. Lewiston, NY: Edwin Mellen, 2000.

Stanley, E. G. "Rhymes in English Medieval Verse: From Old to Middle English." *Medieval English Studies Presented to George Kane*, ed. Edward Donald Kennedy, Ronald Waldron, and Joseph S. Wittig. 19–54. Wolfeboro, NH, and Woodbridge, Suffolk: D. S. Brewer, 1988.

Stanley, E. G. "Studies in the Prosaic Vocabulary of Old English Verse." *Neuphilologische Mitteilungen* 72 (1971): 385–418.

Stanley, E. G. "Unideal Principles of Editing Old English Verse." Sir Israel Gollancz Memorial Lecture. *Proceedings of the British Academy* 70 (1984): 231–73.

Stanley, E. G. "Verbal Stress in Old English Verse." *Anglia* 93 (1975): 307–34.

Steen, Janie. *Verse and Virtuosity: The Adaptation of Latin Rhetoric in Old English Poetry*. Toronto: University of Toronto Press, 2008.

Terasawa, Jun. *Nominal Compounds in Old English: A Metrical Approach*. Anglistica 27. Copenhagen: Rosenkilde and Bagger, 1994.

Whitbread, L. "The Old English Poem *Judgment Day II* and Its Latin Source." *Philological Quarterly* 45 (1966): 635–56.

V. CRITICAL AND OTHER SECONDARY SOURCES

Anderson, Earl R. "The Seasons of the Year in Old English." *Anglo-Saxon England* 26 (1997): 231–63.

Anglo-Saxon Manuscripts in Microfiche Facsimile 6: Worcester Manuscripts, described by Christine Franzen. Tempe, AZ: Medieval and Renaissance Texts and Studies, 1998.

Berkhout, Carl T. "The Pedigree of Laurence Nowell the Antiquary." *English Language Notes* 23.2 (1985): 15–26.

Brett, Caroline. "A Breton Pilgrim in England in the Reign of King Athelstan." *France and the British Isles in the Middle Ages and Renaissance: Essays by Members of Girton College in Memory of Ruth Morgan*, ed. Gillian Jondorf and D. N. Dumville. 43–69. Woodbridge, Suffolk: Boydell, 1991.

Busse, Wilhelm G. "*Swa gað ða lareowas beforan ðæm folce, & ðæt folc æfter*: The Self-Understanding of the Reformers as Teachers in Late Tenth-Century England." *Schriftlichkeit im frühen Mittelalter*, ed. Ursula Schaefer. 58–106. ScriptOralia 53. Tübingen: Narr, 1993.

Caie, Graham D. "Codicological Clues: Reading Old English Christian Poetry in its Manuscript Context." *The Christian Tradition in Anglo-Saxon Teaching: Approaches to Current Scholarship and Teaching*, ed. Paul Cavill. 3–14. Cambridge: D. S. Brewer, 2004.

Caie, Graham D. "The Vernacular Poems in MS CCCC 201 as Penitential Literature." *A Literary Miscellany Presented to Eric Jacobsen*, ed. Graham D. Caie and Holger Nørgaard. 72–78. Copenhagen: Atheneum, 1988.

Clemoes, Peter. "The Chronology of Ælfric's Works." *The Anglo-Saxons: Studies in Some Aspects of Their History and Culture Presented to Bruce Dickins*, ed. P. A. M. Clemoes. 212–47. London: Bowes and Bowes, 1959. Rpr. in *Old English Prose*, ed. Szarmach, 29–72.

Cross, J. E. "Wulfstan's *De Anticristo* in a Twelfth-Century Worcester Manuscript." *Anglo-Saxon England* 20 (1991): 203–20.

Dendle, Peter. *Satan Unbound: The Devil in Old English Narrative Literature*. Toronto: University of Toronto Press, 2001.

Di Napoli, Robert. *An Index of Theme and Image to the Homilies of the Anglo-Saxon Church*. Hockwold cum Wilton, Norfolk: Anglo-Saxon Books, 1995.

Flower, Robin. "Laurence Nowell and the Discovery of England in Tudor Times." *Proceedings of the British Academy* 21 (1935): 47–73.

Frank, Roberta. "Old English *æræt*—'Too Much' or 'Too Soon'?" *Words, Texts and Manuscripts: Studies in Anglo-Saxon Culture Presented to Helmut Gneuss on the Occasion of his Sixty-Fifth Birthday*, ed. Michael Korhammer, with Karl Reichl and Hans Sauer. 293–303. Cambridge: D. S. Brewer, 1992.

Giandrea, Mary Frances. *Episcopal Culture in Late Anglo-Saxon England*. Woodbridge, Suffolk: Boydell, 2007.

Gneuss, Helmut. "Addenda and Corrigenda to the *Handlist of Anglo-Saxon Manuscripts*," *Anglo-Saxon England* 32 (2003): 293–305.

Gneuss, Helmut. *Handlist of Anglo-Saxon Manuscripts: A List of Manuscripts and Manuscript Fragments Written or Owned in England up to 1100*. Tempe: Arizona Center for Medieval and Renaissance Studies, 2001.

Bibliography

Hansen, Elaine Tuttle. *The Solomon Complex: Reading Wisdom in Old English Poetry*. McMaster Old English Studies and Texts 5. Toronto: University of Toronto Press, 1988.

Head, Pauline. "Perpetual History in the Old English *Menologium*." *The Medieval Chronicle*, ed. Erik Cooper. Costerus n.s.120. 155–62. Amsterdam and Atlanta: Rodopi, 1999.

Healey, Antonette Di Paolo, and Richard L. Venezky. *A Microfiche Concordance to Old English: The List of Texts and Index of Editions*. Toronto: Dictionary of Old English Project, Centre for Medieval Studies: University of Toronto, 1980.

Henel, Heinrich. *Studium zum altenglischen Computus*. Leipzig: Tauchnitz, 1934.

Hennig, John. "The Irish Counterparts of the Anglo-Saxon *Menologium*." *Mediaeval Studies* 14 (1952): 98–106.

Hicks, Carola, ed. *England in the Eleventh Century: Proceedings of the 1990 Harlaxton Symposium*. Stamford: Paul Watkins, 1992.

Hill, Joyce. "Monastic Reform and the Secular Church: Ælfric's Pastoral Letters in Context." *England in the Eleventh Century*, ed. Hicks. 103–117.

Howe, Nicholas. *The Old English Catalogue Poems*. Anglistica 23. Copenhagen: Rosenkilde and Bagger, 1985.

Howe, Nicholas. "Rome: Capital of Anglo-Saxon England." *Journal of Medieval and Early Modern Studies* 34 (2004): 147–72.

Jones, Christopher A. "Two Composite Texts from Archbishop Wulfstan's 'Commonplace Book': the *De ecclesiastica consuetudine* and the *Institutio beati Amalarii de ecclesiasticis officiis*." *Anglo-Saxon England* 27 (1998): 233–72.

Kleist, Aaron J. "Anglo-Saxon Homiliaries as Designated by Ker." *The Old English Homily: Precedent, Practice, and Appropriation*, ed. Aaron J. Kleist. 493–506. Turnhout: Brepols, 2007.

Lapidge, Michael. "The Saintly Life in Anglo-Saxon England." *The Cambridge Companion to Old English Literature*, ed. Malcolm Godden and Michael Lapidge. 243–63. Cambridge: Cambridge University Press, 1991.

Lawson, M. K. "Archbishop Wulfstan and the Homiletic Element in the Laws of Æthelred II and Cnut." *English Historical Review* 107 (1992): 565–86.

Letson, D. R. "The Poetic Content of the Revival Homily." *The Old English Homily and Its Backgrounds*, ed. Paul E. Szarmach and Bernard F. Huppé. 140–56. Albany: State University of New York Press, 1978.

Lionarons, Joyce Tally. *The Homiletic Writings of Archbishop Wulfstan: A Critical Study*. Woodbridge, Suffolk: D. S. Brewer, 2010.

Lucas, Peter J. "Abraham Wheelock and the Presentation of Anglo-Saxon: From Manuscript to Print." *Beatus Vir: Studies in Early English and Norse Manuscripts in Memory of Phillip Pulsiano*, ed. A. N. Doane and Kirsten Wolf. 383–439. Medieval and Renaissance Texts and Studies 319. Tempe: Arizona Center for Medieval and Renaissance Studies, 2006.

Lutz, Angelika. "The Study of the Anglo-Saxon Chronicle in the Seventeenth Century and the Establishment of Old English Studies in the Universities." *The Recovery of Old English: Anglo-Saxon Studies in the Sixteenth and Seventeenth Centuries*, ed. Timothy Graham. 1–82. Kalamazoo: Medieval Institute Publications, Western Michigan University, 2000.

Magennis, Hugh. *Anglo-Saxon Appetites: Food, Drink and Their Consumption in Old English and Related Literature*. Dublin: Four Courts, 1999.

Ortenberg, Veronica. *The English Church and the Continent in the Tenth and Eleventh Centuries*. Oxford: Clarendon, 1992.

Parks, Ward. "The Traditional Narrator and the 'I heard' Formulas in Old English Poetry." *Anglo-Saxon England* 16 (1987): 45–66.

Pasternack, Carol Braun. *The Textuality of Old English Poetry*. Cambridge Studies in Anglo-Saxon England 13. Cambridge: Cambridge University Press, 1995.

Randle, Jonathan T. "The 'Homiletics' of the Vercelli Book Poems: The Case of *Homiletic Fragment I*." *New Readings in the Vercelli Book*, ed. Samantha Zacher and Andy Orchard. 185–224. Toronto: University of Toronto Press, 2009.

Richards, Mary P. "Old Wine in a New Bottle: Recycled Instructional Materials in *Seasons for Fasting*." *The Old English Homily: Precedent, Practice, and Appropriation*, ed. Aaron J. Kleist. 345–64. Turnhout: Brepols, 2007.

Sauer, Hans. "Zur Überlieferung und Anlage von Erzbischof Wulfstans 'Handbuch'." *Deutsches Archiv für die Erforschung des Mittelalters* 36 (1980):

341–84. Trans. as "The Transmission and Structure of Archbishop Wulfstan's 'Commonplace Book'." *Old English Prose*, ed. Szarmach. 339–93.

Savage, Anne. "Old and Middle English, Poetry and Prose." *Studies in the Age of Chaucer* 23 (2001): 503–11.

Scragg, D. G. "The Corpus of Vernacular Homilies and Saints' Lives before Ælfric." *Anglo-Saxon England* 8 (1979): 223–77. Rpr. *Old English Prose*, ed. Szarmach, 73–150.

Scragg, D. G. "Dating and Style in Old English Composite Homilies." *H. M. Chadwick Memorial Lectures* 9. Cambridge: Department of Anglo-Saxon, Norse, and Celtic, Cambridge University, 1999.

Semper, Philippa. "Doctrine and Diagrams: Maintaining the Order of the World in Byrhtferth's *Enchiridion*." *The Christian Tradition in Anglo-Saxon England: Approaches to Current Scholarship and Teaching*, ed. Paul Cavill. 121–37. Cambridge: D. S. Brewer, 2004.

Sources of Anglo-Saxon Literary Culture: A Trial Version, ed. Frederick M. Biggs, Thomas D. Hill, and Paul E. Szarmach. Binghamton: Center for Medieval and Early Renaissance Studies, State University of New York at Binghamton, 1990.

Stanley, Eric Gerald. "Old English Poetic Diction and the Interpretation of *The Wanderer, The Seafarer,* and *The Penitent's Prayer*." *Anglia* 73 (1956): 413–66. Rpr. in *A Collection of Papers with Emphasis on Old English Literature*, ed. E. G. Stanley. 234–80. Publications of the Dictionary of Old English 3. Toronto: Pontifical Institute of Mediaeval Studies, 1987.

Stanley, E. G. "The Prose *Menologium* and the Verse *Menologium*." *Text and Language in Medieval English Prose: A Festschrift for Tadao Kubouchi*, ed. Akio Oizumi, Jacek Fisiak, and John Scahill. 255–67. Studies in English Medieval Language and Literature 12. Frankfurt am Main: Peter Lang, 2005.

Swan, Mary. "Constructing Preacher and Audience in Old English Homilies." *Constructing the Medieval Sermon*, ed. Roger Andersson. 177–88. Turnhout: Brepols, 2007.

Swan, Mary. "Memorialized Readings: Manuscript Evidence for Old English Homily Composition." *Anglo-Saxon Manuscripts and Their Heritage*, ed.

Phillip Pulsiano and Elaine M. Treharne. 205– 17. Aldershot, UK: Ashgate, 1998.

Szarmach, Paul E., with Deborah Oosterhouse. *Old English Prose: Basic Readings*. Basic Readings in Anglo-Saxon England 5. New York: Garland, 2000.

Szarmach, Paul E. "Vercelli Homily XX." *Mediaeval Studies* 35 (1973): 1–26.

Toswell, M. J. "The Metrical Psalter and the *Menologium*: Some Observations." *Neuphilologische Mitteilungen* 94 (1993): 249–57.

Treharne, Elaine. "Bishops and Their Texts in the Later Eleventh Century: Worcester and Exeter." *Essays in Manuscript Geography: Vernacular of the English West Midlands from the Conquest to the Sixteenth Century*, ed. Wendy Scase. 13–28. Turnhout: Brepols, 2007.

Treharne, Elaine. "The Life and Times of Old English Homilies for the First Sunday in Lent." *The Power of Words: Anglo-Saxon Studies Presented to Donald G. Scragg on His Seventieth Birthday*, ed. Hugh Magennis and Jonathan Wilcox. 205–40. Medieval European Studies 8. Morgantown: West Virginia University Press, 2006.

Trilling, Renée R. *The Aesthetics of Nostalgia: Historical Representation in Old English Verse*. Toronto: University of Toronto Press, 2009.

Tupper, Frederick. "Anglo-Saxon *Dæg-mæl*." *PMLA* 10 (1895): 111–241.

Upchurch, Robert K. "A Big Dog Barks: Ælfric of Eynsham's Indictment of the English Pastorate and *Witan*." *Speculum* 85 (2010): 505–33.

Upchurch, Robert K. "Catechetic Homiletics: Ælfric's Preaching and Teaching during Lent." *A Companion to Ælfric*, ed. Hugh Magennis and Mary Swan. 217–46. Leiden: Brill, 2009.

Warnicke, Retha M. *William Lambarde, Elizabethan Antiquary 1536–1601*. London: Phillimore, 1973.

Whitbread, L. "Notes on the Old English *Exhortation to Christian Living*." *Studia Neophilologica* 23 (1951): 96–102.

Whitbread, L. "Notes on Two Minor Old English Poems." *Studia Neophilologica* 29 (1957): 123–29.

Whitbread, L. "The Old English Poem *Judgment Day II* and Its Latin Source." *Philological Quarterly* 45 (1966): 635–56.

Bibliography

Whitelock, Dorothy. "Archbishop Wulfstan, Homilist and Statesman." *Transactions of the Royal Historical Society*, Fourth series, 24 (1942): 25–45.

Whitelock, Dorothy. "Wulfstan at York." *Franciplegius: Medieval and Linguistic Studies in Honor of Francis Peabody Magoun, Jr.*, ed. Jess B. Bessinger, Jr. and Robert P. Creed. 214–31. New York: New York University Press, 1965.

Wilcox, Jonathan. "The Dissemination of Wulfstan's Homilies: The Wulfstan Tradition in Eleventh- Century Vernacular Preaching." *England in the Eleventh Century*, ed. Hicks. 199–217.

Wilcox, Jonathan. "The Wolf on Shepherds: Wulfstan, Bishops, and the Context of the *Sermo Lupi ad Anglos*." *Old English Prose*, ed. Szarmach. 395–418.

Willis, G. G. *Essays in Early Roman Liturgy*. London: SPCK, 1964.

Willis, G. G. *Further Essays in Early Roman Liturgy*. Alcuin Club Collections 50. London: SPCK, 1968.

Wormald, Patrick. "Archbishop Wulfstan: Eleventh-Century State Builder." *Wulfstan, Archbishop of York*, 9–27.

Wormald, Patrick. *The Making of English Law: King Alfred to the Twelfth Century*. Vol. 1 Legislation and its Limits. Oxford: Blackwell, 1999.

Wrenn, C. L. *A Study of Old English Literature*. New York: Norton, 1967.

Wright, Charles D. "More Old English Poetry in Vercelli Homily XXI." *Early Medieval Texts and Interpretations: Studies Presented to Donald G. Scragg*, ed. Elaine Treharne and Susan Rosser. 245–62. Tempe: Arizona Center for Medieval and Renaissance Studies, 2002.

Wulfstan, Archbishop of York: The Proceedings of the Second Alcuin Conference, ed. Matthew Townend. Turnhout: Brepols, 2004.

Zacher, Samantha. *Preaching the Converted: The Style and Rhetoric of the Vercelli Book Homilies*. Toronto: University of Toronto Press, 2009.

Zacher, Samantha. "The Rewards of Poetry: 'Homiletic' Verse in Cambridge, Corpus Christi College 201." *SELIM* 12 (2003–2004): 83–108.

Index to Manuscripts

Cambridge, Corpus Christi College
  MS 173 (the Parker manuscript), 4, 9, 12-14
  MS 190, parts A and B, 41, 43, 46, 52
  MS 201, Part 1, 11, 41, 81-83
Exeter, Cathedral Library
  MS. 3501 (the Exeter Book), 13
London, British Library
  Additional MS 34652, 10
  Additional MS 43703, 2, 7-10, 12-17, 83, 85 and all references to Nw
  Arundel MS 60, 134
  Cotton MS
  Nero A.i, part B, 41, 46
  Otho B.xi, 2, 4, 6-10, 12-17, 22, 58, 83, 120-22, 131 and all references to Ot
  Tiberius B.i ("Abingdon Chronicle" C), 58, 120
  Tiberius B.iv ("Worcester Chronicle" D), 120
  Tiberius B.v, 38
  Vitellius A.vii, 46
  Vitellius A.xv (the Nowell Codex), 13
  Royal 12 D.xvii, 7
Rouen, Bibliothèque Municipale
  MS 1382 (U. 109), 40
Oxford, Bodleian Library
  MS Bodley 579 (the Leofric Missal), 38
  MS Hatton 20, 55
  MS Hatton 113, 114, 45, 47-49, 51-52, 82
  MS Junius 121, 22, 45, 47, 51-52, 65
Vercelli, Biblioteca Capitolare
  MS. CXVII (the Vercelli Book), 60, 82, 126

General Index

Ælfric, 1, 19, 36, 45, 50, 54, 57, 69, 72, 74, 81, 84, 111, 113-14, 124, 134
    First Series Homily 2, 129
    First Series Homily 6, 133
    First Series Homily 11, 49-50
    First Series Homily 17, 78
    Second Series Homily 3, 125
    Second Series Homily 7, 49-51
    Second Series Homily 15, 114
    Pope, Homily 3, 113
    Old English Letter to Bishop Wulfsige, 53
    Second Old English Letter to Archbishop Wulfstan, 53
    Sermo de Memoria Sanctorum, 133
Ælfwine's Prayerbook, 36
Alcuin, *Liber de Virtutibus et Vitiis*, 56-57, 69, 80
Aldhelm, 70
Amalarius, *De ecclesiasticis officiis*, 36
Andreas, 115, 125
Anglo-Saxon Chronicle, 58
    Version A, 58
    Version C, 58, 120
    Version D, 120
    Version G, 3, 58
Anonymous Homilies
    Assman 12, 135
    Assman 14, 130
    Homily M 15, 116
    Homily S 9 (Ash Wednesday), 46
    Napier 29, 82
    Napier 55, 49-51
Battle of Maldon, 21, 23-33, 36, 63
Bede, *Historia Ecclesiastica*, 3-4
Benedictine Office, poems, 36, 47, 80
    Creed, 1, 20-23, 30-31, 33, 47, 62-63, 65, 111, 113-16, 122, 124
    Gloria I, 47, 63, 117
    Lord's Prayer III, 47, 63
Benedictine Rule, 118
Beowulf, 28, 70, 115
Bible
    Exodus 3:7-9, 111
    Exodus 9:35, 111
    Exodus 19:18, 122
    Leviticus 8:36, 111
    Numbers 1:54, 111
    Numbers 8:20, 111

Index

Deuteronomy 9:9, 122
Deuteronomy 16:1-2, 114
II Kings 2:11, 125
Bible (continued)
   III Kings 19:4-9, 50, 61, 123
   Isaiah 58:5-6, 124
   Malachi 2:7, 18, 46, 124
   Matthew 4:1-4, 125
   Matthew 21:33-46, 113
   Luke 24:19-21, 113
   Luke 24:46-49, 114
   Ephesians 6:14-17, 126
Boethius, *Consolation of Philosophy* (OE), 112
Burghal Hidage, 3, 8, 11-12
Byrhtferth, *Enchiridion*, 1, 38-40, 44, 57, 62, 128
Cædmon's Hymn, 13
Canones Hibernenses X, 53
Christ I 13
Christ II, 126
Christ III, 127, 32
Chrodegang of Metz, *Enlarged Rule* (OE), 134
Chronicle poems, 11, 13-14, 16
Cleanness, 2
Confessional of Pseudo-Egbert (OE), 47, 125
Cotton, Sir Robert, 2, 6
Cynewulf, 60
Dream of the Rood, 128
Ecgberht, Archbishop of York, *Dialogus ecclesiasticae institutionis*, 37

Elene, 125
Elijah, 45, 50-51, 67-69, 71, 75-76, 122, 127
Ember fasts, 11, 19, 24, 29, 36-44, 59, 63-64, 66-68, 71-73, 76-78, 82, 116-17, 121, 126, 131
Exeter Book, 13, 30
   Riddle 40, 116
Exodus, 111
Flower, Robin, 4, 14-15
Genesis A, B, 115, 122
Gluttony, 56, 132-34
Gregory, Pope (the Great), 1, 8, 37-40, 42, 57-58, 67, 69, 71-72, 74, 118, 122, 124
   Libellus Responsionum, 4, 8
   Regula Pastoralis, 55-56
Guthlac B, 123
Homiletic Fragment I, 82
Judgment Day II, 2, 11, 21, 23, 29, 31-33, 36, 60-63, 65, 82, 111, 113, 124, 129
Lambarde, William, 13
Laws, 1
   II Æthelstan, 3, 8
   Alfred and Ine, 3, 8, 12, 17, 119
   V Æthelred, 119
   VI Æthelred, 38, 119
   Northumbrian Priests, 132
Leechbook, 4, 6-7
Lenten fast, 6-7, 11, 24, 28, 44, 49, 55, 59, 67, 71, 75-78, 82
Leofric Missal, 38

Index

Liber Scintillarum, 111, 125
Lord's Prayer II, 63, 129
Manuscripts. *See* Index to Manuscripts
Menologium, 21, 29, 36, 57-60, 115
Moses, 7, 24, 45, 50, 67, 71-72, 74-77, 111, 121-22
Nowell, Laurence, 2, 8-10, 83, and throughout Commentary
    Life, 12-14
    Traits as Copyist, 15-17, 21-23, 34, 84, 111
Old English Metrical Psalms, 59
Phoenix, 82
Piers Plowman, 2
Prayer, 128
Riming Poem, 30
Smith, Thomas, 6
Soul and Body I, II, 132
Stanzas, 14-15, 21-22

Theodulf of Orleans, *Capitula* (OE), 128
Wanley, Humfrey, 2-4, 6-7, 10-11, 14, 83-84, 111, 116
Wheelock, Abraham, 4-5, 8, 10, 83-84, 120-21
Winchester, 4, 11, 37
Worcester, 11, 37, 41, 45, 55
Wulfstan, Archbishop of York, 1, 11, 19, 36-37, 54, 56-57, 70, 72, 80-81, 121, 126, 130, 134
    Canons of Edgar, 52
    Commonplace Book, 40, 44-46, 52-53, 57
    Homily VIIIb, 51
    Homily VIIIc, 51-52
    Homily XIV, 48
Wulfstan II, Bishop of Worcester, 45
York, 41

About the Author

Mary P. Richards is Professor of English Emerita at the University of Delaware. The author of four books and numerous essays and reviews, she has focused on Anglo-Saxon and early Norman manuscripts and texts, especially those associated with Rochester Cathedral Priory and the Old English laws. Her book *Texts and Their Traditions in the Medieval Library of Rochester Cathedral Priory* (Philadelphia: American Philosophical Society, 1988) drew together all of these interests and laid the foundation for her recent work on *Seasons for Fasting*. Since 1986 she has published eight essays on the laws, three on Rochester materials, and two on *Seasons*: "Prosaic Poetry: Late Old English Poetic Composition," in *Old English and New: Essays in Language and Linguistics in Honor of Frederic G. Cassidy*, ed. N. Doane, J. Hall, and D. Ringler (New York: Garland, 1992), 62–75; and "Old Wine in a New Bottle: Recycled Instructional Materials in *Seasons for Fasting*," in *The Old English Homily: Precedent, Practice, and Appropriation*, ed. Aaron J. Kleist (Turnhout: Brepols, 2007), 345–64.